U0463934

蜀韵古镇

——多维视野下的古镇文化遗产保护与利用

HISTORIC TOWNS IN SICHUAN:
THE CULTURAL HERITAGE PROTECTION AND UTILIZATION
OF HISTORIC TOWNS WITH DIFFERENT DIMENSIONS AND VISIONS

赵春兰　杜　抒　黄运昇/编著

by ZHAO Chunlan　DU Shu　HUANG Yunsheng

四川大学出版社

Sichuan University Press

责任编辑:敬铃凌　余　芳
责任校对:周　洁
封面设计:墨创文化
责任印制:王　炜

图书在版编目(CIP)数据

蜀韵古镇:多维视野下的古镇文化遗产保护与利用＝
Historic Towns in Sichuan:The Cultural Heritage
Protection and Utilization of Historic Towns with
Different Dimensions and Visions:汉英对照 / 赵春兰,
杜抒,黄运昇编著. —成都:四川大学出版社,2018.5
ISBN 978-7-5690-1836-3

Ⅰ.①蜀… Ⅱ.①赵… ②杜… ③黄… Ⅲ.①乡镇－
文化遗产保护－研究－四川－汉、英 Ⅳ.①K297.1

中国版本图书馆 CIP 数据核字（2018）第 088920 号

书名　　蜀韵古镇——多维视野下的古镇文化遗产保护与利用
Shuyun Guzhen—Duowei Shiye Xia de Guzhen Wenhua Yichan Baohu yu Liyong

编　著　赵春兰　杜　抒　黄运昇
出　版　四川大学出版社
地　址　成都市一环路南一段24号 (610065)
发　行　四川大学出版社
书　号　ISBN 978-7-5690-1836-3
印　刷　成都市金雅迪彩色印刷有限公司
成品尺寸　230 mm×210 mm
印　张　18.75
字　数　493千字
版　次　2019年1月第1版
印　次　2019年1月第1次印刷
定　价　148.00元

◆读者邮购本书,请与本社发行科联系。
　电话:(028)85408408/(028)85401670/
　(028)85408023　邮政编码:610065
◆本社图书如有印装质量问题,请
　寄回出版社调换。
◆网址:http://press.scu.edu.cn

版权所有◆侵权必究

序言一
Preface 1

　　一直以来，四川古镇研究都是学界的关注热点。"蜀韵古镇"一书，前后经历了八年时间，选题、调研、研讨、写作、编译，现在终于成书了。这是一项由中美三所学校师生和独立研究者共同完成的成果。

　　作为美国弗吉尼亚大学的教师，我有幸在访问四川大学期间更多了解了关于四川古镇的一些信息，觉得很有特色，于是和四川大学建筑与环境学院的赵春兰老师商定共同推进相关研究。适逢从成都赴美留学的学生王一洲情系故里，遂以四川古镇为独立课题开始双语写作。我们一起进行了两学期的努力，写成一篇研究论文。该论文也成为本书后续不断深入细化的发端。

The topic of historic towns in Sichuan province attracted many scholars. This book is the most updated research on the topic as a collaboration among scholars and students from three Chinese and American schools. It has been an eight-year joint effort from topic selection, investigation, research, writing and rewriting, translation and edition, with contributions from faculties, students, and independent scholars who are all dedicated for the project,.

As a faculty member from University of Virginia (UVa), I had the fortune to visit Sichuan University (SCU) and learned some basics about the historic towns around Chengdu. Thus I discussed with Dr. Zhao Chunlan, the teacher at College of Architecture & Enviroment, Sichuan University, and she agreed to jointly promote the relevent research. It happened that a UVa student Wang Yizhou, who was from this city, liked to do bi-lingual writings about his home province as an independent study project. We worked together for two semesters. A booklet was created as a base for the later development on the topic.

在此基础上，后续所有更深入的文字修订、编译、图片和图纸的删减和重绘等工作都是在赵春兰副教授的组织下完成的。正是这些耗时费力的工作让本书更具学术性和专业性。四川大学建筑与环境学院院长熊峰教授对这项研究工作也给予了大力支持。来自建筑系的研究生同学们参与了部分修订工作，更新美化了书稿的图表。

杜抒女士对中文和英文的运用都十分娴熟。她在攻读哥伦比亚大学硕士学位之余，协助赵老师对本书稿英文部分的文字进行了细致的修订和编辑。

除了对四川古镇的研究之外，本书还进行了四川古镇和江南古镇的对比，以及中国历史小镇和美国历史小镇管理和保护模式的比较。这些内容都让本书的内容更丰富，视野更宽阔。

The academic compilation and rewriting of this book was managed by Ms. Zhao Chunlan, the associate professor from College of Architecture and Environment (CAE) of Sichuan University, who has been in leadership for the whole process to produce this book. With great enthusiasm she has edited texts of all chapters, adding more illustrations and made maps in a more professional manner. It is a tremendous job to enhance the original draft to current academic quality. The Dean of CAE, Professor Xiong Feng, offered all her support for the work. Graduate students of CAE also involved improving the graphics.

Du Shu is skillful for both languages. While she was finishing her Master degree at Columbia University, she carefully checked the text, especially the English part of the book.

In addition to the study of historic towns in Sichuan area, this book also contains articles on the comparisons of historic towns in western China and eastern China. We also have an article comparing the American and Chinese practice of managing the historic towns. All of these efforts are aimed to show the nation-wide and international experiences in maintaining, preserving the historic places.

对于古镇文化遗产的保护，应该引起全社会尤其是年轻人的关注。我们的文稿中，还收录了来自四川大学附属中学国际部中学生的古镇田野调查报告。在高放博士和相关老师的组织下，我作为客座导师，带领学生先后多次采访古镇居民，拍摄传统民居和古镇街景。高中生们对古镇的观察、记录和思考也是本书不可缺少的组成部分。

课题的研究和本书的出版，得到了四川瑞信实业集团有限责任公司董事长李向东先生的慷慨资助，在此深深感谢李先生的义举。本书能得以顺利出版，特别是以如此优雅的双语方式完成排版和印制，也要特别感激四川大学出版社的各位编辑的辛勤工作。

The successful preservation of culture and history needs cares from the whole society, especially from the young generations. Here in the book we have also included the works of high school students from international department of the Affiliated High School of Sichuan University. Dr. Gao Fang heads the American Program who organized students to make field trips to historic towns regularly. Being their project advisor, I had guided them to record the townscapes, vernacular architecture, and teach them to interview the native residents. Their documentation and reflection are also an indispensible part of this original study.

Mr. Li Xiangdong, the director of Sichuan Ruixin Industrial Group Co., Ltd., has kindly funded the research and the publication of this book. We thank him for his support. We are also grateful to the publisher who made this book in such a nice bi-lingual form.

黄运昇

2018 年 7 月于美国夏洛茨维尔（小镇）

Huang Yunsheng

Charlottesville, July 2018

序言二
Preface 2

　　本书缘起于 2012 年 3 月 9 日黄运昇教授到四川大学开办的一次讲座。讲座题目是"世界文化遗产的研究：理论、实践、方法"。自 20 世纪 90 年代起就开始接触中西建筑文化遗产的保护与实践，且一直关注中国传统人居文化遗产保护与更新的我，自然是听众之一。讲座后与黄教授的交流也是愉快的。当黄教授了解到我准备带学生对四川古镇进行测绘调研时，他很兴奋。在他看来，四川古镇的独特韵味是在世界上其他任何地方都找不到的。他当时就提出与我们一起对巴蜀古镇和乡土民居进行合作研究的愿望。

　　The cause of this book can be traced back to March 9th, 2012, the day when Prof. Huang Yunsheng came to give a lecture at Sichuan University. The lecture topic was "Research on World Cultural Legacy: Theory, Practice, and Method." As a scholar who had been introduced to the Chinese and western architectural legacy protection and practice, and who had been paying attention to the protection and regeneration of Chinese vernacular settlements, I was certainly among the audience. The conversation with Prof. Huang after the lecture was pleasant, and when Prof. Huang learnt that I was planning to take students to investigate and survey historic towns in Sichuan, he was very excited. In his eyes, the unique aroma of Sichuan historic towns cannot be found anywhere else in the world. He then proposed that we could conduct collaborative research on the historic towns and vernacular buildings in Sichuan area.

蜀韵古镇

HISTORIC TOWNS IN SICHUAN:
THE CULTURAL HERITAGE PROTECTION AND UTILIZATION OF
HISTORIC TOWNS WITH DIFFERENT DIMENSIONS AND VISIONS
——多维视野下的古镇文化遗产保护与利用

在随后的邮件中我们就合作方式进行了初步沟通与讨论。因为我的日常教学和公共服务的任务繁重，所以在2013 年至 2015 年期间，我只能在每年的暑期带本科生选择一个古镇进行古建测绘和调研。由于绝大多数学生绘制的测绘图纸无法一次性达到科研和出版要求，需要不断修改审核，花费了很多时间，因此科研计划一推再推。当黄教授 2014 年暑期再到成都约我见面讨论合作研究时，我十分惭愧，因为我这边的推进速度实在太慢，当时仅确定了让我的一位研究生围绕已经测绘的一个省级历史文化名镇历史街区进行保护更新策略的学位论文撰写。黄教授听完我的介绍不但没有埋怨反倒安慰我说，古建测绘的工作量巨大，是对历史建筑文化遗产保护进行学术性研究的基础，十分必要。同时，他也特别郑重地告诉我，其实文化遗产保护这个事业除了专业性的学术写作外，还有一个阵地也很重要，那就是面向大众的科普式公众教育。我对此也表示十分认同。

In the following emails, we made some initial communications and discussions regarding ways of collaboration. Yet, due to my rather heavy teaching and administration workloads, I was only able to keep taking my undergraduate students to complete the investigation and survey practices in three successive summers between 2013 and 2015. But because the surveyed drawings of most students could not reach the research and publication requirements in one attempt time, they all need to be checked, revised, and rechecked that took too much time, causing the research plan to be postponed again and again. When Prof. Huang made an appointment with me during his visit in Chengdu in the summer of 2014, I felt so abashed for the delayed research progress on my side, as I was only able to assign one of my graduate students to study the protection and regeneration strategy for one of the surveyed historic towns and its historic districts. After listening to my introduction, Prof. Huang not only didn't complain but also tried to comfort me by stressing the importance and necessity of conducting the historic town and building survey, which has always been a hard and time-consuming work, but an important base for conducting any academic research on historic architectural legacy protection. Meanwhile, he also told me in a serious way that, in addition to academic research and publication, another front is of the same importance, which is the public education through the format of popular science. I also strongly agree with this view.

原本以为相关合作事宜会就此搁置，没想到 2015 年的夏天，我又一次接到黄教授的电话，74 岁高龄的他又独自一人来成都了。原来他接受了四川大学附属中学国际部的邀请，担任中美高中学生"天府古镇研究"自主性研究课程指导教师，并且已带领高中生对成都周边几个古镇进行了调研考察。黄教授激动地将一本激光彩色打印的线圈装订初稿递到我手上，告诉我这是他先后指导他教授的中国和美国大中学生完成的系列古镇研究论文和报告。但他自己知道不管是文字还是图像信息等水平离正式出版还有距离，所以希望我能作为第一主编对内容进行编审把关。诚惶诚恐的我不知道该说什么，因为这实在出乎我的意料。

I thought that our collaboration would be suspended. But when I received Prof. Huang's phone call in the summer of 2015, I was shocked to learn that he came to Chengdu again alone at the age of 74. As he told me, he had been invited by the International Department of the Affiliated High School of Sichuan University to be the academic advisor for a group of high school students who had carried out an autonomous study on the historic towns within the Chengdu Plain. Prof. Huang handed a colorfully printed and coil-bound booklet to me in an excited way, and he told me that this was the first draft of a serial study and research on the historic towns by university students as well as high school students under his guidance. But he knew that there was still a distance between such a draft and a formal publication in terms of its texts and illustrations. So, he wished that I could play the role of the first editor-in-chief to check its content and make necessary revisions, adjustments, and supplements. With profound respect and humility, I didn't know what to say because this was really something I had never expected.

看出我的犹豫后，黄教授特别真诚地对我说，他年事已高，精力有限，身体在走下坡路，正是通过几次接触，他看到我对四川古镇文化遗产研究有着特别的执着和严谨，认为我是最合适的主编人选。的确，如果按照我对学术出版物发表的标准，这个初稿需要修改补充和完善的地方实在太多。但当我看到黄老先生期盼的眼神，当他一再强调这并非是学术性专著，而是一部面向公众的科普式读物时，当他表达希望在他结束教书生涯光荣退休之前能完成出版时，我实在不忍心推辞。

接下来的一年多时间里，我先邀请了在美国哥伦比亚大学建筑系求学的杜抒女士对初稿各部分的双语文字进行初步校对，再请我指导的 2016 级研究生瞿颖、周宏健、张振兴同学以及我远在美国的大学同窗陈为人、赵铁铮两位好友对文中涉及的图示和图片进行补充绘制、拍摄和处理。在此基础上，我再逐篇进行所有中英文以及图片资料的复核审校。这个过程没想到是如此漫长，加之因为 2016 年年底突发疾病，我被医生和家人勒令休养了半年多，所以直到 2018 年 4 月初，我才得以向出版社提交第二次修改后的书稿。

Aware of my hesitation, Prof. Huang explained to me in a sincere way about why he considered me as the best person to be the first editor-in-chief. He was getting old with limited energy and not so optimistic health condition, while I was the one who had been dedicated to and rigorous in the cultural research on Sichuan's historic town legacy. Indeed, according to my own standard of academic publication, such a draft was far from ready and needed huge amounts of revisions, adjustments, and supplements. But when I saw the expression in Prof. Huang's eyes, when he kept on stressing that this book was not aimed to be an academic work but a public education material for popular science audience, which he wished to see its publication before his retirement, I could not say no.

In the following year, I invited Ms. Du Shu, who is studying architecture at Columbia University, to make initial proofreading upon all parts of bilingual texts, and then asked my graduate students, Qu Ying, Zhou Hongjian and Zhang Zhenxing, my college friends and classmates, Chen Weiren and Zhao Tiezheng (now living in America) to help take additional photos and make necessary drawings. Based upon such initial efforts, I started to double-check all texts and illustrations page by page for necessary revisions and adjustments. The process was already unexpectedly long, and on top of that, an unexpected health problem at the end of 2016 forced me to recuperate for half a year before I could work again. Therefore, I could only manage to submit the second proofreading and editing version to the publisher by early April of 2018.

在此，首先真诚地感谢黄教授及其指导的所有学生的付出，弗吉尼亚大学建筑学院前古镇研究小组的王一洲、伍秋帆、黄辰颖、田阳、杨莽华、Megan Glynn 完成了本书上篇及中篇初稿，感谢四川大学附属中学中美高中古镇研究项目组的老师王桂芳、王婧以及学生刘瑞楷、郭昊、许愿、王馨之、蔡依言、黄维浩、张玉婷、杨雷晚秋、万国婕、吴颖、范松琪、罗佳明、吴铭洋、曾心怡、陈沁瑜、田涵瑶、刘羽昆、黄兆瑜、马子林、高崇浩、胡锦烨、段昊明、吴采翼、杜亚熹、曹磊、程荟铭、刘宇豪、王韵琪、韩雨扬、周子暄、程皖津、刘思宇、吴杭、张澜川、刘一、宋鑫宇、韩旭、鲍秋留洋、Peiwen Jiang、高川翔、陈柯伊、张丝怡、何艾青、宋佳洋、张婉旎、林莹莹等完成了下篇书稿。

特别感谢李向东先生对本书出版的慷慨赞助，感谢四川大学建筑与环境学院熊峰院长的大力支持，感谢四川大学出版社王军社长、邱小平总编等对本书的高度认可。感谢家人在我生病时无微不至的关怀和照顾，在我熬夜加班时的理解和包容。

I would like to firstly and sincerely thank Prof. Huang and all his students who had contributed greatly to the formation of this book. They are Wang Yizhou, Wu Qiufan, Huang Chenying, Tian Yang, Yang Manghua, and Megan Glynn, members of the historic town research group at the College of Architecture, University of Virginia. Teachers and students from the Affiliated High School of Sichuan University who carried out the historic town research project, including teachers, Wang Guifang, and Wang Qian, and students, Liu Ruikai, Guo Hao, Xu Yuan, Wang Xinzhi, Cai Yiyan, Huang Weihao, Zhang Yuting, Yang-lei Wanqiu, Wan Guojie, Wu Ying, Fan Songqi, Luo Jiaming, Wu Mingyang, Zeng Xinyi, Chen Qinyu, Tian Hanyao, Liu Yukun, Huang Zhaoyu, Ma Zilin, Gao Chonghao, Hu Jinye, Duan Haoming, Wu Caiyi, Du Yaxi, Cao Lei, Cheng Huiming, Liu Yuhao, Wang Yunqi, Hao Yuyang, Zhou Zixuan, Cheng Wanjin, Liu Siyu, Wu Hang, Zhang Lanchuan, Liu Yi, Song Xinyu, Han Xu, Baoqiu Liuyang, Peiwen Jiang, Gao Chuanxiang, Chen Keyi, Zhang Siyi, He Aiqing, Song Jiayang, Zhang Wanni, and Lin Yingying, etc.

Special thanks to Mr. Li Xiangdong, who is so generous in sponsoring the publication of this book. Thanks to Prof. Xiong Feng, Dean of College of Architecture & Environment, Sichuan University, who has provided me with great support in the editorial and publication process. Thanks to Mr. Wang Jun, Director of Sichuan University Press, and Ms. Qiu Xiaoping, Chief Editor of Sichuan University Press, who have given high recognition to the edited draft. Thanks to my family who have provided meticulous care and attention when I was sick and who have shown great understanding and tolerance when I had to stay up late and work overtime.

当书稿经过四川大学出版社张晶、敬铃凌两位编辑以及周明倩、金谷曼两位年轻实习编辑的认真修订和排版师傅的努力变得如此赏心悦目时，我终于可以长舒一口气，觉得自己前前后后所做的一切工作或许可以不负黄教授的重托，不负相关人士的期许。希望这本书的出版可以帮助更多的人关注中国古镇的发展与文化遗产保护，对四川地区其他特色古镇在未来得到更加理性、负责、创新的保护和利用尽绵薄之力。

When the revised book draft had become enjoyable to read with the help of my two editors, Ms. Zhang Jing and Ms. Jing Lingling, and two young intern editors, Ms. Zhou Mingqian and Ms. Jin Guman, in addition to the effort of the composing master, I could finally relax, feeling that all work that had been done in the whole process was worthwhile, and able to live up to the trust and expectation of Prof. Huang and all related people. I sincerely hope that the publication of this book will help draw more people's attention to the cultural legacy protection and development of Chinese historic towns, and especially promote a more rational, responsible and creative protection and utilization of those unique historic towns in the Sichuan region.

赵春兰

2018 年 8 月写于成都

Zhao Chunlan

Chengdu, August 2018

Contents

目录

中篇 Part II：

对比阅读 Comparative Reading

下篇 Part III：

关于文化遗产的公众教育 On the Public Education of Cultural Heritage

上篇：
天府古镇考察

Part I:
Investigations on
Tianfu Historic Towns

　　本篇是对十个比较有代表性的四川古镇的综述，包括代表客家移民文化的洛带古镇，反映独特山水环境下聚落民居特征的黄龙溪、柳江、街子古镇等，反映独特建筑形态和类型特征的罗城和安仁古镇，反映主导产业特征的罗泉古镇，作为茶马古道重要驿站的平乐和上里古镇，以及因抗战作为临时全国科研中心的李庄古镇……走进本篇，读者可从历史沿革、文化渊源、建筑景观、节庆活动、美食民俗等不同的角度，认识和了解每个古镇独特的内涵和气质，帮助大家更好地理解为何成都平原这块土地上会涌现出如此风韵独特的古镇。

　　In this part, ten representative historic towns in Sichuan are reviewed, such as Luodai, which reflects the Hakka immigrant culture; Huanglongxi, Liujiang and Jiezi, which contain unique settlement and vernacular building features affected by unique environmental conditions; Luocheng and Anren, which are featured in their unique architecture forms and typologies; Luoquan, which reflects its main industry; Pingle and Shangli, which used to be the key posts along the Ancient Tea-Horse Trading Route; and finally Lizhuang that was once the temporary national science and research center during the period of Anti-Japanese War.... Let's walk into these historic towns to try learn and understand their unique meanings and qualities through different angles such as historic evolutions, cultural origins, architecture and landscape, holidays and activities, gourmet and folklores, thereby helping people understand why and how so many special historic towns could emerge from the soil of the Chengdu Plain.

I 总论：
概念定义和研究场地

Introduction:
Definitions and Research Sites

　　为了确保此次对天府古镇的研究工作富有针对性，在研究伊始我们就对研究对象和研究范围做出了明确的定义。被定义的内容包括"历史古镇"、研究场地成都平原以及关于李庄的特例研究。在明确这些定义时，我们着重参考了中华人民共和国住房和城乡建设部（简称"住建部"）的现行法律法规，结合历史保护研究的具体意义和实际情况，以期达到历史与实际相结合、开发与保护相融合的目的。

　　In order to make our research and exploration precise and highly focused, we have to clearly and selectively define our research objects and sites from the beginning. These concepts include "historic towns," the Chengdu Plain, our research sites, and the special case study about Lizhuang. While formulating these definitions, we have paid particular attention to the current laws and regulations of the Ministry of Housing and Urban-Rural Development of the People's Republic of China (MOHURD) with references to the practical conditions of the historic preservation. We hope to accomplish our purpose to reach the common ground between the history and today, as well as between development and preservation.

1. "历史古镇"定义 Definition of "historic towns"

根据中华人民共和国住房与城乡建设部和国家文物局的相关规定，考虑到实际情况，本次研究的"历史古镇"将按照以下标准定义：

(1) 历史价值：该历史古镇拥有的建筑遗产和文物古迹能较完整地反映某一历史时期的传统风貌、地方特色和民族风情。

(2) 时间性：该历史古镇的大致形成时间应处于夏朝（约公元前 21 世纪—前 16 世纪）以后，五四爱国运动（1919 年）以前的时间段内。

(3) 规模：该历史古镇现存的历史传统建筑的建筑面积须在 5000 平方米以上，且分布较为集中。

(4) 原状保存程度：镇内历史传统建筑、建筑细部及周边环境基本上原貌保存完好；或因年代久远，原建筑群、建筑物和周边环境虽曾倒塌破坏，但已按原貌整修恢复；或原建筑群和周边环境虽部分倒塌破坏，但主要部分尚存且部分建筑细部保存完好，其余部分已依据实物的结构、构造和样式原貌修复。

According to the regulations of the Ministry of Housing and Urban-Rural Development of the People's Republic of China and China's State Administration of Cultural Heritage and considering the practical situation, "historic towns" in this research are defined by:

(1) Historic Value: the historic town shall have the architectural heritage, historic sites, and cultural relics that can be a relatively complete reflection of the traditional features, vernacular characters, and ethnic customs of a certain historical period.

(2) Time: the approximate formation time of the historic town shall fall between the Xia Dynasty (c. 21st century B.C.–16th century B.C.) and the May 4th Movement (1919 A.D.).

(3) Magnitude/Scale: the extant traditional architectural heritage shall have a building area larger than 5,000 square meters with considerable extent of concentration.

(4) Current Condition of Original State: the historic architectural complex, architectural elements, and surrounding sites of the historic town are mostly well preserved, the original complex and site were collapsed or destroyed due to time but have already been reconstructed in accordance with original appearance, or the complex and site are partially undermined, but the main component and some architectural elements are well-preserved, and the rest is restored in accordance with the original appearance, styles, and structures.

HISTORIC TOWNS IN SICHUAN:
THE CULTURAL HERITAGE PROTECTION AND UTILIZATION OF
HISTORIC TOWNS WITH DIFFERENT DIMENSIONS AND VISIONS
——多维视野下的古镇文化遗产保护与利用

2. 研究场地：成都平原的定义　Research site: Definition on "Chengdu Plain"

广义的成都平原位于龙泉山脉、龙门山脉和邛崃山脉之间，北起江油市，南至乐山五通桥区，包括北部的涪江冲积平原，中部岷江、沱江冲积平原和南部的青衣江、大渡河冲积平原，总面积约 23 000 平方公里。因位于平原中部的成都市而得名。

以下所列古镇仅仅是大四川地区众多历史古镇中很小的一部分。事实上，在成都平原之外还有很多值得我们关注的古镇，它们的文化和历史价值不容忽视。因此，我们也选择了位于成都平原之外，但在四川省内的另一特色古镇进行对比考察。李庄有着 1460 年的建置历史，位于宜宾东郊和长江南岸，被称为"万里长江第一古镇"。在抗日战争时期，李庄是同济大学、中国营造学社等高校和科研机构内迁之地，成为中国人民不屈不挠的民族精神象征地。

Geographically, Chengdu Plain is broadly defined as the area surrounded by Longquan Mountain, Longmen Mountain, and Qionglai Mountain. The area starts from the city of Jiangyou on the north and ends at the District of Wutongqiao of Leshan on the south. It primarily includes Fujiang River Fluvial Plain in the north, Minjiang-Tuojiang River Fluvial Plain in the center, and Qingyijiang-Daduhe River Fluvial Plain in the south. The overall area is 23,000 square kilometers. It is named as "Chengdu Plain" because the city of Chengdu was situated in the middle of the plain.

The major sites chosen below are only a very small portion of the historic towns of the grand Sichuan area. In fact, some other historic towns beyond Chengdu Plain also strongly caught our attention, as they do have strong cultural or historical values that we can't afford to ignore. Therefore, this text will select a few distinctive historic towns outside Chengdu Plain but within Sichuan Province to be studied, with comparisons to the sites above. Lizhuang, with a history of 1,460 years, is situated on the east suburb of Yibin Municipality and on the south bank of Yangtze River. It is widely known as "the first historic town on the endless Yangtze River." During the Anti-Japanese War period, Lizhuang hosted several important universities and institutions including Tongji and the Society for the Research in Chinese Architecture. It has become a representation of China's national ethos of perseverance.

我们将主要考察位于成都平原地区的几个历史古镇（图 1）。它们的一个共同特点是：它们都保留和反映了当地独特的地域文化和传统。

洛带古镇　于三国时期（220 年—280 年）创建，后以其独有的客家文化著称。古镇上的传统建筑面积达到 2 万平方米。

平乐古镇　最早建镇于西汉时期（前 206 年—25 年），现在保留的明清时期的传统建筑面积约 23.54 万平方米。它不仅因其古街和川西民俗而闻名，还有"茶马古道第一镇""南丝绸之路第一驿站"的美誉。

安仁古镇　始建于唐朝（618 年—907 年），现存的传统建筑和街道成型于晚清和民国时期。除了历史性的街道和传统木构建筑，它还拥有约 30 万平方米的公馆建筑。

黄龙溪古镇　有 1700 余年的历史，曾经是古蜀国的重要军事要冲。现今保存的传统建筑达 3.12 万平方米，同时还保留着各式各样当地的民间艺术，是成都平原休闲文化的代表。

罗城古镇　始建于明崇祯元年（1628 年），它是中国唯一一个将街道建成船形的古镇，也是四川井盐贸易中心之一。

罗泉古镇　始建于秦朝，作为古镇的历史已超过 1700 年。罗泉是四川盐文化的一个重要据点，也是中国唯一建有盐神庙的古镇。

柳江古镇　始建于南宋绍兴十年（1140 年），以"柳江烟雨"著称，有大量保存完好的明清时期的传统建筑。

上里古镇　其历史超过了 1500 年。自唐朝起，它就是南方丝绸之路和唐蕃古道上的一个重要驿站，保留有大量明清时期式样的木构民居建筑。

街子古镇　在五代时期就已经十分繁华，是清代西南地区小镇的最好代表之一。古镇有大量保存完好的庙宇和民居，其建筑与当地的自然环境和文化融合紧密。

This research will mainly focus on several historic towns on the Chengdu Plain (Fig. 1). These towns share the characteristics of strong historic connection to the local area and proper reflection of distinct local culture and traditions.

Luodai was initially built during the Three-Kingdom Period (220 A.D.–280 A.D.). Luodai is famous for its Hakka Culture. The total building area of traditional architecture reaches over 20,000 square meters.

蜀韵古镇
HISTORIC TOWNS IN SICHUAN:
THE CULTURAL HERITAGE PROTECTION AND UTILIZATION OF
HISTORIC TOWNS WITH DIFFERENT DIMENSIONS AND VISIONS
——多维视野下的古镇文化遗产保护与利用

Pingle was initially formed as a town in West Han Dynasty (206 B.C.–25A.D.). The major area has traditional architecture from Ming and Qing dynasties with a total building area exceeding 235,400 square meters. It is famous for not only its ancient streets and vernacular convention of West Sichuan, but also for its being the first post house on the South Silk Road and the first town on the Ancient Tea-Horse Route.

Anren was initially built during the Tang Dynasty (618 A.D.–907 A.D.). Anren's current traditional architecture and streets were erected in the late Qing Dynasty and the early period of the Republic of China. It has historic streets, traditional architecture in wooden structure, and a manor with a total building area of approximately 300,000 square meters.

Huanglongxi has a history of more than 1,700 years and was the key military place of Ancient Shu Kingdom. Currently, it possesses a group of well preserved traditional architecture with a total floor area of around 31,200 square meters. Huanglongxi has kept a myriad of old vernacular conventions or folkloric arts and is the representative of the Leisure Culture in the Chengdu Plain.

Luocheng was initially built during the Ming Dynasty during the first year of Chongzhen (1628 A.D.). It has the only boat-shaped traditional street in China. It was also an important trading center for Sichuan well salt.

Luoquan was initially formed during the Qin Dynasty and has a history as a town for over 1,700 years. Luoquan is the focal point of the salt culture of Sichuan, where the Temple of the God of Salt is located, a unique temple in honor of the God of Salt.

Liujiang was initially built during the Song Dynasty, in the tenth year of Shaoxing (1140 A.D.). It is famously known as "Liujiang in the Misty Rain." Liujiang has considerable amounts of well preserved traditional buildings from the Ming and Qing Dynasties.

Shangli has a long history spanning more than 1,500 years. Starting from the Tang Dynasty, Shangli had been an important post house of the South Silk Road and the Tang-Tibet Ancient Trading Route. It has well preserved the Ming-Qing styled traditional houses in wooden structure.

Jiezi has prospered since the Five-Dynasties Period (907 A.D.–960 A.D.). Jiezi well preserves considerable amounts of old temples and vernacular houses. It is also the best representative of small towns in the southwest part of the Qing Dynasty, whose architectural development was closely integrated with nature and local culture.

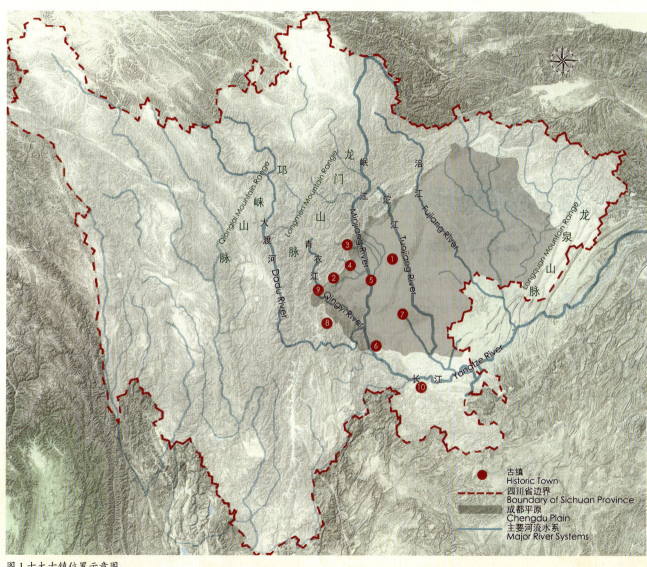

图 1 十大古镇位置示意图
Fig. 1 Location map of ten historic towns

1 洛带 Luodai
2 平乐 Pingle
3 街子 Jiezi
4 安仁 Anren
5 黄龙溪 Huanglongxi
6 罗城 Luocheng
7 罗泉 Luoquan
8 柳江 Liujiang
9 上里 Shangli
10 李庄 Lizhuang

II 分论
十个古镇

Ten Historic Towns

洛带 Luodai

　　洛带古镇坐落于成都市龙泉驿区以北 10 公里处，属龙泉山脉中段的二峨山山麓。因位于亚热带季风气候区，冬无严寒，夏无酷暑。洛带靠近中国中西部地区经济最发达的地区，与地区内的高速公路、机场、铁路、经济技术开发区接近，拥有得天独厚的区位优势。

　　Luodai is situated 10 kilometers north of the Longquanyi District of Chengdu, at the foot of Er'e Mountain, which belongs to the middle part of the Longquan Mountain Range. Located in the region of subtropical monsoon climate, Luodai enjoys a weather without bitter winters or scorching summers. Luodai is close to the most developed area of mid-west China and therefore akin to the economic and communications resources, including expressways, airports, railways, and economic technical development areas.

广东会馆 Guangdong *Huiguan*
湖广会馆 Huguang *Huiguan*
江西会馆 Jiangxi *Huiguan*
川北会馆 North Sichuan *Huiguan*
—— 主要道路 Main Road
古镇边界 Historic Town Scope
绿地 Green Land

图 2 洛带古镇范围及主要建筑分布示意图
Fig. 2 Diagram of Luodai historic town's scope and its major buildings

洛带（图2）在三国时就已有街，名"万景街"；后于三国时蜀汉丞相诸葛亮兴市，更名为"万福街"。"洛带"原作"落带"，因此地有一"天落之水状如玉带"之河，故称"落带"。镇名的另一说法与蜀汉后主刘禅相关：相传其身佩玉带落入镇旁八角井而更名为"落带"，后演变为"洛带"。洛带在唐宋时期已发展为成都府灵泉县（今成都市龙泉驿区）一个较大的地区性集镇。至此，外来人口逐渐增加，并建立各自的会馆，体现了不同区域的文化精神内涵。自明清时期起，由于"湖广填四川"，客家人开始大量由广东地区迁入并定居，在语言、建筑、饮食、服装、音乐等方面融入当地文化并影响塑造了新的洛带本土文化。

Luodai (Fig. 2) formed its first street during the Three-kingdom Period. Initially named "Wanjing Street," it later evolved into a town when Zhuge Liang was the prime minister, and the street was renamed as "Wangfu Street." The name "Luodai" (in Chinese translated as "a dropped belt") came from the river nearby described as "the water dropped from the sky like jade belt." Another version came from the last emperor of Shu-Han Dynasty, Liu Chan, who dropped his jade belt into the octagonal well. The dropping belt then evolved into another homonym called "Luodai." Luodai turned into Lingquan County of Chengdu (today's Longquanyi District of Chengdu) during the Tang and Song dynasties. From then on, the external population started to increase and brought with them their own culture in the form of *Huiguan* (assembly halls for fellow provincials). In the period of the Ming and Qing Dynasties, due to the movement known as "Hu-Guang Fills Sichuan," the Hakka people migrated from the Guangdong Province and settled in Luodai, bringing their culture and blending it into the locality of Luodai in the domains of language, architecture, food, clothing, music, etc.

图 3 湖广会馆面向老街的立面
Fig. 3 Street facade of the Huguang *Huiguan*

　　客家人最早伴随着"湖广填四川"西进进入四川，定居于成都东郊洛带镇。在此以后，洛带逐渐发展成为中国西部客家人最为集中的小镇。目前洛带超过 90% 的人口为客家人，他们仍然说客家方言，沿袭客家习俗。

　　The Hakka people first appeared in Luodai during the migration from Hunan and Guangdong to Sichuan. From then on, Luodai gradually developed into the most intensive habitat for the Hakka people in western China. Currently, Hakka inhabitants form over 90 percent of Luodai's population, and they are still speaking the Hakka dialect and practicing Hakka customs.

随着大量客家人从外地涌入，洛带本地的文化也受到了影响并发生改变，最为明显的即是会馆。会馆，原是一批同乡人在外地生活工作之时所建的居住、办公兼休闲场所，通常为来客提供客房和会议室，大的会馆甚至还有戏楼。洛带现存的客家会馆建筑群是客家同乡聚会议事和祭祀的中心，是移民们的聚集地。

洛带客家会馆建筑群规模宏大，布局考究，既反映了客家文化的建筑风貌，又融入了四川当地的建筑特色。总体而言，这些会馆建筑内部结构细腻精巧，雕饰图案栩栩如生，技艺精湛。客家会馆以中轴线对称布局，并由于移民的缘故，在朝向上坐北朝南，寓意对岭南故乡的无限思念之情。会馆的入门楼即为戏楼或大型戏台，也有将戏楼设于内院的，其两侧多为两层厢房，中为大坝，这是举行大型祭祀或开展娱乐活动的场所，它们既相对独立，又与正堂主厅紧密相连。目前洛带有四大客家会馆，分别为广东会馆、湖广会馆（图3）、江西会馆和川北会馆。

With considerable numbers of Hakka people migrating into Luodai, its local culture and fabric have been altered and influenced. The most salient proof is the construction of *Huiguan*. *Huiguan* was usually built by a group of people from the same place but living in a non-native area. Usually a complete building complex, such club houses in Luodai function as a gathering center for Hakka people to meet, discuss, and hold rituals. They are equipped with residential facilities, official areas, and recreational utilities. Normally, it is composed of guest rooms, meeting rooms, and some large ones even have theater buildings.

Hakka *Huiguan* complexes in Luodai are built in monumental scale with elaborate composition. They not only embody the architectural styles and features of Hakka culture but also incorporate the characteristics of Sichuan local culture. In general, these buildings have subtle internal structure and components that serve both mechanical and ornamental purposes. The carving and engraving decoration in these buildings are highly lifelike with exquisite craftsmanship. Hakka *Huiguan*s implement all this in a symmetrical layout. Thanks to the migration, these buildings sit in the north facing the south, resembling their endless homesickness for their hometown in the southern area of the Five Ridges. The entrance building of these *Huiguan* complexes is a huge theatrical stage, which can also be placed in the inner area. The side architecture is usually made up of two-story wing rooms, with a large open-ground space in the middle for large-scale rituals or entertainment activities. They are either independent themselves or attached tightly with the principle hall. At present, Luodai has four Hakka *Huiguan* unique spaces: Guangdong *Huiguan*, Huguang *Huiguan* (Fig. 3), Jiangxi *Huiguan,* and North-Sichuan *Huiguan*.

图 4 洛带老街街道
Fig. 4 Old street scene in Luodai

广东会馆于康熙十一年（1672年）由广东籍客家人出资修建，供奉在南华寺弘法的禅宗六祖慧能，故又名"南华宫"。整个建筑群建筑面积达3310平方米。该会馆大部分建筑于清朝末期毁于火灾，于1913年重建。为表达对岭南故乡的思念之情，广东会馆的总体朝向为坐西北朝东南。由于洛带镇的主街（图4）位于会馆以北，为遵循这一特定朝向的传统，会馆不惜牺牲交通的便利性而背部临街。广东会馆所处的位置位于该区域内的相对高点，这样其使用者向北可以俯瞰洛带古镇全貌，向南可以远眺龙泉山脉的自然风光。

Guangdong *Huiguan* was funded by Hakka people from Guangdong in 1672. It is also named as Nanhua Palace, as it offers oblation to Huineng, the sixth Patriarch of Zen Buddhism at the Nanhua Temple. The overall building area of the complex is 3,310 square meters. The majority of the compound was damaged by a fire during the late Qing Dynasty and was rebuilt in 1913. The basic orientation of the Guangdong *Huiguan* strictly follows the Hakka tradition facing south-east to express the homesickness of the Hakka people. Since the major street of Luodai (Fig. 4) is to the north side of the building, the complex even sacrifices the convenience of transportation with its back facing the street in order to keep such an orientation rule. The site is located on a relatively highland comparing to the surroundings, which allows people in this building compound to have the chance to enjoy a panoramic view of the entire historic Luodai town and the natural landscape of the Longquan Mountain.

蜀韵古镇

HISTORIC TOWNS IN SICHUAN:
THE CULTURAL HERITAGE PROTECTION AND UTILIZATION OF
HISTORIC TOWNS WITH DIFFERENT DIMENSIONS AND VISIONS
——多维视野下的古镇文化遗产保护与利用

整个会馆建筑群的复四合院布局为传统的轴对称状，主要建筑如戏台、乐楼、耳楼、前院以及三座大殿均沿对称轴线性分布。为了保持整个布局的完整性，尤其是戏台的宏伟，会馆的正门开在戏台下方净高仅有两米左右的空间中，通向前院。作为大多数建筑群的共同特点，一个开阔的前院通常是不可缺少的，因为大家可以方便地在此交流聚会。洛带广东会馆的前院（图5）面积约为500平方米，是大多数会馆活动举行的场所，比如聚会、交谈、民俗文化表演和祭祀拜祖等。这样的功能和会馆本身作为客家民族在西部的聚集地的作用是密不可分的。在人们进入前院之前，他们的视线会被戏台底部低矮的通道限制，通过之后，一个宽广的前院会突然呈现在他们眼前，这种强烈的视觉和心理的差异能够更加突出前院的宽阔，强调它的空间功能。

图 5 广东会馆前院 *
Fig. 5 Front courtyard of Guangdong *Huiguan*

The basic multi-quadrangle composition of the *Huiguan* compound is traditional with axial symmetry. Major building structures, including theater stages, orchestra buildings, wing buildings, courtyards, and three grand halls, are arranged linearly along the axis of symmetry. In order to keep the integrity of this composition, especially the grandiosity of the theater stage, the entrance of the facade is located under the stage with very limited height of some two meters. As one of the universal precedents of the architecture complex, the expansive front courtyard is often indispensable for social function of public gathering and communication. The front courtyard in Guangdong *Huiguan* (Fig. 5) behind the theater buildings has an approximate area of 500 square meters. It plays an important role for public meetings, conversation, folk culture shows, and certain rituals which are all in accordance with the function of *Huiguan*, a gathering place for Hakka people. Before entering this courtyard, people's vision will be severely constrained by the passageway under the theater buildings. Afterwards, the open courtyard will suddenly show up in front of their eyes. This huge visual and psychological contrast strongly emphasizes the spatial expansiveness and function of the courtyard.

　　前院后面是会馆的单檐卷棚式硬山瓦顶前殿。硬山顶出现时间较晚，宋朝论述建筑工程的官方著作《营造法式》中并无记载。据推测，这种五脊二坡式屋顶可能是随明清时期砖石结构的兴起而开始大量使用的。硬山顶利于防风火，其最大的特点在于其两侧山墙把檩头全部包封住，使其屋檐不出山墙。然而客家人在建造前殿的同时考虑了洛带的气候特点，洛带位于亚热带季风气候区，降水充沛，而硬山顶本身不利于防雨，故广东会馆前殿的硬山式屋顶结构又加入了卷棚顶的变形，使其在雨季的防雨性能更好。

At the back of the front courtyard is the front hall with a single-cornice, round-shed, Yingshan tile roof. This Yingshan roof appears relatively late; at least it was not recorded in the *Official Treatise on Architectural Methods and State Building Standards* of the Song Dynasty. Such a five-ridge and double pitch roof was likely to get popular during the Ming and Qing periods with the prevalence of masonry construction. It is known for being good at preventing damage from wind and fire. The most salient feature of this five-ridge, double-slope roof is that the side gables completely contain the purlin so that the cornice does not exceed the gable. However, the Hakka people have made significant changes to the prototype of Yingshan roof. Because Luodai is situated in the subtropical monsoon climate region with abundant rainfalls and Yingshan roof is weak at preventing rain runoff, this round-shed roof helps to improve the performance during the rainy season.

蜀韵古镇

HISTORIC TOWNS IN SICHUAN:
THE CULTURAL HERITAGE PROTECTION AND UTILIZATION OF
HISTORIC TOWNS WITH DIFFERENT DIMENSIONS AND VISIONS
——多维视野下的古镇文化遗产保护与利用

　　会馆前殿（图6）并不是一个独立的封闭空间，它没有门，而是直接面对开放的前院。这种空间的开放性使前殿极大地延伸了前院的空间和其作为公共聚会场所的社会功能。同时为从前殿进入中殿的人们提供了一个空间缓冲。从前殿进入中殿之前还有一个天井，天井中央有一个小水池，这个水池和池中的假山以及盆景植物一起为这里的开放空间营造了一处别致的景观，为前殿和中殿增添了生机和魅力。

　　中殿制式类似于前殿，由青瓦做顶，沿整个建筑群的中轴线轴对称布局。中殿的主体结构由一排正面双列廊柱和一道承重墙支撑。墙柱之间形成一个正交的议事空间，并以主次座的方式布置有桌椅，供客家长辈举行正式会议和讨论时使用。

　　The front hall of *Huiguan* (Fig. 6) is not a closed independent space. It doesn't have doors or gates and faces directly toward the front yard. This openness extends the social function of the courtyards for public gathering while providing a buffer for people entering the middle hall. In front of the middle hall, there is a small courtyard with a pond in the center. This pond, together with the rockwork and vegetation, creates an exquisite landscape that enhances the liveliness and attraction of the front and middle halls.

　　Similar to the front hall, the middle hall has a roof composed of gray tiles and is symmetrical. The structure of the middle hall is supported by facade dipteral columns and a single load-bearing wall at the back. Therefore, the space between the columns and the wall forms a completely orthogonal parlor with chairs arranged hierarchically for the formal meetings and discussions of Hakka leaders.

图 6 在广东会馆前殿门廊里休息的客家人
Fig. 6 The Hakka people sitting in the corridor of the front hall of Guangdong *Huiguan*

最后也是最恢宏的建筑就是广东会馆的正殿（图7）。这座正殿面阔 23 米，通进深 11.13 米，全高 16 米，屋面覆有黄色的琉璃瓦，为三层木质结构，重檐歇山顶。这种九脊歇山顶的上部为硬山或悬山顶，下部为庑殿顶，两层之间由中部"折断"。歇山顶融合了直线和斜线，造成棱角分明、结构清晰的视觉效果。在中国古代等级森严的建筑规格下，歇山顶规格极高，尤其是重檐歇山。在很长一段时间内，只有五品以上官吏的住宅正堂才被允许使用。同时，其正殿屋顶所使用的金黄色琉璃瓦在中国古代很长的一段时间内一直是皇家独享的颜色和材质，广东会馆使用这种逾制的屋顶体现了客家人在当地经济文化中举足轻重的地位。正殿的楼上是粤王台，人们可循梯而上遥望自己远在广东的故乡。

The last but the grandest structure in Guangdong *Huiguan* is the main hall (Fig. 7). The main hall has a width of 23 meters, a depth of 11.13 meters, and an overall height of 16 meters, with its major surface covered with golden glazed tiles. It is a three-floor wooden structure with multi-cornice *Xieshan* roof. This high-level roof style has nine ridges with Yingshan or *Xuanshan* on the top and Wudian roof at the bottom. Between these two levels is a kink that combines the straight lines and oblique lines. This style would provide a visual style of high angularity and clear hierarchy. In the strict traditional Chinese architectural hierarchy, this *Xieshan* style is considered very noble in most periods; only the main residential building of fifth-rank officials or above was allowed to use it. Besides, the color of the glazed tiles, gold, has been reserved for the royal family exclusively in ancient China. The frequent use of these high-level architectural and decorative components in Guangdong *Huiguan* reflects the significantly influential status of Hakka people in the local area. The upper part of the main hall is the Stage of Yuewang (the King of Guangdong), where Hakka people can climb up along the stairs to look afar to their hometown in Guangdong.

图 7 广东会馆正殿
Fig. 7 The main hall of Guangdong *Huiguan*

　　广东会馆各殿在结构上均入乡随俗，采用了四川当地典型的穿斗式结构。这种结构房屋的进深方向按檩数立一排柱，每柱上架一檩，檩上布椽，屋面荷载直接由檩传至柱。每排柱子靠穿透柱身的穿枋横向贯穿起来，成一榀架构。每两榀架构之间由斗枋和纤子连在一起，形成一间房间的空间构架。由于柱头直接接檩，而无须通过梁去传递载荷，故穿斗式结构比其他木质结构承重力更好。然而，这种结构在中国北方极少出现，因为其用料偏纤细，对砖结构的厚重屋面承载力不足，同时落地柱较多，不宜形成较大的完整空间。然而，穿斗结构在中国南方被大量使用，尤其在长江流域的四川地区，是一种典型结构。

The structures of Guangdong *Huiguan*'s several major halls incorporate the local character of Sichuan by implementing the *Chuandou* structure. Along the depth, buildings with this structure have rows of column according to the amount of purlins, which lies above each column and under the rafter. *Chuandou* structure will pass the load of the roof from purlins to columns directly without the beam as media. Each row of columns is attached horizontally with the square pillars penetrating through. These components thus form a structure of "Ping," while every two of the Ping structures are connected by wooden pillar, hence constituting a complete space. *Chuandou* structure usually performs better than normal roof structures in bearing weight, but it hardly withstands the heavy brick structure due to its slim materials. What is more, the complete *Chuandou* structure requires a considerable amount of columns landing on the ground. This demanding condition hinders this structure from being able to form large interior space. Therefore, the style rarely appears in northern China. Instead, it is widely used in the southern China, especially in the Yangtze River basin with Sichuan as the typical representative.

这三殿相互之间由庑廊相连，构成两个天井。这种三殿两井的结构侧面由高大厚重的砖砌封火山墙（图8）组成。这些山墙都是动感十足的腾龙造型，这样的构型不仅丰富了主要结构庄严肃穆的感觉，而且为洛带古镇勾勒出了优美流畅的天际线，逐渐成为古镇的标志性结构。从文化融合的角度来讲，封火山墙是地域文化交融的典型明证。明清以前巴蜀等地的建筑墙体无论是官式还是民间都未有如此鲜明的风格。正是由于"湖广填四川"这种大规模的移民运动，才会使封火山墙随着会馆建筑群整体在四川地区流行起来，以至在后来，更多地出现在会馆和公馆等建筑群落中。

These three halls are connected by hip galleries (Wulang) constituting of two courtyards. On both sides of such compositions are the lofty and massive brick fire-sealing gables (Fig. 8). These gables are all in the highly dynamic shape of dragons that enrich the solemn styles for the major halls and roofs. Furthermore, these dragon-shaped walls define the curvature and elegant skylines of Luodai. As a result, they have gradually become the landmark structures of Luodai. From the perspective of cultural fusion, fire-sealing gables are the typical proof of regional cultural interaction. Before Ming-Qing period, the wall structures didn't have such sharp characteristics in neither official styles nor civil use in the grand Sichuan area. It wasn't until a massive migration movement like "Hu-Guang Fills Sichuan" that the fire-sealing gables would rise in popularity along with the entire *Huiguan* architectural complex, and later with more prominence in other *Huiguan* compound and villa residences.

图 8 从街道看广东会馆的封火墙
Fig. 8 The fire-sealing gable wall of Guangdong *Huiguan* viewed from the main street

平乐古镇（图 9）坐落于成都西南部，地处亚热带湿润性气候地区，降水充沛。发源于天台山玉霄峰的白沫江流经古镇，平乐拥有良好的生态环境。作为四川最重要的历史文化名镇之一，平乐深受各级政府的重视，规划保护方案和体系完善，目前 85% 的古建筑仍保存完好或被复建。

Pingle (Fig. 9) is situated to the southwest of Chengdu. Located in the subtropical humid zone with the Baimo River winding through, Pingle enjoys a great ecological ambience with abundant precipitation. As one of the most culturally important towns in Sichuan, Pingle is carefully protected and meticulously planned by various levels of government. 85 percent of the traditional architecture in this town is well preserved or restored.

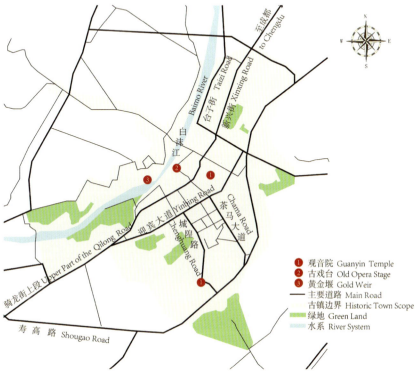

观音院 Guanyin Temple
古戏台 Old Opera Stage
黄金堰 Gold Weir
主要道路 Main Road
古镇边界 Historic Town Scope
绿地 Green Land
水系 River System

图 9 平乐古镇范围及主要建筑景物示意图
Fig. 9 Diagram of Pingle historic town's scope and its major buildings

平乐，古称"平落"，古蜀开明王时期（前 7 世纪初—前 316 年）兴修水利形成聚落。公元前 150 年西汉时期开始形成集镇。伴随着南丝绸之路（成都至印度 / 孟加拉国 / 越南 / 西亚）和茶马古道（雅安至印度 / 尼泊尔 / 不丹）的发展，平乐成为这两条商贸通道上第一个重要驿站，络绎不绝的人流和商品贸易极大地推动了平乐的发展。公元 970 年平乐正式成为火井县治所所在地。

Pingle used to be called "Pingluo." It was initially formed as a settlement during the period of Ancient Shu Kingdom thanks to the hydrological projects. In 150 B.C. during the West-Han Dynasty, Pingle started to evolve as a market town. Later with the development of the South Silk Road (Chengdu-India/Bangladesh/Vietnam/West Asia) and the Ancient Tea-Horse Trading Route (Ya'an-India/Nepal/Bhutan), Pingle became the first important posthouse in these two routes. The endless stream of people and trades brought great momentum for the growth of this town. In 970 A.D., Pingle was established as the government center of Huojing County.

平乐古镇的繁荣对成都地区的发展贡献极大，同时古镇的经济也随着成都的发展而得到进一步发展。成都自古以来就是中国西部地区的经济和文化中心。正是这样的社会经济以及地缘政治区位使成都成为欧亚大陆最大的商品集散地，辐射整个藏区以及东南亚、南亚和西亚。两条重要的商业通道——南丝绸之路与茶马古道正是从这里出发。南丝绸之路的主要功能是：将中国的丝绸、贵重金属、药材和盐出口，再从印度、中东和东南亚地区进口棉花、珍珠、服装、宝石等。茶马古道则主要将中国内陆地区生产的茶叶、丝绸、盐以及日用品与西藏地区的马匹、骡子、毛皮和药品进行交换。这两条商贸通道不仅历史悠久，而且贸易量巨大，为沿途各处的经济文化提供了得天独厚的发展机遇。

平乐正是在这一过程中发展成为两条古道上的第一驿站的。白沫江穿平乐镇，北上经锦江（原府南河）流向成都，南下沿岷江出川，同时南丝绸之路经平乐出川入缅甸。如此丰富的交通资源与号称"天下第一囷"的平乐花楸茶一起使这个小镇成为两条商贸大动脉上的重要集镇。

The prosperity of Pingle was a very important contributor to the Chengdu area: Chengdu has been the economic and cultural center of western China in most historical periods. This socio-economic position of Chengdu and the dominant geopolitical position of old China made this city the greatest origin for and destination of commodities at the center of the Euro-Asia continent, radiating Tibetan areas and countries of southeast Asia, as well as south and west Asia. Two significant commercial channels starting here, the South Silk Road and the Ancient Tea-Horse Trading Route, formed with time. The former was utilized for the trade of silk, noble metal, drugs, salt from China and cotton, pearl, jewelry, and cloth from India, Middle East, and southeast Asia. The latter functioned as the pathway for barters between tea, silk, salt, daily necessities from inland China, and horses, mules, furs, and drugs from Tibetan areas. These trade channels not only have a long history but also bear considerable commodity volume, which has provided matchless opportunities for economic and cultural development along these channels.

With this vital economic environment, Pingle developed with great momentum and became the first major posthouse along the two routes. The Baimo River that crossed Pingle connected up to Chengdu through the Jinjiang River (formerly the Fu-Nan River) and down beyond Sichuan through the Minjiang River. The South Silk Road also pass through Pingle towards Myanmar. Such unique resources of transportation, combined with Pingle's famous Huaqiu Tea from "The Finest Tea Orchard" led this small town to become the first major trade market on these commercial channels.

图 10 平乐古街道
Fig. 10 Old street in Pingle

平乐古镇 33 条古街道（图 10）保存完好，其古典及传统建筑的建筑面积达到了 235 400 平方米。平乐的古建筑展现了浓郁的川西民居风格，其临街的一楼一底的木结构建筑以一楼为居室，一底做铺面，展现了明清时期的传统民居风格。这种亦居亦商的房屋功能配置反映了在明清时期资本主义萌芽阶段中国市民阶级典型的生活状态。

作为商贸繁荣之地，平乐历来受到富豪乡绅的青睐，又尤以纸商、茶商和船户居多。他们通常选取风景秀美之地建起自家大院，如山顶和江边。这些私家大院大多规模宏大且技艺精美，带有非常明显的明清时代建筑风格的烙印。同时，这些大院也是当地民俗文化得以传承保留的重要场所。

作为繁荣的船运码头，白沫江沿岸的吊脚楼同样具有当地古老的风情：为了抵御江水的侵袭，这些明清时期风格的吊脚楼直接矗立于圆木之上，同时整个建筑群落的布局随着江岸地势地形而蜿蜒回环，错落有致。这样典雅而富有诗意的建筑和江边挺立千年的古榕树一起构成了平乐如诗如画的江景（图 11）。

With 33 old streets (Fig. 10) and 235,400 square meters of well preserved traditional architecture, Pingle reveals the rich style of the West Sichuan area from the Ming-Qing period: most houses along street banks are in two-floor wooden structures with one for a living room and one basement level for shops. This composition of living and business functions reflects the typical lifestyle of the bourgeois class in China's budding stage of capitalism in this period.

As a rallying point of commercial trade and commodity production, Pingle was favored by the noble class and rich people, especially merchants from paper industry, tea production, and shipping industry. They normally chose places with spectacular sceneries as their own housing compound, for instance, the hill tops and the river banks. These architecture compounds share the characteristics of large scale and delicate building techniques with a very typical imprint of the Ming-Qing period. Simultaneously, they became, during that time, the places where the folk culture could be preserved for successive generations.

As a prosperous shipping harbor, the architecture erected along the bank of the Baimo River is also highly characteristic of the local old traditions. These Diaojiao buildings of Ming-Qing styles (stilted buildings) along the river were established upon piles to avoid the erosion near the river during flood seasons. The overall composition meanders along the crooked river, thus shaping a picturesque disorder. The elegant and poetic architectural scenery, combined with the thousand-year-old banyans constitute the marvelous river bank landscape of Pingle (Fig. 11).

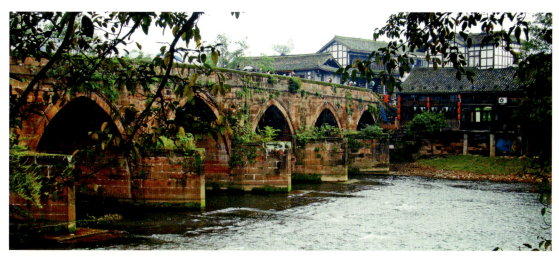

图 11 白沫江上的长桥和江边的榕树与吊脚楼
Fig. 11 Long bridge on the Baimo River with banyan trees and pile dwellings along the river

作为富豪乡绅的聚集之地，平乐成了众多商贾官员的安家之处。这些社会上流阶层的成员通常会选择风景优美、风水顺和的地方修建自己的居所、大院。大院是中国古典家族文化在建筑领域最直接具体的投射，通常它们在结构上一丝不苟，多呈封闭、幽深状，且一般都用高大的院墙与外界隔离。典型的大院群落多以传统的四合院为单元构架，院院相扣并沿总体中轴线左右延伸开来。房间的布局通常主次分明而且内外有别，反映了礼制、等级和纲常等中国古典思想观念。

As a place gathered by myriads of the noble class and rich people, Pingle is the residence for considerable numbers of officials and merchants. These people from the upper class of society usually chose places with magnificent scenery and favorable environment to build their home residences. These compounds are the direct and concrete reflection of Chinese traditional family culture in the domain of architecture. In general, these residence compounds follow meticulous structural precedents, most likely in enclosed shape, deep, and serene. These compounds are separated from the outer world with tall walls. The typical compound utilizes the traditional quadrangle as the basic unit that links each other and extends outwards to both the left and right along the axis of symmetry. The composition of rooms has a strict hierarchy in accordance with the traditional Chinese social institutions of order and etiquette.

图 12 俯瞰李家大院 *
Fig. 12 A bird's eye view upon Li's Family Compound

　　李家大院（图 12），始建于清咸丰末年（1860 年—1861 年）英法联军入侵国家的动荡之时，系清代名商李洪楷所建。明万历年间（1573 年—1620 年），李氏家族因政治原因从浙江西迁，避祸于平乐，其十一代孙洪楷因经营造纸发家致富，择地以典型的清代民居风格修建李家大院。整个建筑群落占地面积为 13 000 余平方米，建筑面积达到 4 164 平方米，房屋 149 间。李家大院的选址极为考究，在深山之麓，四周被青山所环抱，少寒风。大院正面紧临山溪，便于取水，而背面则是山路交汇之处，交通便利。此处地势为向阳坡，风势顺畅，坡形有助于排污，风水极佳。大院本身坐西朝东，取"紫气东来"之意，总是能够有朝阳普照，同时暗示了李氏家族对东部祖籍的思念。类似于广东会馆，李家大院整个建筑群沿中轴线对称分布，空间结构上同样具有线性的"三进两天井"结构，两侧搭配有南北厢房，外接南北偏院，以门、廊相连。

　　Li's Family Compound (Fig. 12) was initially built in the late years of Xianfeng (1860 A.D.–1861 A.D.) during the French-British invasion and belonged to Li Hongkai, whose family moved to Pingle from Zhejiang Province during the years of Wanli (1573 A.D.–1620 A.D.) due to political reasons. Li Hongkai, the 11th descendant of Li's family, became rich thanks to the paper production business of the time. Therefore, he started building the compound for his family with the typical residential style of the Qing Dynasty. The whole compound occupies the area of some 13,000 square meters and building areas of 4,164 square meters and has 149 rooms. The site of Li's Family Compound is highly selective. The compound was situated in the deep piedmont surrounded by deep mountains with rare chilling winds. In addition, the façade of this compound is close to creeks for water, and the back is next to roads for transportation. Furthermore, the compound is located on an adretto, where the wind and civic pollution discharge are unhindered. As a result, Li's Family Compound has wonderful *Fengshui*. The compound sits on the west facing the east, taking the concept that a propitious omen comes from the east and that the compound should receive the sunlight from the east every morning. In the meantime, this orientation also implies the homesickness of Li's family to their old homes in east China. Similar to the Guangdong *Huiguan*, the whole compound is arranged symmetrically along the axis. Also, the spatial composition has the linear structure of three halls and two courtyards. Both sides have wing rooms with north and south remote halls connected with doors and galleries.

蜀韵古镇
HISTORIC TOWNS IN SICHUAN:
THE CULTURAL HERITAGE PROTECTION AND UTILIZATION OF
HISTORIC TOWNS WITH DIFFERENT DIMENSIONS AND VISIONS
——多维视野下的古镇文化遗产保护与利用

　　虽然李家大院和广东会馆同为大型建筑群落,总体结构也有相似之处,然而其主人的社会地位存在明显的差异。这一关键性的差异导致这两处建筑群落在规制和功能上也有不同。李家大院虽也是三进结构,但其前院房屋 8 间提供给门卫,后院给仆人,所以这两院的规制很低。而其单檐悬山顶木质正殿也远低于广东会馆的重檐歇山顶。这样的规制正是清代时期平民建筑群落的典型构架:整个群落功能齐备,包括下人的生活需求也能被满足,因此其总体建筑等级规格较低。

　　Even though both Li's Family Compound and Guangdong *Huiguan* are large-scale architectural complexes and their major compositions are similar, they serve different purposes for people at different social levels. This essential discrepancy determines that the architectural formats and function vary in these two compounds. In Li's Family Compound, the front hall of eight rooms is provided for guards and the back hall for servants. Therefore, these structures are in relatively low form. The major hall in single-cornice *Xuanshan* wooden roof is also far lower in form than the multi-cornice *Xieshan* roof of Guangdong *Huiguan*. However, this was the most typical architectural format for a residence compound during the Qing Dynasty: they had complete functions for the whole family, including the servants, therefore, the format and architectural hierarchy would be relatively plain.

　　正堂作为整个李家大院建筑群落最为核心的部分，是李氏宗族举办各种重大活动的场所。其本身以及周围关键建筑的构造和布局相当精巧。正堂占地很大，且直面同样开阔的主天井（图13）。在后者的烘托下，前者越发显出威严和气势。堂外由檐廊相连进入天井，其屋檐较宽，在天井转角处更大。这种结构在形态上近似一棵大树，寓意为李家后嗣遮风避雨。同时这种结构本身便于迅速扩建成完整的房间，可作为储备空间，一旦李家子嗣众多有需求即可扩建使用。正堂两侧南北各有厢房四间，且均由门廊与正堂相通，形成多房向心的格局，进一步突出了正堂在整个建筑群中的重要地位。同样的思想也体现在各门的布局方向上，其整体基本形成了"正门正，偏门隐"的风格。

As the most important structure of the whole complex, the main hall has the responsibility of hosting all the significant events of Li's family. The composition that the main hall and related rooms follows is therefore genuinely conceived. The main hall occupies a large interior space with an even larger courtyard affront (Fig. 13). The scale of the open and enclosed spaces enhances the prestige and monumentality of this major structure. The main hall extends outwards along the sides of the courtyard with galleries roofed by wide eaves, which grow significantly at the corner of the courtyard. This structure morphologically resembles trees with meanings that it will provide shelter for the descendants of Li's family. It is also a reserved place that could easily be developed into complete roofs if necessary due to the growing population. On the north and south side of the main hall are four wing rooms, respectively. They all have doors and paths connected to the main hall, forming an arrangement with centrality that emphasizes the noble status of the main hall in the whole residence compound. This idea is also visible with the layout of the doors, that in this compound, the main door is open to the front direction, whereas the remote doors are open towards obscured directions.

蜀韵古镇

HISTORIC TOWNS IN SICHUAN:
THE CULTURAL HERITAGE PROTECTION AND UTILIZATION OF
HISTORIC TOWNS WITH DIFFERENT DIMENSIONS AND VISIONS
——多维视野下的古镇文化遗产保护与利用

图 13 李家大院大天井
Fig. 13 Big courtyard of Li's Family Compound

图 14 门窗上的精美木雕
Fig. 14 Elegant wood sculpture in windows and doors

作为私家住宅，李家大院使用了大量的雕饰，然而不同于当时流行的砖雕和石雕，李家使用的都是朴素的木雕（图 14）。考虑到李家祖上受到政治迫害的原因，我们可以揣度李家后人如此低调可能是为了避免灾祸。这些朴素而又精致的雕饰被广泛用于李家大院的门、窗和屏风。这些雕饰大多线条流畅，造型优美，制造技艺精湛。同时，它们大多采用了吉庆呈祥的图案，反映了儒家教化的内容，体现了中国传统劳动人民对财富、幸福、长寿、欢乐的美好憧憬。李家大院大部分木雕内容取材于中国古代典故，如"和合二仙""双凤朝阳""寿星跨鹤""八仙过海""麒麟仰凤"等。另外很多雕饰选用了各种植物主题，寓意美好。比如，很多雕饰描绘了芙蓉、桂花和万年青，谐音寓意"万年富贵"；一些雕饰取材松竹，寓意挺拔、坚毅、一身正气；还有一些雕饰描绘了成串的葡萄，象征蔓长多子。

李家大院主体材料使用的空斗砖，是一种中国传统建筑材料，常用于民居和寺庙建筑。空斗墙体结构的优点在于用料节约，自重较轻，隔热和隔音效果较好。自明代以来，空斗墙在四川以及中国西南其他一些地区得到广泛运用。传统的空斗墙由特制的薄砖平、侧交替砌成，其中形成的中空部分通常会由碎砖、炉渣和泥土填充以改善其热工性能，这样对建筑过程中产生的边角余料也进行了充分的利用。

As a private residential compound, Li's Family Compound is decorated with numerous carving ornamentations. However, these elaborate carving works used plain wood as material, rather than the then fashionable tile and stone carving (Fig. 14). Considering the family history of political persecution, we could make reasonable conjecture that the descendants of Li have been intentionally keeping low key to avoid unnecessary troubles. These plain but delicate carving decorations are widely used in the doors, windows, and screens. These carvings share the characteristics that they are all highly curvaceous with fine techniques. They implement considerable numbers of motifs or patterns depicting Confucian culture, presenting the great wishes for fortune, welfare, longevity, and happiness. One major portion of the carving motif is the historical stories from ancient China, such as Twin Fairy He-He, Two Phoenixes Flying to the Sun, the Immortal Riding on the Crane, the Eight Immortals Crossing the Sea, and Kirin Looking Up to Phoenix. Also, a large number of carvings are in vegetated motifs. For instance, some carvings depict lotuses, osmanthus, and Rhodea japonica, which phonetically represent "eternal richness and nobleness"; some are for pines and bamboo, which traditionally represent the moral integrity; some are for grapes growing on vines, which stand for the flourishing of a family with growing sons.

Li's Family Compound is primarily built from rowlock bricks, which is a very popular and traditional building material for civil residences and temples in China. The rowlock wall structure is good for its economical consumption of materials, small self-deadweight, spectacular heat insulation, and noise deadening. From the Ming Dynasty, rowlock walls rose in popularity in Sichuan and some other southwest areas of China. Traditional rowlock wall structure is made of tailor-made thin bricks which are laid out in a method of alternating standing and sleeping bricks. In the hollow space formed by this alternation of bricks, rubble, slags, and clay are inserted to enhance the thermodynamic engineering performance, which makes full use of construction tailing.

安仁 Anren

　　安仁古镇（图 15）坐落于成都平原西部，虽始建于唐朝，但现在完好保存的是大量建于清朝末年和民国初年的古建筑。封建社会的文化余脉和西方文化的影响共同交汇于安仁，深刻地影响了它的建筑风格。目前，安仁古镇保存有超过 300 000 平方米的传统建筑，27 处公馆建筑群和 3 条古街。

　　Anren (Fig. 15), the historic town, is situated in the west of the Chengdu Plain. Initially built during the Tang Dynasty, Anren preserves an amazing amount of architectural heritage from the years between the late Qing Dynasty and the period of the Republic of China. Therefore, vestiges from both feudal society and western culture are largely seen in Anren, greatly influencing its architectural styles. Currently, Anren has over 300,000 square meters of traditional architecture, 27 old *Gongguan* complexes, and three old streets.

安仁古镇，原名为安仁县治，建于唐高祖武德三年（公元 620 年），据北宋时期的乐史《太平寰宇记》记载，古镇名取"仁者安仁"之意，直至公元 1284 年撤销县的建置。清末至民国时期，安仁涌现了以刘氏家族为代表的军政要员和富豪乡绅，因而中华人民共和国成立前安仁又有"三军九旅十八团"之称。这些富甲一方的军政要员在安仁建起了成片成群的公馆建筑作为自己的安家行乐之所。这些公馆建筑群大多数不仅继承了川派建筑的特点，又融入了房主人故乡的建筑样式。同时，这些建筑还或多或少地受到了西式建筑的影响，各种风格交融在一起，形成了安仁独特的川西文化建筑群落。

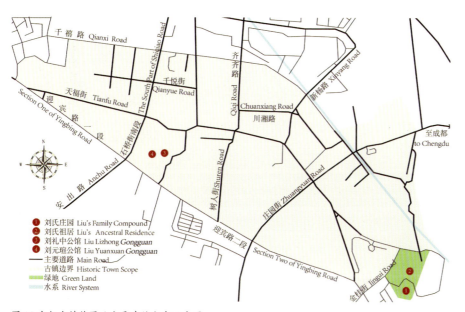

图 15 安仁古镇范围及主要建筑分布示意图
Fig. 15 Diagram of Anren Historic Town's scope and its major buildings

Anren was called Anren County until 1284 A.D. It was established in the third year of Wude years of the Tang Dynasty (620 A.D.). According to *Taiping Huanyu Ji* [*Universal Geography of the Taiping Era* (976 A.D.–983 A.D.)], Anren was named after the Confucian concept that the benevolent delight with benevolence. During the late Qing Dynasty and the era of the Republic of China, a considerable number of important figures from military affairs and political domains settled in Anren, which therefore got an alias as "Center of Military Corps." The arrival of the rich and the powerful brought to Anren huge areas of *Gongguan* architectural compound land as their home of comfort. These compounds not only inherited the characteristics of Sichuan-style architecture but also incorporated styles and formats from the owners' original hometown. Furthermore, these constructions also assimilated the ideals from western architecture. These various styles bind in Anren, forming its unique "West-Sichuan Architectural and Cultural Quintessence."

公馆原是中国古代帝王的离宫别院，而在封建社会的晚期和民国初年，大量政府高官或军队要员开始在自己的家乡修建公馆建筑群，用于居住和享乐。由于其拥有者通常具有很深厚的军政界背景，这些公馆通常规制高档，风格华贵，其装饰多带有强烈的个人喜好，而且整个群落中通常会配备有完整的娱乐设施，因而这些公馆群落本身的建筑风格多会成为当地最为华丽出彩的一类。

以刘文彩、刘文辉和刘湘为代表的刘氏家族于清初从安徽移民入川。民国初年，刘氏家族凭借其横行四川的军政实力积累起了惊人的财富和土地。同时他们也在老家安仁修建起了大量公馆以享受奢靡的生活并以此为据点盘剥当地的百姓。刘氏兄弟在安仁陆续修建起了五座公馆，连同刘氏祖宅一起构成了中国现存保存最为完整、规模最大的地主私人庄园。刘氏庄园（图 16）分为南北两大建筑群，总占地面积 7 万余平方米，建筑面积 2.1 万余平方米，房屋共 545 间。

Gongguan ("great mansion") used to be the detached palace of ancient emperors. During the late period of China's feudal society and the inception period of the Republic of China, a large amount of wealthy people from the high offices or with military powers started to build *Gongguan* as residential compounds at their hometown for their own enjoyment. Thanks to their official or military background, these *Gongguan* complexes, were usually built in very noble and extravagant formats. The *Gongguan* complexes were usually decorated with strong personal taste and equipped with recreational facilities. Their architectural styles were the most attractive ones in their local areas.

Liu's family, represented by Liu Wencai, Liu Wenhui, and Liu Xiang, initially immigrated to Sichuan during the early Qing Dynasty. In the first years of the Republic of China, Liu's family started to gather huge wealth and land with their dominant military and political powers in Sichuan. In the meantime, they began to build various *Gongguan* complexes for their luxury and enjoyment in Anren, their hometown, and to use their mansions as their base to exploit the people in this area. They built five *Gongguans*, and together with their ancestral home, they formed the largest and best preserved private residential compound of China. Liu's family compound (Fig. 16) is composed of north and south portions, occupying a total area of some 70,000 square meters with a building area of 21,000 square meters, as well as 545 rooms.

图 16 刘氏庄园俯瞰 *
Fig. 16 A bird's eye view of Liu's *Gongguan* compound

图 17 刘氏祖居大门
Fig. 17 Main gate of Liu's ancestral house

　　"文化大革命"时期，相当一部分古建筑受到严重破坏，不过刘氏公馆建筑群却被完好地保存下来。刘氏公馆被当作爱国主义教育基地和地主恶霸阶级的反面典型，这在客观上对保护这一特色公馆群落起到了巨大的作用，使其免遭损毁。

　　During the period of the Cultural Revolution in China, quite a few traditional architectural compounds were damaged. However, Liu's *Gongguan* compound was well preserved as a major base for patriotic education and a negative example of typical evil landocracy, which actually made significant contributions to the protection of this architectural heritage.

刘氏祖居始建于清道光元年（1821年）前后，其最初的主人是刘家第六世先祖刘仕识，目前占地总面积约1300平方米，建筑面积约480平方米，房屋20余间，其间历经三次大规模扩建，由最初的单进三合院简单结构发展成目前宏大的传统建筑群落。刘氏祖居建筑采用中国传统住宅普遍型制，结构标准化，且遵循封建礼仪制度和阴阳五行思想，具有明显的地方特色：刘氏祖居位于成都平原西部，受川西潮湿多雨、日照稀少等自然气候影响，特别是受风水学说的深厚影响，始建时格外重视宅址的地点及朝向选择。根据"阴阳五行"理论，祖居主体建筑坐西向东的朝向布局与刘氏姓氏高度契合。因此，根据地理风水师的建议，刘氏先祖在此建造"吉宅"。

刘氏祖居主体上采取极富四川特色的穿斗木柱排架式结构，极个别承重较大的房间采取了抬梁式结构。四周的维护结构为木板墙裙，辅以竹编夹泥墙套白。整个祖居从主体建筑到附属用房，屋面均采用小青瓦覆盖，营造出了一种融合统一的视觉效果。

Liu's ancestral home was initially built at around the early years of Daoguang of the Qing Dynasty (1821 A.D.). It first belonged to Liu Shishi, the sixth generation of ancestor of Liu's family. The compound occupies a total area of over 1,300 square meters with building areas of around 480 square meters and has around 20 rooms. Starting from the original single-hall triple-room composition, the compound has experienced three large-scale expansions and has become a monumental architectural complex. Liu's ancestral home implemented the typical format of a traditional residence with standardized structures, which is in close accordance with feudal etiquette and the theory of *Yinyang Wuxing*. This complex is located at the west part of the Chengdu Plain, an area that is highly humid and rainy with scarce natural sunlight. Besides, Liu's family was deeply influenced by *Fengshui* theory. Based on these backgrounds, the site selection and complex orientation was very carefully determined. According to the theory of *Yinyang Wuxing*, the orientation of sitting on the west facing the east is highly suitable for Liu's surname. Following the advice of geomancer, Liu's ancestors chose to build their house compound at this auspicious location.

The major building structure in Liu's ancestral house is the *Chuandou* type with wooden columns in bent structure, a very typical Sichuan-style structure. A few rooms bearing significant weight are constructed with post and lintel frame. The surrounding structure is constructed with plank dado with a bamboo plating wall covered by ashes. The surface of the house is covered by blue roofing tiles, expanding the whole complex from major hall to the supplementary rooms, which created a united visual effect.

　　刘氏祖居采取前后两进式四合院结构，中为天井，住宅正门（图17）开于正中，自其进入便是前堂，兼作客厅和饭厅使用，第二进便是正堂。第二进整体地基略高，取"步步高升"之意。正堂房屋朝天井开，厢房由长辈居住，前堂厢房分由晚辈或客人居住，均以左为大。各类附属的房屋，包括厨房、仓储室、酿酒房等，围绕建筑主体而建（图18）。大门（四川民居称"龙门"）是统领整个建筑总体风水的重要组成部分，因此，传统民居建造时往往要请地理风水师依据自然环境选择大门的方位及朝向。在风水师的建议下，刘氏祖居大门在偏东北方一侧。另外，因大门是一幢宅子的门面，体现主人的身份、地位和文化修养，故刘氏主人对此特别重视，采用了木构门罩式大门，而非当时普通民居所普遍使用的土砖牌坊式或简单门罩式大门。

　　天井（图19），作为一个开放的空间，不仅是宅院的交通枢纽，还很适应四川潮湿多雨、日照较少的气候，满足了对外封闭、对内开敞的围合空间的需求，有利于各房屋的通风和采光。天井周围的檐廊向中心有明显延伸，创造出更多的廊下空间，使得各种日常活动更为便利。如此纳天地之灵气、阴阳平衡的居住环境，占有"四水归堂"之利。天井中还特设一太平缸，缸中盛满水，既有消防功能，亦是对风水中"水聚财"的一种向往，故又称"风水缸"。

图 18 刘氏祖居的院子
Fig. 18 Courtyard of Liu's ancestral house

图 19 刘氏祖居天井
Fig. 19 Sky well in Liu's ancestral house

HISTORIC TOWNS IN SICHUAN:
THE CULTURAL HERITAGE PROTECTION AND UTILIZATION OF
HISTORIC TOWNS WITH DIFFERENT DIMENSIONS AND VISIONS
——多维视野下的古镇文化遗产保护与利用

The basic building format is in the quadrangle shape with two primary halls and a courtyard in between. The main entrance (Fig. 17) is located at the center of the front gate that leads to the front hall through the courtyard. The front hall serves the purposes of living room and dining room. The second hall is the major hall of Liu's ancestral house, with three rooms aligned linearly. The foundation is slightly higher than that of the front hall, which suggests the meaning of "rising step by step" in Chinese. The major hall opens towards the courtyard, and its wing rooms are for the elderly to live, while those of the front hall for the young and the guests. In both cases, wing rooms on the left side (if seen from the hall) are generally higher than those of the right side. All the supplemental rooms, including the kitchen, storage room, brewery room, etc., are built around the major complex (Fig. 18). The front gate, so-called "Dragon Gate" in the Sichuan area, is the most important architectural component that dominates the overall *Fengshui* of this compound. Therefore, during the design and construction phases of Chinese traditional residential complexes, people will often consult *Fengshui* masters to determine the location and orientation of the front gate in accordance with the natural ambience. Guided by these principles and this ethos, the front gate of Liu's ancestral house is oriented towards the north-east direction. In addition, the front gate is the face of the whole family, reflecting the owner's identity, social status, and cultural accomplishments. The owner of Liu's ancestral home highly emphasized the format of the front gate, thus implementing the monumental wooden-cover type for the gate rather than the popular single-cover door or the adobe *Paifang* style.

The courtyard (Fig. 19), as a piece of open space, is not only the transport hub of the whole residential compound but also for the humid, rainy, and sunlight-deficient climate of the grand Sichuan area. The existence of this courtyard satisfies the need of enclosed open space, which is enclosed on the outside, but open on the inside. This spatial character helps the ventilation and lighting for each individual room. The corridor under the eaves around the courtyard has been significantly extended towards the center, providing more space for everyday activities. The courtyard would simultaneously draw from the natural essence of the universe and *Yin-Yang* balanced living environment. Additionally this composition, takes the auspicious meaning "water from all directions will gather in the center." The center of the compound also puts a Taiping Gang (peace tank), which serves the purpose of firefighting and reflects the profound influence from the theory of *Fengshui*, in which water is considered an auspicious element for accumulating wealth.

图 20 刘文辉公馆大门
Fig. 20 Main gate of Liu Wenhui's *Gongguan*

图 21 刘文辉公馆大门细部
Fig. 21 Details of the main gate of Liu Wenhui's *Gongguan*

　　刘氏庄园这一传统建筑群落在建筑特点上具有旧中国地主阶级生活方式向普通日常生活方式融合的明显趋势。它集中反映了清中晚期至民国初年川西农村建筑形态、技艺及哲学思想、民俗传统、社会变迁以及刘氏家族本身发展的兴衰。以这一建筑群落为代表，类似的建筑都具有高大明亮的正厅，配以高档奢华的装饰，以便为地主阶级提供奢侈舒适的生活环境（图 20、图 21）。同时，这样的建筑群还建有完备的家庭作坊用以自给自足和扩大经济来源。更具特色的是整个建筑群落中密布暗藏了很多枪眼炮位，具有明显的自卫作用和军事意义，而这也反映出当时社会危险和动荡不安的一面。

This residential compound has the typical characteristics of the lifestyle of landocracy in the old China, which was also blended with a strong civil tendency. It intensively reflects the architectural styles, prototypes, construction techniques, building philosophy, folk culture, social vicissitude of west Sichuan, and the evolution of Liu's family during the mid and late period of the Qing Dynasty and the early years of the Republic of China. Like this residential compound similar kinds of architecture all have monumental halls with luxury decoration, providing comfortable living conditions and recreation utility for the land owners (Fig. 20, Fig. 21). In addition, this compound had for the time a complete family handcraft workshop to widen economic profit and self-sustenance, including family brewery and crop production. What is unique is that there are quite a few secret embrasures installed in the compound, which clearly define the danger and instability of that special epoch.

蜀韵古镇

HISTORIC TOWNS IN SICHUAN:
THE CULTURAL HERITAGE PROTECTION AND UTILIZATION OF
HISTORIC TOWNS WITH DIFFERENT DIMENSIONS AND VISIONS
——多维视野下的古镇文化遗产保护与利用

图 22 刘文彩公馆的一个庭院
Fig. 22 A courtyard in Liu Wencai's *Gongguan*

作为刘氏庄园建筑群落中始建年代最早的一座，刘氏祖居明显保留了当地的建筑风格，体现了当地的建筑理念。而作为整个庄园中最为宏大和保存最为完好的一座，刘文彩公馆（又名"老公馆"）虽然始建时间（1928 年）略晚于中国新民主主义革命开始的时间，但仍然具有非常明显的中国古典建筑风格，体现了中国古典哲学思想。不过，由于建于特殊历史时期，刘文彩公馆又受到了西式建筑思想的影响，因此整体风格中西合璧、传统大气、秀美精致（图 22）。

刘文彩公馆占地面积达 12 300 平方米，建筑面积约 7650 平方米，房屋 160 余间，拥有大小天井 27 个。在建造过程中，刘文彩一共霸占了 23 户农民的房产土地，而且每霸占一户，整个院落就会增加新的结构、墙体和门廊，因此整个刘文彩公馆重墙夹巷，后门铁锁，布局错综复杂，迂回曲折，且四周均以 6 米余高的封火山墙围成，显得格外阴森复杂，布局凌乱如迷宫，从侧面反映了刘文彩蚕食土地、扩建庄园的过程。这样的扩建过程使整个群落的形态比较多样化，常见的有长方形、正方形、梯形和菱形等。

As the oldest structure in the whole of Liu's residential compound, Liu's ancestral home still keeps very obvious traditional style and architectural philosophy of the region. On the other hand, as the largest and best preserved one in the compound, Liu Wencai *Gongguan* (also named as "the Old *Gongguan*"), although built slightly later than the China's New Democratic Revolution (in 1928 A.D.), still has a strong imprint of traditional Chinese architectural forms and styles. However, due to the specialty of the historical period, Liu Wencai *Gongguan* had also been influenced by the western architectural philosophy. Therefore, the overall style of this *Gongguan* blends the east and the west while looking grand and magnificent but delicate and graceful at the same time (Fig. 22).

Liu Wencai *Gongguan* has a total area of over 12,300 square meters with a building area of some 7,650 square meters, around 160 rooms, and 27 courtyards. During the construction phase of this residential complex, Liu Wencai had forcibly seized the land and property of 23 peasants. After each forcible secures, this compound would expand with new structures, walls, doors, and eaves galleries. Therefore, the whole composition of the compound was highly intricate and complicated, built up with thick walls and firm locks everywhere in considerable twists and tortuosity. The whole compound is surrounded with fire-sealing gables of some 6 meters of height. This approach of formation adds up to the formal diversity of the complex, such as rectangles, squares, trapezoids, and rhombuses. This compositional characteristic also implies the process of Liu Wencai as landlord nibbling on property of ordinary peasants.

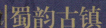
刘文彩公馆同样十分重视大门的修建和规制，融合了西方和东方的建筑技艺：公馆大门采用西式建筑中的竖向直柱装饰，然而却坚持使用中国传统的动植物装饰。大门背后是一个古典中式民居中不可缺少的方形天井，其西侧设有中西两种风格和样式的会客厅，主人可依据客人的身份和地位进行接待。大厅上高悬着一副长联——"大展经纶，由商而政而军扶摇直上；全膺福禄，既富且贵且寿矍铄永康"，与南端一对红砂雅石花缸相得益彰，对庄园主的权势进行了极力的恭维和颂扬。刘氏公馆的核心区域仍然使用了中国古典民居群落的四合院构架，融入了一些独特的个人风格。

图 23 刘氏庄园的风水墩
Fig. 23 The *Fengshui* Pier in the Liu's Family Compound

四合院的主体是刘文彩一家供奉祖先的祖堂和祝寿的寿堂，院内四周挂满金碧辉煌的匾额和对联，室内安放着各式各样描金嵌玉的家具和当时高质量的生活用品，存放着大量的金银珠宝和古玩字画。庄园主刘文彩的卧室陈放着一张金龙抱柱大花床，占地面积达 9 平方米，形制独特且做工精良，表现出较高的工艺水平，同时也反映了刘家奢华的生活方式和较高的社会地位。从内院房屋的建筑规制和布局来看，堂屋供奉祖先，老爷居住正房，妻妾居于一侧，厢房安排子女，紧邻内院的群房群厢则供贴身佣人居住或用作他途，充分反映出封建地主家庭的父严子孝、男尊女卑的等级关系和纲常伦理。

在四合院主体的周围有一些功能特殊的结构，最典型的如内花园中的吸烟室，即是专供刘文彩夏季乘凉吸食鸦片的地方；与之对应的是"水窖"，这个面积约 22 平方米的长方形砖石结构地下室是刘文彩用于存放备用鸦片和烟叶的地下仓库，通流水以保持整个仓库湿度和温度的恒定。另外，小院的正堂还特设佛堂一处，皆因庄园主刘文彩晚年笃信佛教，每日必到此颂经念佛。最为独特的是院落中有一处独特的"风水墩"（图 23）。在古代中国人看来，若能求得能够藏风、得水和具有生气的吉地，用于安葬逝者或修建住宅等，可以达到趋吉避祸、福荫子孙的目的。而刘文彩庄园中这块高出周围地面的土墩子原被称作"刘墩子"，后来被刘文彩当作发家致富的宝地，逢年过节都要召集全家对"风水墩"顶礼膜拜，其胞弟刘文辉打仗之前，也会在此祈祷求吉。

Similar to Liu's ancestral house, Liu Wencai *Gongguan* also emphasizes the format of the front gate. It incorporated styles and forms from both the west and the east. The front gate is constructed with vertical columns with western style, while the ornament is still adherent to China's traditional animal and vegetated motifs. Behind the front gate is the rectangular courtyard that is indispensable in conventional Chinese residences. On the west side of the courtyard, two meeting rooms decorated respectively in Chinese and Western styles are installed in order to receive visitors according to their social status and identities. In the main hall, an extraordinarily long couplet is put together with a couple of red-sand ornamented stone flower tanks paying significant flattering compliment to the owner of the house. The core structure of this *Gongguan* style still implements the traditional quadrangle shape, but it also incorporates some likely uniquely personal characteristics.

The major part of this quadrangle is given to the family shrine hosting the ancestors and the mourning hall for longevity. Around the structure, the inner walls are decorated with countless inscribed boards and couplets made of gold and jade. The house is full of a considerable amount of luxury furniture with huge numbers of jewels, curios, calligraphy, and paintings. In Liu Wencai's personal bedroom, there is a nine-square-meter bed with golden dragons around the pillar. It reflects the highly refined skill level with superior techniques. The architectonics and composition embody the rigid family hierarchy and feudal virtues with ethical codes. Therefore, the major building hosted ancestors, the main room was for the owner (with wives living aside) with wing rooms for younger generations, while surrounding rooms were for servants and other services. This hierarchy is a close view of the lifestyles and ethics of the landowner class in the early period of modern China.

Outside the quadrangle were some functional rooms. For example, the summer divan in inner garden was exclusively used for Liu Wencai to enjoy the cool in opiophagy. Correspondingly, there was a water storage that he used for his opium. The water storage is a 22-square-meter rectangular underground storage unit made of bricks to store opium and tobacco. The water is infilled to keep the humidity and temperature constant. Additionally, a little hall for the worshipping Buddha was set in the main hall of the compound because in Liu Wencai's later life, he had a deep belief in Buddhism. Hence, he would come to this little hall to pray the classics and to worship the Buddha. The most inimitable of the whole compound was the unique "*Fengshui* Pier" (Fig. 23). In the traditional Chinese viewpoint, a place hidden from wind, holding water with lively air, if built for houses or tombs, will bring welfare and avoid disasters for their later generations. The *Fengshui* Pier, also called Liu's Pier, was regarded by Liu Wencai as the most important factor for his rising up. He would summon the whole family on holidays to pay tribute and homage to this pier. Also, before his brother Liu Wenhui went to war, he would also come to the pier to pray for the auspicious.

黄龙溪 Huanglongxi

　　黄龙溪古镇（图24）地处成都平原南部，境内平坝、丘陵、河流交错，是府河下游最为重要的集镇之一。黄龙溪古镇历史悠久，约形成于2000多年前，至今仍保存着各朝各代的历史遗迹。作为距成都很近的名胜之处，黄龙溪古镇成为当下成都市区的人们休闲放松的理想去处。

　　Huanglongxi (Fig. 24), filled with plains, hills, and rivers, sits on the south part of the Chengdu Plain. It is one of the most important commercial towns in the lower reaches of the Fu River. With its time-honored history of more than 2,000 years, Huanglongxi has preserved most of the historic heritage. As a place of interest so close to Chengdu, Huanglongxi is now an ideal place where people from the metropolitan area of Chengdu search for relaxation and comfort.

黄龙溪形成于 2000 多年前的古蜀王国时期，原为屯兵习武之所，后有汉代古墓群遗留于此。据《水经注》载："武阳有赤水其下注江。建安二十四年，有黄龙见此水，九日方去。"从唐宋时期起，由于府河和鹿溪江带来的交通便利，黄龙溪逐渐成为南丝绸之路上一个重要的集散地。自明清以来，黄龙镇逐渐演变得更加生活化、悠闲化，因此有很多民居和戏台在此时期集中出现（图 25）。同样，很多佛教寺庙沿老街修建，形成了寺中有街、街中有寺的奇特景观（图 26）。

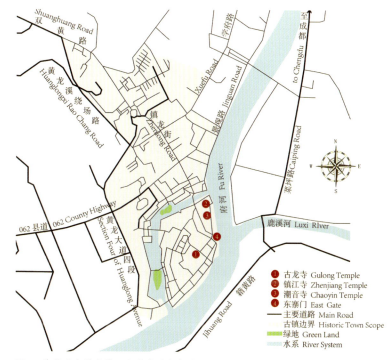

图 24 黄龙溪古镇边界及主要建筑分布图
Fig. 24 Diagram of Huanglongxi Historic Town's scope and its major buildings

Huanglongxi was formed more than 2,000 years ago during the ancient Shu Kingdom period as a military bastion, and ancestors of the Han Dynasty left tomb compounds there. Starting from the Tang-Song period, Huanglongxi became an intensive trading place on the South Silk Road thanks to the convergence of the Fu River and the Luxi River winding through. At the Ming-Qing period, Huanglongxi had gradually transformed into a more peaceful place closer to the expected daily lifestyle. Therefore, more civil residences in typical Ming-Qing architectural formats were erected, with wood theater stages centered to formulate large-scale residential complexes (Fig. 25). By the same token, with the influence of Buddhism, more temples and religious practice installations have been established along the old street, forming a unique landscape of temples on streets, with streets in temples (Fig. 26).

图 25 保留的老民居
Fig. 25 Preserved old dwelling

成都平原地区的休闲文化拥有悠久的历史，极富地方特色，体现出明显的大众性、娱乐性和多样性。显然，这样的文化特点，其成因、发展和普及并非偶然，它与成都平原得天独厚的地域条件和长期以来稳定而优良的经济发展水平是密不可分的。

公元前 4 世纪，古蜀国王开明九世于"广都樊乡"（今双流）"徙治成都"，以"周太王从梁止岐，一年成聚，二年成邑，三年成都"的典故，取名成都，沿用至今。公元前 256 年，蜀郡太守李冰父子率岷江两岸人民兴建都江堰水利工程。从此以后的两千余年，成都水旱从人，少历旱涝，土地肥沃。受到亚热带季风性湿润气候的影响，自古成都平原便物产丰富，形成了"两年三熟"的农作物熟制，更以织锦业驰名。同时，成都平原被众多高原山脉所拱卫，少有战火。不仅资源丰富，历来也为各朝所重视，西汉公孙述、三国刘备、西晋李雄、东晋李寿、五代前蜀王建、后蜀孟知祥等封建王朝均建都成都。成都还一直是各朝代的州、郡、县治所，元、明、清为四川省治所。民国初年，成都是四川省省会，中华人民共和国成立前后为川西行政公署驻地及省会。

优越的自然环境和稳定的社会政治环境催生了成都繁荣的经济和高速发展的工商业。早在秦代，成都就已经成为全国有名的商业城市；汉代又是全国五大都会（洛阳、邯郸、临淄、宛、成都）之一；唐代更有"扬（州）一益（成都）二"之称；北宋时期，成都已是除汴京外的第二大都会。在此期间，成都的经济不仅在规模上实现了飞跃，在制度上也敢为先行。唐宋时期成都的商业已突破了历史上传统的坊市制的束缚，兴起了临街设店和前店后坊（手工作坊）的格局，进而发展为城内有东市、南市、新南市、西市和北市，城外有草市的布局。不仅如此，各种专业性市场也纷纷兴起，如灯市、花市、锦市、扇市、香市、酒市等。

The leisure culture in the Chengdu Plain has rich and varied local characteristics. This culture has a long-established history and embodies obvious traits of popularity, recreation, and diversity. Undoubtedly, this cultural feature, together with its formation, popularity, and development, is far from accidental, as it is inseparable from the unique natural conditions, especially geographical ones, and the long-term stable and eminent economic factors of the Chengdu Plain.

At the fourth century B.C., the ancient Shu emperor, Kaiming the 9th, started migrating people to Chengdu with its new construction. Chengdu ("becoming a city") was named with the meaning "one year the settlement becomes a complex, two years a town and three years a city." In the year 256 B.C., the procurator of Shu province of the Qin Dynasty, Li Bing, and his son led the people living near the Minjiang River to construct Dujiangyan Weir. From then on to more than two thousand years later, Chengdu has been enjoying fertile land and the rarity of drought or flood. Moreover, situated in the area of a humid subtropical monsoon climate with the cropping system of "three-ripe-in-two-years," Chengdu has been suitable and thusly superabundant in various products, especially the famous tapestry, baldachin, and embroidery. Meanwhile, the Chengdu Plain is defended with multiple plateaus and mountains, resulting in very rare incidents of invasion or combat. Not only blessed in natural resources, the Chengdu Plain has been politically favored by every dynasty. Gongsun Shu in West Han, Liu Bei in the Three-Kingdom period, Li Xiong in West Jin, Li Shou in East Jin, Wang Jian in Former Shu, and Meng Zhixiang in Later Shu established feudal dynasties in Chengdu; it has also always been the center for state, province, county, and administrative offices until the Republic of China and the People's Republic of China.

These paralleled conditions both naturally and politically rapidly helped Chengdu to develop the prosperous economy and highly advanced industry and commerce. In the Qin Dynasty, Chengdu was the nationally renowned commercial city; in the Han Dynasty, it was one of the five national metropolis areas (Luoyang, Handan, Linzi, Wan, and Chengdu); during the Tang Dynasty, Chengdu was compared with Yangzhou with the saying "Yang Yi Yi Er" (Yangzhou the first; Chengdu the second); in the Northern Song Dynasty, Chengdu had already become the largest city, inferior only to Bianjing, the capital. The economic leap of Chengdu is calculated not only in scales but also in mechanism. In the Tang-Song period, the Chengdu Plain broke the shackles of the traditional workshop-market system and erected the retail businesses at the street frontage and the system of "stores in front and factories behind," which later evolved to the different markets of eastern market, southern market, new southern market, western market and northern market in the city, and the Caoshi market in the suburbs. Furthermore, a myriad of professional markets also emerged, including lantern fairs, flower markets, embroidery fairs, fan markets, incense markets, wine markets and so on.

蜀韵古镇

HISTORIC TOWNS IN SICHUAN:
THE CULTURAL HERITAGE PROTECTION AND UTILIZATION OF
HISTORIC TOWNS WITH DIFFERENT DIMENSIONS AND VISIONS
——多维视野下的古镇文化遗产保护与利用

图 26 黄龙溪古镇街景
Fig. 26 Street scene in Huanglongxi

　　这样发达的经济所带来的先进生产力水平为成都的休闲文化提供了优越的物质条件。同时，长期和平安定的生活也为当地文化、教育和道德精神的发展提供了一个天然的温室。早在公元前 141 年，蜀郡太守文翁在成都兴学，开学馆，设讲堂，建文翁石室，从而使蜀地之人才辈出于两汉。作为当时全国地方办学的首创，文翁石室至南宋时期已发展为规模近千人的地方高等学府。唐宋时期，成都地区的音乐、歌舞、戏剧已非常繁盛，有"蜀戏冠天下"之称。地方戏川剧更以其独特的高腔，以及变脸和吐火等技艺而闻名于世。

　　另外，不得不提的还有四川独特而卓越的饮食文化。川之饮以川之茶和川之酒而傲视天下。成都新津是整个四川最早进行茶叶贸易的地区。唐宋时期，成都平原是全国茶叶生产的主要地区，也是茶叶贸易的集散中心。清代以来，成都的茶馆文化别具一格，相沿至今，其茶馆之多，闻名世界。左翼作家萧军 1938 年到成都，惊讶于茶馆之多，曾感叹道："江南十步杨柳，成都十步茶馆。"时至今日，伴着蜿蜒的锦江，在熙熙攘攘的茶馆中，呷一口盖碗茶，和街坊邻居摆摆龙门阵仍然是成都人休闲生活中重要的一部分。

The prosperous economy brought an advanced level of productive forces that guaranteed the superior conditions of materials. In the meantime, the long-time peaceful and settled life created a natural ambience for the growth of the local culture, education, morale, and spirit. As early as 141 B.C., the procurator of Shu Province, Wen Weng, began to build schools and lecture halls in Chengdu, known as Shi Shi ("Stone House") as the first precedent of local education that promoted the personnel development in Sichuan. By the Southern Song Dynasty, Shi Shi had already evolved as a large scale higher education center. In the Tang-Song period, the Chengdu Plain had a significant blossoming of music, dance, and operas, with the reputation of "Shu's Opera is unsurpassed!" The local Sichuan Opera is considerably eminently known for high pitched tune, *Bian Lian* (Face-Changing), and Fire Breathing.

The cooking culture here is also a magnificent treasure, to which we cannot afford our indifference. Sichuan's drinking culture is hardly rivaled with not only its tea but also its spirits. Xinjin, a small town on the Chengdu Plain, is the earliest trading center of the tea businesses amongst the entire Sichuan area. In the Tang-Song era, the Chengdu Plain had become the major tea production and trading location of the whole of China. From the Qing Dynasty, the culture of teahouses started emerging in the urban areas of the Chengdu Plain to worldwide acclaim. When famous writer Xiao Jun visited Chengdu in 1938, he could not help saying that "Jiangnan is filled with willows, while Chengdu is filled with teahouses." Even today, it is still one of the greatest pleasures for Chengdu people to sit in an old teahouse that winds along the Jinjiang River, take a deep sip of lidded-cup tea, and talk about the ups and downs of life with the old folks.

蜀韵古镇

HISTORIC TOWNS IN SICHUAN:
THE CULTURAL HERITAGE PROTECTION AND UTILIZATION OF
HISTORIC TOWNS WITH DIFFERENT DIMENSIONS AND VISIONS
——多维视野下的古镇文化遗产保护与利用

川之酒也是成都平原休闲文化的重要体现，其中川人的酿酒以五粮液和剑南春为典范。川人嗜酒的历史源远流长，旅居成都的唐代伟大诗人杜甫在《八哀诗·赠太子太师汝阳郡王琎》中曾写道"岂无成都酒，忧国只细倾"，唐及五代诗人孙光宪在笔记小说集《北梦琐言》中也提到"蜀之士子，莫不酤酒"。

川之食，以麻辣见长，多重油盐，虽取材丰富，但仍以"三椒"（花椒、辣椒和胡椒）为多，口感上讲求"一菜一格"，国际烹饪界素有"食在中国，味在四川"之说。川菜"上河帮"，即"蓉派川菜"，主要流行于成都平原地区，起源于传统官家川菜，精致细腻，多为流传久远的传统川菜。受其影响，成都平原地区也孕育出口味浓重的各类小吃，包括众多面点、羹汤和肉食等。做法从蒸煮烘烤到油酥油炸，琳琅满目，各味俱全，种类不下200 种，大街上随处可见。这些小吃，多半是早年由小商小贩肩挑手提，沿街摆摊设铺经营起家的。它们往往由小商贩的姓氏和设店开业的街道为名，招牌丰富多彩，紧扣行业特点和店址风光，既满足人们的味觉要求，又为成都平原添上了一道靓丽的风景线。

Sichuan alcohol is also a significant embodiment of the leisure culture on the Chengdu Plain. As for its brewing, Wuliangye and Jiannanchun are the best examples of Sichuan's alcohols; in terms of drinking, people here share an incredibly long history of drinking. The famous poet Du Fu once wrote that the melancholy for the nation evaporates with Chengdu's alcohols. Later, poet Sun Guangxian also wrote down that no scholars in Sichuan could resist the fondness of drinking.

The dishes in Sichuan are perceptibly magnificent with the spicy and pungent style and heavy usage of oil and salt. Even though they draw materials from plentiful sources, three kinds of peppers (Pericarpium Zanthoxyli, Capsicum, and Piper Nigrum) are always in heavy use with the pursuit in "one flavor in one course." The cuisine trade has the saying that "The best food is in China, while the best flavor is in Sichuan." The largest branch of Sichuan cuisine, Shanghebang cuisine, also called Rong style cuisine is mostly popular in the area of the Chengdu Plain. It originated from the conventional cuisines of government, with demand of delicacy and long-standing history. Under this influence, this area also produced a multitude of snacks with strong flavors, including wheaten food, thick soups, and meats. With more than two hundred types of snacks, the cooking methods, include frying, steaming, baking, and so forth. They are oftentimes widely dispersed along the streets, some of which are carried with hands and trolleys, others in primitive stalls. They usually take their names from the people or the streets with rich and varied signs while closely related to the characteristic of the snacks. These foods and snacks not merely satisfy the taste buds of the people but moreover create the interesting scenery on the Chengdu Plain.

图 27 黄龙溪暮色
Fig. 27 Evening scene in Huanglongxi

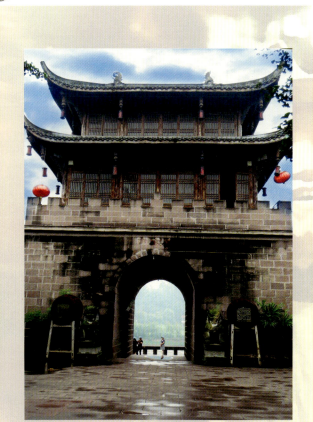

图 28 东寨门内侧
Fig. 28 Inner side of the east gate

在各种优越的自然和人为条件的滋养下，成都平原地区自古以来就崇尚安逸生活与休闲文化。在金沙遗址和三星堆遗址中，有大量以黄金、玉、象牙和青铜为材料制成的休闲用的纯装饰物。不仅如此，成都历史上众多的文人墨客诸如扬雄、张载、左思、司马相如、薛涛等在大量的赋体文章中也充分反映并讴歌了历代成都人对休闲安逸的生活追求。这种长期富庶的生活条件以及根深蒂固的生活态度对这一区域本身的城市肌理和社会风貌也带来了深刻而全面的影响。随着时间的推移和社会财富的积累，这种休闲文化在成都平原地区逐渐扩散开来，而诸如茶馆、老街一类的这种文化的外在体现更是得到保护和修复。黄龙溪古镇便深受这种休闲文化的影响。古镇本身被河流环抱，风光旖旎（图 27），唐宋时期水道运输繁荣以后聚集了很多商贾，建屋筑园，依江景，兴茶馆，搭戏台，立古树，张酒肆，古镇的气息由商品货物集散地迅速向休闲、安逸和市井演变。作为茶叶产区以及茶马古道和南方丝绸之路的必经之路，黄龙溪被浓厚的茶文化氛围包裹，路旁、堤上和竹下四处可见古典的茶馆，飘着茉莉花、竹叶青和峨眉雪蕊花茶的清香。这样的生活和当地的明清民居相融合，黄龙溪既有阁楼窗棂，又有临河吊脚楼，具有明显的古蜀干栏式建筑文化特色（图 28）。在这些物质文化的映衬下，黄龙溪还孕育出了休闲文化中非物质的一类，它们多呈现出丰富的表演形式，比如火龙、狮灯、船工号子、打更等，与古老的城镇和建筑交相辉映，给黄龙溪古镇打磨出了独特的休闲风貌。

Such superior natural and human conditions bring to the Chengdu Plain the long-established cultural deposits and living habits. In the excavation of the Jinsha Ruins and Sanxingdui Ruins, a large number of purely decorative components made of gold, jade, ivory, and bronze are found to demonstrate the leisure lifestyle then. What is more, a great bunch of poets, refined scholars, and literature practitioners of Chengdu in ancient times like Yang Xiong, Zhang Zai, Zuo Si, Sima Xiangru, Xue Tao, etc., eulogized this lifestyle and living conditions of Chengdu in their poetic essays in the Fu (the descriptive prose interspersed with verse) style. This lifestyle and the ingrained life attitude towards leisure profoundly and holistically engraved the urban fabric and social features. With the passage of time and the accumulation of social wealth, this leisure culture has been gradually expanded geographically in the area of the Chengdu Plain and accumulatively in every aspect of life, with some external features like teahouses and old streets being intentionally protected and restored. Huanglongxi Historic Town is therefore deeply influenced by this leisure culture: the town itself is surrounded by rivers, creating a charming and enchanting scenery. From the prosperity of the water communication during the Tang-Song period, Huanglongxi gathered a massive pile of wealthy merchants, who were highly successful in their business and shifted their concentration to enjoying their lives. They erected mansions, fenced gardens, built teahouse with the popular scenic river view, set up theater stages, planted old and precious trees, and opened up pubs. They transformed the overall air of the town from a commercial spot to a place of leisure, comfort, and coziness (Fig. 27). As a tea production area and an inevitable spot on the Ancient Tea-Horse Trading Route and the South Silk Road, Huanglongxi is covered by strong tea culture with old teahouses scattered along the road, the dam, and under bamboos and fragrance from jasmine, Zhuye Qing, and E'mei Xuerui drifting. This life is meshed with the local residence from the Ming-Qing period, not only the attics with mullion, but also the stilted buildings along the rivers, reflecting the typical wood-railing styled architecture of ancient Shu culture (Fig. 28). With these tangible material culture markers, Huanglongxi also nucleates the intangible and dematerialized side of this leisure culture with abundant formats of performances, such as fire dragon, lion lantern, sailors' work song, night watches, etc. Together with the historic town and architecture, these cultural forms have been supplementing each other and shaping the unique leisure fabric of Huanglongxi historic town for many years.

罗城 Luocheng

　　罗城古镇（图 29），地处四川省乐山市犍为县以东，位于成都平原的南部边缘地带。罗城古镇坐落于一个椭圆形的山丘顶上，因而其主街构成为船形结构，不仅符合地理特征，又暗合其"旱码头"的别称。整个船形布局东西略长，南北略短，状似一个织布的梭子，故又名"云中一把梭"。

　　Luocheng Historic Town (Fig. 29) is located on the east of Qianwei County of the city of Leshan on the south edge of the Chengdu Plain. Luocheng sits on the top of an elliptical hill. Therefore, the major street is constructed as a boat shape, not only fitting the topographical character but also reflecting its reputation as "Dry Wharf." Like a shuttle, the overall composition of the boat is slightly wider in the direction of east-west, shorter on the north-south side. Therefore, Luocheng is also named as "A Shuttle in the Clouds."

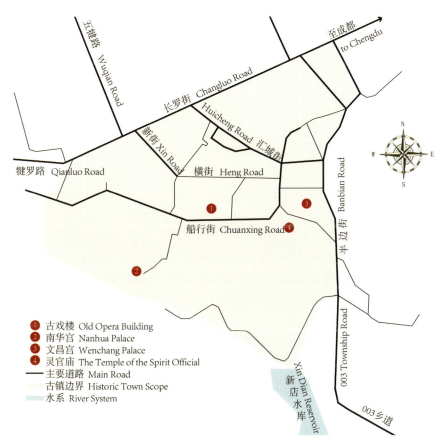

① 古戏楼 Old Opera Building
② 南华宫 Nanhua Palace
③ 文昌宫 Wenchang Palace
④ 灵官庙 The Temple of the Spirit Official
— 主要道路 Main Road
古镇边界 Historic Town Scope
水系 River System

图 29 罗城古镇范围及主要建筑分布图
Fig. 29 Diagram of Luocheng Historic Town's scope and its major buildings

罗城古镇始建于明崇祯初年（1628 年），成型于清代。建镇之初即作为军事要地扼守西南边陲，因此明清时期均是屯兵制夷（西南少数民族）的"军事铺"，故又称作"罗城铺"。古镇西部的营盘山即为当年的屯兵之所。

Luocheng was initially built in the years of Chongzhen of the late Ming Dynasty (1628 A.D.) and maturely formed in the Qing Dynasty. As soon as it was established, it became an important military point to defend against the minority groups in the south-west China. Therefore, Luocheng has been called "Luocheng Pu," which means "Luocheng Military Base." The Yingpan Mountain on the west of Luocheng was the place where military camps were located.

罗城古镇沿主街凉亭街两侧延伸发展，从北向南先逐渐加宽，至主街中部开始逐渐收窄直至穿过古戏台彼此交汇而终止（图30），整个古镇呈船形主体布局，从空中俯瞰尤为明显，故又有"山顶一只船"的别名。关于这条"船形街"的来历，历史上有两种说法。一说古时罗城多雨，洪涝频繁，古人在修建街道时采取两头窄中间宽的船形街道以祈求平安。另一说崇祯时期罗城镇上缺水。某日，一张姓秀才路过罗城，偶听得镇上老人叹息，大吃一惊，便念道："罗城旱码头，客商久难留。若要不缺水，罗城修成舟。"随后全镇人民就在张秀才的带领下将整个古镇修成了船形。从此以后，世世代代的罗城人便居住在"船"中。

Luocheng expands along the main street of Liangting Street in both directions. The town initially widens from north to south until it reaches the middle portion. From there, the town starts narrowing till the two sides converge after traveling through the ancient stage (Fig. 30). Therefore, the whole layout of Luocheng clearly reveals the shape of a boat, especially when looking from the aerial views. This formal character gains it a name of "A Boat on the Mountain Top." There are two major versions of history explaining the origin of this unique town shape. One version states that Luocheng was severely harried by the excessive raining in the old days, which brought too much flooding. Therefore, people intentionally built the street in a format that widened in the middle while shrinking at both ends to symbolize the pursuit of peace and welfare which eventually evolved into a boat shape. On the contrary, the other story tells that during the years of Chongzhen (1628 A.D.–1644 A.D.) Luocheng was suffering from a water shortage. The story goes that one day, a scholar with the surname Zhang, passed by Luocheng, and heard the deep sigh from some old folks there. He was shocked and said that "Luocheng is a dry wharf and naturally lacks in guests and business people. If water shortage is to be avoided, Luocheng has to be shaped into a boat." From then on, all people living there started reshaping the town into a boat under the leadership of this scholar.

图 30 船形街宽廊下的茶馆街市
Fig. 30 Teahouses and small business within the wide corridor along the boat-shaped street

　　在以上两种历史传说中，后者的说法目前较为通行，而且得到了佐证：罗城镇周边的定文镇、白鹤镇和南阳镇等降雨明显比罗城充沛，且常出现罗城周边地区大雨倾盆，而罗城本身却滴雨未见的现象。然而以此即断定该镇船形的成因仍然难以自圆其说。其主要疑点在于：第一，参照当时的生产力水平，整个城镇的修建或改建工程十分浩大，可能需要几年甚至数十年的时间，而考虑到缺水问题的迫切性，修建一个船形古镇显然既不省时又不省力。即使真有必要兴师动众，其船形的选择仍然值得商榷，毕竟中国古代的鱼形、龙形或河形等更为贴合求雨的寓意。第二，罗城古镇的船形布局并不规范，而且其不规范的区域较大，不是仅用建筑误差就能解释的。最明显的一点就是其左侧街面高于右侧街面，差距最小处达到 0.5 米，最大处达到 3 米左右。这样的差距对于通常平坦的船底而言是一个巨大的问题。同时左右街道弯曲的方向很怪异，两街均向右弯曲凸出，形成一个弧度很大的侧拱形，远非左右对称的基本形态。这种形状的"船"在实际中是不可能存在的。第三，古戏楼附近通常被视作罗泉船形古镇的"船舱"，然而该处的地势却比周围的街面平均高出 0.5 米左右。通常船舱应该是整个船体中最底部的结构，更应明显低于船头和船尾。然而罗城的船形则是本应平坦低矮的船舱却成了整个"船体"中最高的部分，且街面明显不平整（图 31）。

The latter version seems to be more popular. In fact, it also gains some side proof that towns conterminously around Luocheng, including Dingwen, Baihe, and Nanyang, have much more abundant precipitation than Luocheng does. Sometimes, Luocheng will be totally dry while these neighbor towns are under huge rainfall. However, these phenomena are far from enough to address all the doubtful points about this version. Firstly, considering the level of productive forces of around four hundred years before, neither the construction nor rebuilding for the whole town could be finished without at least a couple of years of input. Confronted by an imperative and acute issue like water shortage and drought, it was certainly not practical to rebuild the whole town for this single symbolic purpose. Even if it were worth the effort, the boat shape would not even be the best choice, for in traditional Chinese culture, the motif of fish or dragon, or the direct mimicry of a river, would be closer to the actual meaning in this situation. Secondly, the boat-shape layout of Luocheng is far from standard in the vast majority of areas, which cannot be accounted for by mere inaccuracy. The most discerned problem is that the left side of the street is higher than the right one, with the difference ranging from 0.5 meters at the minimum and three meters at the maximum. For the "bilge" that is supposed to be flat, this level of height difference is outrageous. Meanwhile, the orientation to which both sides of the street is bent is also aberrant, for both sides are curving out towards right, creating a side arch with a massive radian, rather than the basic form of axial symmetry. This "boat" constructed in this shape is definitely impractical in real life. Thirdly, the old stage building is normally regarded as the central bilge of the boat; what is inconceivable is that the height of this area is higher than the surroundings by an average edge of 0.5 meters. In real life cases, bilges should be the lowest part of the whole structure and should be considerably lower than both the bow and the stern. Nonetheless, in the "boat" shape of Luocheng, the bilge becomes the highest part of the whole "boat" with its own street surface drastically uneven. This way of layout in terms of height is unrealistic as well (Fig. 31).

蜀韵古镇

HISTORIC TOWNS IN SICHUAN:
THE CULTURAL HERITAGE PROTECTION AND UTILIZATION OF
HISTORIC TOWNS WITH DIFFERENT DIMENSIONS AND VISIONS
——多维视野下的古镇文化遗产保护与利用

图 31 罗城最具特色的船形街
Fig. 31 The most unique boat-shaped street in Luocheng

　　事实上，如果把镜头拉得远一点，我们可能会得到一些有用的线索。整个罗城古镇位于山丘的顶上，因而其建设和发展都受到了这种地理条件的影响。尤其是从罗城古镇的东侧沿东南指向新店水库的方向上，从南华宫开始，外侧地势迅速下沉，几乎形成悬崖。而整个罗城东侧的建筑就是沿着崖边而建的。所以，我们可以据此推测，罗城古镇独特布局的主要原因很可能是地形和地势，古镇只是恰巧比较接近一艘船的形状而已。

　　In fact, if one were to draw back the lens, one may be able to dig out some useful clues. Luocheng is situated on the very top of a mountain. Therefore, its construction and development should have been in accordance with this pre-condition of the site. On the east site of the town, in the southeast direction pointing towards the Xindian Reservoir, the topography plummets starting from the outside surface of the Nanhua Palace. This topographical change demanded the east side of construction to follow the meandering of the cliff's edge. Based on this analysis, one makes plausible conjecture that the unique layout is formulated in accordance with the topographical conditions. The outlined shape might be, therefore, resembling that of a boat by coincidence.

罗泉 Luoquan

罗泉古镇（图32）位于资中县西部，随着珠溪河蜿蜒而下，呈龙形布局，故古时又称"龙镇"。罗泉镇不仅是四川历史文化名镇，也是中国100个千年古镇之一。

Luoquan Historic Town (Fig. 32), set at the west part of Zizhong county, winds along the Zhuxi River, forming a dragon shape and giving Luoquan another name, "Long Town" (the town of dragon). Luoquan is not only a cultural and historic town highly valued by Sichuan Province but also one of China's hundred historic towns that have over one thousand years of history.

图 32 罗泉古镇范围及主要建筑分布图
Fig. 32 Diagram of Luoquan Historic Town's scope and its major building

根据《盐法志》和《资中县志》记载，罗泉镇于秦朝因采盐业的兴起而创镇，距今有 1700 多年的历史。三国时，蜀丞相孔明兴师南征曾扎营罗泉镇营盘山，因凿井时井中泉水涌出，似箩筐大小，即命名此井为"箩泉井"，后来便逐渐演变成"罗泉"。历经南北朝、隋、唐、宋、元历代的发展，到明先祖洪武年间，罗泉镇已有一定规模，并于清雍正八年（1730年）设立资州罗泉分州府。其间，罗泉的盐业开发日趋繁盛。清同治七年（1868 年），商贾云集、热闹非凡的罗泉建起了世界上独一无二的盐神庙。至清光绪年间已有盐井 1515 眼，其所产井盐在 1925 年巴黎世界博览会上获得金奖。

According to the records from *Yan Fa Zhi* (*The Record of Salt Production*) and *The County Annals of Zizhong*, Luoquan was established during the Qin Dynasty due to the prosperity of salt production, with a history of over 1,700 years. Developed through the Northern and Southern Dynasties, Sui, Tang, Song and Yuan Dynasties, Luoquan evolved with considerable scale during the Hongwu Years of the founding father of the Ming Dynasty. In the eighth year of Yongzheng of the Qing Dynasty (1730 A.D.), Luoquan officially became the branch provincial capital of the Zi province. In this period, the salt industry in Luoquan was significantly developed, and in the years of Tongzhi of the Qing Dynasty (1868 A.D.), the boisterous Luoquan, filled with business people, erected the unique Temple of the God of Salt. There had been altogether 1,515 salt wells established up till the years of Guangxu. The salt production even won the golden prize in the World Expo in Paris in 1925.

图 33 井盐图说*
Fig. 33 Illustrated handbook of well salt

　　四川自古以来就有产井盐的传统。四川的井盐制作利用一种古老而独特的方法，由凿井、汲卤、煎制而成（图 33）。明朝科学家宋应星的科学技术著作《天工开物》记载："滇、蜀两省远离海滨，舟车艰通，形势高上，其成脉即蕴藏地中。凡蜀中石山去河不远者，多可造井取盐。"因而早在战国末年，秦蜀郡太守李冰就已在成都平原开凿盐井，汲卤煮盐。彼时的盐井口径大，井壁脆，且无保护措施，极易坍塌。加之其深度普遍较浅，因而只能汲取浅层盐卤。至北宋中期后，川南自贡、宜宾、泸州等地区出现了卓筒井，"凿地植竹，为之卓筒井"。卓筒井发明于北宋庆历年间（1041 年－1048 年），比西方早 800 多年。卓筒井是一种小口径深井，凿井时，使用"一字形"钻头，采用冲击方式舂碎岩石，然后注水或利用地下水，以竹筒将岩屑和水汲出。卓筒井的井径约碗口大小，井壁厚实且不易崩塌。同时，川人还将大楠竹去节，首尾套接，外缠麻绳，涂以油灰，下至井内作为套管，防止井壁塌陷和淡水浸入。取卤时，以细竹作汲卤筒，插入套管内，筒底以熟皮作启闭阀门，一筒可汲卤数斗，井上竖大木架，用辘轳、车盘提取卤水。卓筒井工艺复杂精巧，它的出现标志着中国古代深井钻凿工艺的成熟。此后，盐井深度不断增加。清道光十五年（1835 年），四川自贡盐区钻出了当时世界上第一口超千米的深井——燊海井。

Sichuan has the deeply rooted tradition of producing well salt in an ancient but unique method starting from shaft sinking, brine exhaustion, and salt baking (Fig. 33). According to *Tian Gong Kai Wu*, a scientific and technological book written by Song Yingxing, a scientist of the Ming Dynasty: "Sichuan and Yunnan are far from the seaside with high elevation and tough transportation. Therefore, salt resources here are stored in the deep underground of the local areas. With wells, most areas on stone mountains close to rivers in Sichuan are able to become a salt source." As early as late years of Warring States Period (453 B.C.–221 B.C.), Li Bing, the governor of Shu County of the Qin Dynasty had already drilled wells and produced salt on the Chengdu Plain. At the time, the well opening was relatively large, which makes the sidewall too thin to hold the structure without any protection device. Therefore, wells of that period frequently collapsed. Besides, limited by the materials and techniques, the well depth was prevalently shallow, resulting in the fact the salt production could only rely on the bittern on the lamina superficially. From the mid Song Dynasty (960 A.D.–1127 A.D.), Zhuotong Well appeared in southern Sichuan, including Zigong, Yibin, and Luzhou. Zhuotong Well, drilling the well and planting the bamboo, was invented at the Qingli years (1041 A.D.–1048 A.D.) of Song Dynasty, more than eight hundred years earlier than western world. Zhuotong Well is a kind of deep shaft of small caliber. When used to drill the well, the in-line Zhuotong Well aiguille will pound against the rock by percussion. Then, infilled water or underground water will be implemented in the bamboo tube to pump out the rock debris. The caliber of Zhuotong Well is about the size of a normal bowl, which thickens the sidewalls and lessens the risk of collapse. Simultaneously, salt producers in Sichuan decap the bamboo that are then connected from head to end with hemp rope surrounded and putty painted. These bamboo tubes are extended towards the well in order to further prevent well collapse and fresh water seepage. During the process of extracting the brine, people use thin bamboo tubes intruded into the cannula with barks at the bottom serving as the valve. One such cannula will extract several buckets of brine. Above the well stands the large wood scaffold with windlass and hull lift to do the extraction work. Zhuotong Well has a delicate technique and complicated devices. Its mergence indicates the mature of China's tradition deep-well drilling technology. With its help, the depth of salt wells in Sichuan increased significantly. In the fifteenth year of the Daoguang years of the Qing Dynasty (1835 A.D.) the salt producers in the Zigong area succeeded in drilling the first well with a depth of more than one thousand meters, which was called Shenhai Well.

制盐技术的进步为整个制盐产业以及相关产业的发展打下了坚实的基础。然而真正奠定制盐业在四川地区经济地位的是其井盐业经营制度的开放和发展。西汉汉武帝时期（前140年—前87年）以来，食盐的制造、运输和销售均由官方以官家器皿施行，并且严厉打击民间制盐。据《史记·平淮书》记载，"敢私铸铁器煮盐者，钛左趾，没入其器物"。盐业专卖制度形成的原因可能有增加政府收入、稳定食盐价格和流通、减缓民间财富的积累并压榨民间财富、对食盐实行质量控制等。在这项专制制度实施的上千年过程中，皇家财富得到了极大的积累，却在社会中下层引起了很大的矛盾。西汉桓宽《盐铁论》便记载了以御史大夫桑弘羊为代表的中央利益和以贤良文学为代表的地方利益之间的论战博弈。从宋朝中后期开始直至明朝，北方少数民族对中原地区的骚扰使得官方运输粮盐的路途不堪重负，尤其使得明朝初期政府对北方防御的后勤补给变得极为困难。官府因而不得不以合法贩卖"官盐"的资格来换取民间商贾尤其是燕蓟和山西等地商人的运力和财富支持。然而四川地区社会安定，久无战事，其本身的井盐产业得到了充足的发展空间，官府对盐业的掌控却没有被明显减弱，与北方官民之间半合作半竞争的态势形成了鲜明的对比。清朝以前，四川井盐产区遍及各个州县，但所有产业均由官府控制，难以为百姓生活水平的提高和地方经济的发展提供足够的助力。明朝末年，由于长期战乱，四川地区的盐井夷塞殆尽，生产难以恢复。清康熙年间开始，在资本主义萌芽和政府对恢复

图 34 安静的盐神庙大门
Fig. 34 Quiet main gate of the Salt God Temple

盐业生产的需求等多重因素的推动之下，清政府改变了四川井盐业的经营方式，允许民间自由开采。至清乾隆年间，政府先是对新开盐井减轻赋税，直至完全免除。这样的举措让四川地区的井盐业的产量迅速增加，在不到100年内产量最高翻了八番，从雍正时期的9000余万斤上升至嘉庆时期的7亿余斤。

The huge technical leap in salt production laid firm foundation for the development of the salt production industry and the related industries. However, it was the stark reform and improvement of the management mechanism that propelled the salt manufacturing to an indispensable economic place in Sichuan. Starting from Emperor Wu of West Han Dynasty (140 B.C.–87 B.C.), the production, transport, and sales were all exclusively conducted by the government with the official measurement. Civil salt production was severely punished. Recorded in *Shi Ji: Ping Huai Shu* (*Records of the Grand Historian: Book of Huai's Equalization*), all people who dared to cast iron and produce salt had to be fettered with their vessels and tools confiscated. The possible factors of this exclusive mechanism include increasing the governmental revenue, stabilizing the salt price and circulation, retarding and suppressing the accumulation of private wealth, and carrying out the quality control of salt production. With the practice of this mechanism for over a thousand years, the royal wealth had increased significantly, yet it incurred considerable social contradictions in the lower half of society. *Yan Tie Lun* (*Discourses on Salt and Iron*) by Huan Kuan in the West Han Dynasty recorded the controversy and reencounter between the interest groups in central government and those in the local, respectively represented by the Grand Censor Sang Hongyang and Confucian scholars. Starting from the latter half of the Song Dynasty till the Ming Dynasty, the military harassment from the northern minority groups made the official communications of foodstuff and salt unbearable. In the early years of the Ming Dynasty, the logistic services for the northern frontier defense were especially difficult. Therefore, the government had to transfer the qualifications of legal salt sale to get the support of transport and wealth from the merchants, particularly from Yan, Ji, and Shanxi. However, in Sichuan, the overall social structure was highly stable without major warfare. This social serenity somehow helped the development of the well salt industry, but the governmental control was kept strict and effective, a stark contrast with the half-cooperative and half-competitive methods in northern China. Before the Qing Dynasty, even though the production units were scattered throughout Sichuan, the entire industry was at the hands of the central and local governments, unable to assist the enhancement of the living standards of the mass public and the local economic development. During the last period of the Ming Dynasty, owing to the enduring warfare, most of the salt wells were blocked, and the industry in Sichuan was close to collapse. In the reign of Kangxi (1661 A.D.–1722 A.D.), with the imperative need to restore the well salt production and the development of capitalism, the Qing government reformed the management mechanism of salt manufacturing in Sichuan, allowing the non-governmental people to start drilling the new wells freely. Later, in the reign of Qianlong (1735 A.D.–1799 A.D.), the Qing government began to lessen the taxation of the newly-drilled salt wells until totally canceling the tax. These progressive measures incurred a skyrocketing increase in the production and its impact in the entire economical chain, with the salt outcome of Sichuan expanding eight-fold within a century, from around forty-five thousand tons during the Yongzheng period (1722 A.D.–1735 A.D.), to around three hundred and fifty thousand tons during the Jiaqing period (1796 A.D.– 1820 A.D.).

自清政府放开了沿袭千年的盐业专卖制度并允许私人投资凿井以后，社会资本开始大量进入这个行业。四川井盐产区的投资者主要是商人，其中尤以陕、晋商人为多。他们多以经营盐业或典当起家，多从控制川盐运输领域入手，以"租引代销"手法，获取大量利润，继而进一步控制广大川盐销售口岸，在各地开设盐店，积累巨额财富；最终这些外地商人多与四川本土的盐商合伙，将商业资本投向盐业井灶，转化为产业资本。四川盐业在走向商业化和资本化的过程中自身的技术水平快速发展，至 20 世纪初已做出了向近现代化工业过渡的尝试。

After the Qing government freed the thousand-year mechanism of salt production exclusive sales and allowed individuals and groups to open wells and production, social capital entered this industry on a massive scale. Most of the primary investors of well salt production industry were merchants from Shaanxi and Shanxi, who were growing and thriving from running salt-related business or pawns in a method of rent and sale with consignment. They usually started from controlling the communication channels to generate great profit, then expanding to the market ports, and finally opening up the salt shops. These merchants most likely ended up cooperating with the local salt business people by transferring commercial capital into industrial capital by means of pouring it into the physical process of salt production. During the process of commercialization and industrialization, the well salt industry upgraded its technology at a fast pace. In the first period of the twentieth century, some effort in developing into modern industrialization even appeared in this industry.

图 35 盐神庙内的戏台
Fig. 35 Opera stage in the Salt God Temple

蜀韵古镇

HISTORIC TOWNS IN SICHUAN:
THE CULTURAL HERITAGE PROTECTION AND UTILIZATION OF
HISTORIC TOWNS WITH DIFFERENT DIMENSIONS AND VISIONS
——多维视野下的古镇文化遗产保护与利用

图 36 从戏台看盐神庙大殿
Fig. 36 The main hall seen from the opera stage

　　四川井盐业的发展历经上千年的历史，在这期间，盐业产地本身和盐业运输沿途的城镇经济都得到了发展。罗泉古镇集产地和集散地于一身，当仁不让地迅速提升了自身的经济文化水平，不仅形成了完整的城市化架构，而且孕育出了丰富多彩的盐业文化。这一脉独特的文化以盐神庙的修建为标志达到了巅峰。盐神，为春秋时期齐桓公上卿管仲，他在齐国大力发展盐业，并制定了中国历史上首部盐政法典《正盐荚》，影响了其后两千余年的中国盐业。盐神庙的建立体现了盐业对罗泉当地文化和思想的深刻浸透，也反映了盐业文化的成熟和丰富以及对当地风貌的深刻影响。

　　盐神庙（图34-36）坐落于罗泉古镇子来桥东隅，于清同治七年（1868年）由当地制盐业大家钟氏家族筹资1.8万两白银修建，以供奉盐神管仲并方便盐商集会。1925年，罗泉井盐荣获巴黎世博会金奖以后，中华民国政府赠予官制走铜金粉字"盐神庙"大匾一块。罗泉盐神庙占地1964平方米，建筑面积达2700余平方米。盐神庙自建成之日起就成了四川东部井盐产区广大盐业生产经营者祈祷神灵保佑的精神寄托之地。

　　The well salt industry in Sichuan has been evolving for over a thousand years, during which both the manufacturing location of the salt and the towns along the salt transport routes had good opportunities to develop themselves. Luoquan Historic Town was not only a manufacturing spot but also a distributing center, which seized the opportunity to promote its own economic and cultural development. It formulated the complete urban structure, while conceiving a rich culture centering the salt industry. This unique cultural branch reached its peak when Salt God Temple was erected. Salt God is Guan Zhong, the senior minister of the Qi Kingdom in the Spring and Autumn Period (770 B.C.–476 B.C.). He significantly developed the salt production and drew up *Zheng Yan Jia*, the first salt administration code that has been influential to salt industry for more than two thousand years. The erection of the Salt Gold Temple resembles the profound permeation of salt production into the local culture and ethos of Luoquan, while also symbolizing the maturity and richness of the salt production and its influence on the local fabric.

　　Salt God Temple (Figs. 34-36) is situated on the east side of the Zilai Bridge in Luoquan. It was initially built in the seventh year of Tongzhi in Qing Dynasty (1868 A.D.). Funded by the local salt merchant, Zhong's family, with 18,000 tales of silver, this temple pays homage to the Salt God, Guanzhong, and provides a place for the salt merchants to gather. After winning the gold award in the 1925 World Expo in Paris, the government of the Republic of China donated a copper tablet with the characters "Yan Shen Miao," meaning "Temple of the Salt God." The temple occupies an area of 1,964 square meters with the building area of some 2,700 square meters. Since its erection, the Salt God Temple has become the spiritual ballast for a massive number merchants in salt production and sales industry in eastern Sichuan.

蜀韵古镇

HISTORIC TOWNS IN SICHUAN:
THE CULTURAL HERITAGE PROTECTION AND UTILIZATION OF
HISTORIC TOWNS WITH DIFFERENT DIMENSIONS AND VISIONS
——多维视野下的古镇文化遗产保护与利用

图 37 盐神庙层次丰富的建筑屋顶
Fig. 37 Layered roof shapes of the Salt God Temple

作为一个完整的建筑群落，盐神庙包括庙门、牌坊、戏台、耳楼、侧房和戏坝等部分（图 37）。它沿袭了中国古典建筑群落的传统布局方式，并融合了道教宫观的布局思想：根据八卦方位，乾南坤北，即天南地北，整个群落坐北朝南并沿南北方向纵深发展；左右侧根据日东月西、坎离对称的原则沿一条长达 52 米的地基中轴线呈对称分布，既有"尊者居中"的等级思想，又体现了平稳、持重和静穆的审美情趣。庙门临街，院落左右两侧各有一个约 150 平方米的临街店铺，分别作为盐商的现货交易之所

和品茶聊天之地。盐神庙院落错落有致，与古街浑然一体。盐神庙布局类似于一个大四合院，除正殿以外的其余结构均参照一楼一底的模式修建。进入庙门后即是一个由青石板铺成的宽敞的露天坝，面积超过 300 平方米，东西两侧均配有环廊，供罗泉人尤其是罗泉盐商观摩戏剧。露天坝后紧接着就是主戏楼，其建筑面积达到 132 平方米，由八根圆形木柱托起。戏台两侧各有五间小屋供演员休息准备，穿过戏台沿石阶向上即到达正殿。正殿坐落于整个盐神庙群落的最高处，由四根雕刻有金龙的大木柱支撑，整个庙宇的主神管仲和副神关羽、火神李冰就供奉在这四根龙柱的正中央。正殿两侧由山墙封边，但各有一道小门连通至一个小天井，天井四周各有一间小屋，供盐神庙管事及贵宾下榻。

盐神庙的正殿是整个庙宇的精华之所在，其构架和布局同样参照了道教宫观建筑的风格，整体规格极高，属于中国古代建筑中规格最高的殿式建筑，高于大式建筑和小式建筑。正殿四柱的方正结构贴合了道家平稳自持的审美心理，且利于建筑本身聚四方之气，迎四方之神。四根木柱以金龙雕刻缠绕，象征着建筑规格极高和崇高的地位（在中国古代一般非帝王后妃使用的建筑中均严禁描龙画凤）。

As a comprehensive architectural complex, the Salt God Temple is composed of the front gate, *Paifang*, theater stage, wing rooms, and central courtyard (Fig. 37). Inherited from the conventional composition of classical Chinese architectural compounds, while also taking rich references from the traditional Taoism architecture, the Temple of the Salt God was developed along the north-south orientation. According to the orientation of the Eight Diagram, Qian (Sky) stands for the south and Kun (Earth) is for the north, and the compound should sit on the north (Earth) facing the south (Sky). Meanwhile, learning from the natural composition of Sun (Kan) on the east and Moon (Li) on the west, the complex is laid out following a 52-meter-long axis of symmetry to reach the balance of Kan and Li. This layout not only reveals the hierarchical idea of "the noble sits in the middle" but also reflects the aesthetical pursuit of calmness, prudence, and solemnity. The front gate is close to the old street directly, with two 150-square-meter stores on both sides, one for the trade of salt products, another for the merchants to rest and meet. The complex is not only developed in a sophisticated manner but also meshed perfectly into the old street. The composition of the temple is close to a huge quadrangle residence complex. All constructions but the main hall were built with two floors. Behind the front gate there is a spacious courtyard, with an area of over 300 square meters covered by indigo slates. It is surrounded by rounded galleries on both the east and west sides for the Luoquan people, especially the salt merchants, to sit and watch the opera. The major theater stage supported by eight round logs stands next to the courtyard, with the building area of 132 square meters. On each of the two wings of the stage are five rooms provided for the opera cast to rest and prepare. At the back of the stage is the main hall reached by the stone stairs. The main hall commands the very height of the entire compound. It is surpported by four huge wood columns engraved with golden dragons. The principle god, Guanzhong, and the secondary gods, Guan Yu and Li Bing (the God of Fire), are enshrined at the exact center of these four dragon-columns. The two sides of the main hall are enclosed by the mountain walls, but there are small gates open to a little courtyard surrounded by a small guest room on each side.

The main hall, whose composition and frame also took reference from the precedents of the palace-temple architecture of Taoism, bears the quintessence of the whole temple compound. The formal level of the main hall is ultimately high and belongs to the Palace Architecture, which is superior to the other two forms of traditional Chinese architecture, Big Architecture (wooden frame with a bucket arch) and Small Architecture (wooden frame without a bucket arch). The orthogonal structure of the four columns of the main hall complies with the reposeful and self-restraining aesthetic pursuit. Furthermore, this structure will facilitate the architecture to gather the air and welcomes deities from all four different directions. The engraved decoration in the motif of golden dragon symbolized the high level and noble status of the architecture, whereas in ancient China, the dragon and phoenix related ornament is exclusively reserved for the emperors and his queens.

柳江 Liujiang

　　柳江古镇（图 38），位于四川省洪雅县城西南花溪河的支流柳江沿岸。柳江是洪雅县的几何中心，将洪雅分为南北两部。因此，古镇自然就成了南北的必经之地，加上位于瓦屋山北口，交通十分便利。明代以后水利开发较为充分，柳江经济较为发达。柳江古镇自然资源丰富，尤以竹木资源为甚，森林覆盖率达到 67%。

Liujiang (Fig. 38) is in the south-west part of Hongya County of Sichuan. Since it is at the geometric center of Hongya County, Liujiang divides Hongya County into two parts on the north and the south. Therefore, Liujiang naturally becomes an important point of the traffic going between the north and the south. Meanwhile, it is at the north porch of the Wawu Mountain, enjoying wonderful transport conditions. From the Ming Dynasty, this area started leaping up economically due to the exploitation of hydrological resources. Liujiang historic town has abundant natural resources, especially forests and bamboos, with the forest covering up to 67%.

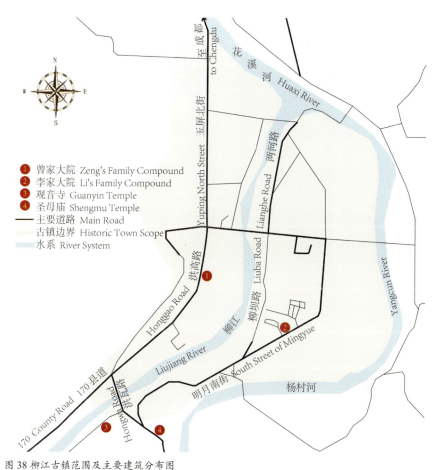

图 38 柳江古镇范围及主要建筑分布图
Fig. 38 Diagram of Liujiang Historic Town's scope and of its major buildings

① 曾家大院 Zeng's Family Compound
② 李家大院 Li's Family Compound
③ 观音寺 Guanyin Temple
④ 圣母庙 Shengmu Temple
— 主要道路 Main Road
古镇边界 Historic Town Scope
水系 River System

柳江古镇古代为芦村，南宋绍兴十年（1140 年）始建为镇，原名"明月镇"。清代中期，小镇上柳、姜两姓族人合资修建起一条石板长街而更名为"柳姜场"。清乾隆四十五年（1780 年）正式定名为"柳江镇"。

In the old days, Liujiang historic town was a little village named Lucun Village. In the years of Shaoxing of the South Song Dynasty (1140 A.D.), Liujiang was established as a town, with the original name called "Mingyue" town ("bright moon" in Chinese). In the mid years of the Qing Dynasty, two families in this town, the Lius and the Jiangs, contributed cooperatively to build a stone street. This town therefore changed its name to "Liujiang Field." In the forty-fifth year of Qianglong (1780 A.D.), this town was officially given the name of "Liujiang."

蜀韵古镇

HISTORIC TOWNS IN SICHUAN:
THE CULTURAL HERITAGE PROTECTION AND UTILIZATION OF
HISTORIC TOWNS WITH DIFFERENT DIMENSIONS AND VISIONS
——多维视野下的古镇文化遗产保护与利用

图 39 柳江边的古榕树和吊脚楼
Fig. 39 Banyan trees and pile dwellings along the river

图 40 柳江的老街
Fig. 40 Old street in Liujiang

　　柳江古镇坐拥秀丽旖旎的自然风光，在瓦屋山、五凤山和玉屏山的环抱之中，受到花溪河和杨村河的滋养。这样优厚的自然条件孕育了柳江独特的自然景观和生态景观，这些景观成了柳江古典建筑中不可分割的一部分。景观和建筑相辅相成，相存相依，缺一不可（图 39-41）。比如，在曾家大院中，最为明显的标志就是一棵奇特的古树。

　　Liujiang is intensively blessed with splendid and charming natural scenery. Surrounded by Wawu Mountain, Wufeng Mountain, and Yuping Mountain while nourished by the Huaxi River and the Yangcun River, Liujiang has been enjoying a unique natural landscape and ecological environment, which has meshed smoothly with the classic architecture of Liujiang by becoming an indispensable part of it. Therefore, the landscape and the architecture beautify each other and blend as one (Figs. 39-41). For instance, the most discernible feature of Zeng's Compound is a peculiar old tree that blends seamlessly into the scenery.

图 41 环抱柳江的山与水
Fig. 41 Mountains and rivers around Liujiang

蜀韵古镇

HISTORIC TOWNS IN SICHUAN:
THE CULTURAL HERITAGE PROTECTION AND UTILIZATION OF
HISTORIC TOWNS WITH DIFFERENT DIMENSIONS AND VISIONS
——多维视野下的古镇文化遗产保护与利用

图 42 曾家大院的西式元素
Fig. 42 Western elements in Zeng's Family Compound

柳江历史上曾有四大家族，传言"曾家房子、杨家顶子、张家女子、何家谷子"，其意为曾家有最好的家族庄园，杨家做官势力最大，张家的女子最为美丽，而何家拥有最多的良田。曾家大院正是柳江古镇乃至整个洪雅地区保存最为完好的庄园。曾氏家族的发迹人曾壁光（约 1795 年—1875 年），字枢元，柳江本地人，曾师从张带江，后官至贵州巡抚等封疆大吏，谥号"文诚"。曾家大院便是曾留学法国主修建筑的后人柳江名绅曾艺澄先生设计建造的（图 42-43）。由园中匾铭可知，曾家大院始建于 1927 年，历时十年建成。

In the history of Liujiang, there have been four major families: the Zengs famous for their architectural compound, the Yangs who held significant power in politics, the Zhangs with beautiful girls, and the Hes who held large number of crop fields. In fact, it is Zeng's Family Compound that has been best preserved in Liujiang and even throughout the entire Hongya County. The Zengs gained their eminence from Zeng Biguang. Zeng Biguang (c. 1795 A.D.–1875 A.D.), with the courtesy name Shuyuan, was a Liujiang local. He used to study under the great trecentist Zhang Daijiang. He went on to peak as the Governor of Guizhou and ended with the posthumous title "Wen Cheng," meaning loyalty to literature. Zeng's Compound was initially designed and constructed under the leadership of his progeny Zeng Yicheng, who had studied architecture in France (Figs. 42-43). According to the recordings from the tablet and stone inscriptions left behind, Zeng's compound was built during 1927 and underwent ten years of construction.

图 43 曾家大院里的建筑
Fig. 43 Buildings in Zeng's Family Compound

蜀韵古镇

HISTORIC TOWNS IN SICHUAN:
THE CULTURAL HERITAGE PROTECTION AND UTILIZATION OF
HISTORIC TOWNS WITH DIFFERENT DIMENSIONS AND VISIONS
——多维视野下的古镇文化遗产保护与利用

图 44 曾家大院内的戏台
Fig. 44 Opera stage in Zeng's Family Compound

曾家大院坐西向东，始建占地面积为 11 621 平方米，总建筑面积 5402 平方米。整体呈"四院三戏台"布局，从前到后共有四套四合院，穿插着三个戏台（图 44），周围搭配观景台、八字龙门、小姐楼、书房和牌坊等结构，另配有牡丹园和荔枝园等供院主人歇游赏玩。这座复合四合院建筑群落按繁体字"壽"布局，尤其是外墙临河出位顺应此字的笔画布局，严格地一拐一弯，状如锯齿，这样独特的布局体现了设计者和院落主人对长寿安康的精神追求。

作为传统的民居建筑，曾家大院普遍采用了木结构配以穿斗梁架，各处楼台以通廊式转角相连，并与各檐廊相接，连缀成一个统一的有机整体。整个大院以正厅（图 45）为最重要的部分，其正厅面阔五间 29 米，进深五间 18.7 米，通高 11 米，主楼高 4.5 米，整体从地面垫高 0.7 米，位于一座素面台基上，因而配有四级垂带踏道，往上立有悬柱廊，廊宽 2.5 米，柱间栅栏高 1 米，旁有飞来椅，上施浮雕。正厅屋顶采用单檐歇山的制式，全木结构配六穿七柱式的穿斗梁架，迎面主体为仿砖式装饰，并施以仿砖格图案，用捶灰木框架塑形，形成了方梁方柱的视觉效果。而各个窗户和檐角下均配有相应的以浆塑工艺制成的花卉或瑞兽图案。正厅两侧通过走马转角廊连通的对称等高的左右厢房，均面阔四间宽 12.9 米，通进三间 10.2 米，通高 8.2 米。正厅以后由院坝与戏楼相连。戏楼规格为单檐歇山顶，采用木结构配五穿五柱的穿斗梁架，面阔三间宽 11.9 米，进深三间 10.2 米。整个戏楼建筑面积约为 990 平方米，其中有花斋 50 平方米，歌榭 285 平方米。

Zeng's Family Compound oriented horizontally by sitting at the west facing to the east. The original complex occupies an area of 11,621 square meters in total with a building area of 5,402 square meters. The major composition is formulated with four yards and three stages (Fig. 44). They aligned linearly with the three stages and interluded into the four quadrangles. Around this main structure is the sightseeing platform, " 八 "-shaped dragon building, lady's building, studyroom, and memorial arches. Besides, some components including the Garden of Peony and the Garden of Litchi were constructed for the delight of the compound owners. This multi-quadrangle residential compound is arranged in the form of the traditional Chinese character " 壽 " (Shou, longevity). This design is especially visible for the part of the external walls near the river, where the construction is severely deformed and jagged. It is said to befit the character of the composition. This unique design of the compound reveals the spiritual pursuit of longevity and welfare.

As the typical residential housing complex, Zeng's Family Compound widely utilizes wooden frames with *Chuandou* structure. Various buildings and standards are connected to the manner of gallery, while also connected to different eaves and verandas. They cooperatively formulate an organic unity. The Main Hall (Fig. 45) is the most significant component of the compound, with the five-room width of 29 meters and five-room depth of 18.7 meters. The overall height of the Main Hall reaches 11 meters, with the major building height of 4.5 meters. The construction is set off 0.7 meters from the ground upon a plain surface podium, therefore forming a four-step *Chuidai* (vertical) path. Above are rows of hanging colonnade with a 2.5-meter in-between space, which is filled with the one-meter-high rack stakes. Attaching to the building are several flying chairs decorated with relief sculpture. The roof of the Main Hall implements the formal of the single-cornice *Xieshan* style, while the entire wood frame is structured with the six-beam-seven-column *Chuandou* structural system. The major facade is decorated with checkered quasi-brick techniques, and formed by the ash-loading wooden truss. They jointly create the visual experience of rigidly square beams and square columns. Under every window and eaves corner is decorated with sculptures of either flowers or beasts as motifs produced in the manner of pulp modeling. The two sides of the Main Hall are connected to the symmetrical and equal-height wing rooms through corner galleries. Both wings are built to the four-room width of 12.9 meters, the three-room depth of 10.2 meters, and the height of 8.2 meters. Behind the Main Hall is the courtyard, which points to the stage building. The stage building, erected in a format of single-cornice *Xieshan* roof, incorporates the wood frame with the five-beam-five-column *Chuandou* structure system. The building has a three-room width of 11.9 meters and three-room depth of 10.2 meters. The overall building area for the entire stage building complex is approximately 990 square meters, of which 50 square meters are for the flower studio and 285 square meters are designated to the singing and dancing platform.

蜀韵古镇

HISTORIC TOWNS IN SICHUAN:
THE CULTURAL HERITAGE PROTECTION AND UTILIZATION OF
HISTORIC TOWNS WITH DIFFERENT DIMENSIONS AND VISIONS
——多维视野下的古镇文化遗产保护与利用

图 45 从庭院看曾家大院正厅
Fig. 45 The main hall viewed from the courtyard in Zeng's Family Compound

　　由于所处时代背景的特殊性和开放性，曾家大院呈现出了中西建筑风格和建筑形式融合的特点。就群落的整体布局而言，曾家大院继承了中国古典家族建筑群落的特点：封闭森严，具有较强的对外隔绝性。然而其对几何形式和线条的运用又体现了欧式建筑舒缓流畅的柔和感。大院的主要装饰部件多采用中国古典雕刻和制造技巧，其中体量较小的窗棂反映了中式艺术技法的精巧雅致，体量较大的栅栏和廊柱体现了中式正统建筑群落的庄重和肃穆。而其回廊、楼梯以及墙面天花和地面等装饰则受到了西方建筑哲学、美学以及壁画工艺艺术的启发。值得注意的是，虽然曾家大院的主人曾艺澄有过留洋背景，在中国封建社会的遗留桎梏未去的情况下，大院的核心设计理念仍然遵循中国传统文化和思想。例如中部天井中太平缸的应用，又如整个群落的南部紧邻被视为"风水宝地"的杨村河，而曾家在大院该部分清一色地采用了纯正的中式古典建筑风格和形式。

　　Due to the openness and particularity of the historic background it fell into, Zeng's Family Compound reflects the character of integration of both Chinese and Western architecture in terms of styles and form. As far as the overall composition, Zeng's Family Compound inherited the typical architectural traits of the Chinese classical family compound that is considerably exclusive to the external. Nonetheless, the implementation of geometric forms, especially lines, embodies the sense of gentle flow and smoothness of European architecture. A great portion of the decorative components of the compound utilized the traditional Chinese technique of sculpture and of the making. Those small-volume window panels reflect the delicacy and elegance of Chinese artistic techniques, while the large-volume fences and columns unveil the solemnity and gravity of the orthodoxy of the Chinese architectural compound. On the other hand, the embellishment of corridors, stairs, walls, ceilings, and floors is inspired by the western architectural philosophy and aesthetics, including the mural painting techniques. What is noteworthy is that, even though the owner and designer Zeng Yicheng had a background of studying abroad, the core design ideals of Zeng's Family Compound still developed in accordance with the traditional Chinese culture and ethos, with the remaining shackle of Chinese feudalism, such as the application of the Tank of Peace. For another instance, the southern part of the compound neighbor, Yangcun River, was considered the "blessed land" of *Fengshui*. Therefore, all structures in this section were built in the purest Chinese traditional styles and formality.

上里 Shangli

　　上里古镇（图 46）坐落于四川雅安市北部，位于成都平原中心西南部，东接名山和邛崃山，西连芦山，群山环抱，更是两河相交的夹角之处，是四川省"十大古镇"之一。上里既是南方丝绸之路临邛古道进入雅安的重要驿站，又是唐蕃古道上茶马司所在地，亦是红军长征时过境之地。

　　Shangli (Fig. 46) is situated to the north of the city of Ya'an, at the mid-southwest of the Chengdu Plain. It connects with Mingshan Mountain and Qionglai Mountain to the east and reaches Lushan Mountain to the west. Shangli is not only surrounded by mountains but also enclosed by two rivers. As one of the "Ten great historic towns of Sichuan province," Shangli is an important posthouse of the Linqiong Ancient Route connecting to the South Silk Road towards Ya'an. Besides, it is also where the Tea-Horse trading spot on the Tang-Tibet Ancient Route is located. In addition, the Chinese Red Army also passed through Shangli during the Long March.

to Chengdu 至成都

Yashang Road 雅上路

016 Township Road 016 乡道

Maoxi River 茅溪河

Yashang Road 雅上路

① 韩家大院 Han's Family Compound
② 文峰塔 Wenfeng Tower
③ 双节孝牌坊 Shuangjiexiao *Paifang*
④ 二仙桥 Two Immortals Bridge
—— 主要道路 Main Road
古镇边界 Historic Town Scope
水系 River System

图 46 上里古镇范围及主要建筑分布示意图
Fig. 46 Diagram of Shangli Historic Town's scope and its major buildings

上里在最早期为民族聚集区，主要以本地的青衣羌族为主。秦灭赵国以后将赵国臣民迁于此，后来汉代建立以后又将西楚的臣民迁来，至明末清初又有大量移民随"湖广填四川"来到这里。不仅如此，由于南方丝绸之路的日渐繁华，往来客商等也来此定居，各地文化同当地文化融合成了统一的汉文化。古镇初名"罗绳"，取昔日古道上的驿站、关隘之意，是巴蜀平原通往外民族地区的关卡之一。中华人民共和国成立后，依据陇西河的流向，上游所在的乡被划为上里。

At the very beginning, Shangli was the rally point of the minority groups, primarily the local Qingyi Qiang People in the local Ba-Shu region. After the Qin Kingdom defeat of the Zhao Kingdom, the Qin migrated many people from former Zhao Kingdom to Shangli. Later, after the Han Dynasty was established, many people from former West Chu went to Shangli as well. In the late Ming and early Qing period, even more people came here from the migration movement "Hu-Guang Fills Sichuan." Besides these official movements, more commercial people and merchants from along the South Silk Road came to settle at Shangli with the rising prosperity of this trading route. These various cultures have been incorporated with the local one to form a uniformed Han culture. Shangli was originally named as "Luosheng," meaning "the old post on ancient route." After P.R. China was established, this area on the upstream of Longxi River was named "Shangli."

蜀韵古镇

HISTORIC TOWNS IN SICHUAN:
THE CULTURAL HERITAGE PROTECTION AND UTILIZATION OF
HISTORIC TOWNS WITH DIFFERENT DIMENSIONS AND VISIONS

——多维视野下的古镇文化遗产保护与利用

　　中国历史文化名城研究所川西北调研组朱晓林博士在《中国古镇游》一书中写道：（上里古镇）镇内石板铺街、木屋为舍，建筑群高低错落、古风宛然；大院建筑雕梁画栋、飞阁流丹、镂空细作、曲尽其妙，均为清代佳作。就现状总体风貌与居住建筑群规模而言，上里镇是保护得相当完整的乡土聚落（图48）。然而，上里古典建筑的风韵远非这几句简单的话就能概括。虽然很多精美的艺术在岁月的侵蚀下失去了光鲜的色泽，但其古建筑中青瓦飞檐、木窗、枋等以浮雕、镂空雕和镶嵌雕组合而成的部件仍以其精湛的工艺和精巧的构图凸显出深厚的民族文化。从空间格局上看，上里古镇的建筑聚落主要为民居，风格以明、清时期为主，街道均采取"井"字布局，辅以木结构建筑，寓意"井中有木，水火不容"，以水制火孽，祈愿平安（图47）。

　　Dr. Zhu Xiaolin, a senior research fellow for the Research Institute of China's Historic and Cultural Towns, once wrote in *China's Historic Towns* that Shangli has streets paved with stone slate, dwelling houses made of wood. The architecture compounds that are scattered in various manners, are accompanied with decoratively carved beams, beautifully painted rafters, and flying attics with flowing water landscape in a subtle and elegant way. They resemble the splendid architectural techniques and construction ideals of the Qing Dynasty. From the perspective of the entirety of the architectural appearance and the scale of the architectural compounds, Shangli has relatively well preserved vernacular complexes. (Fig. 48) However, the charm and grace of Shangli's architectural heritage can never be summarized by these simple sentences. A considerable amount of artistic masterpieces were eroded by the time lapsing and lost their bright glamour. However, architectural components including green-tale cornice, wood window frames and rafters with relief sculpture, hollowed-out sculpture, and mosaic sculpture are still resembling the profundity of the vernacular culture using the exquisite techniques and elaborate composition. From the perspective of spatial order, the main architectural compound in Shangli is the dwelling residence with styles of the Ming-Qing period, while streets are laid out in the format of the Chinese character "井" (Jing, meaning "water wells") with wood buildings. They cooperatively articulate a layer of meaning that "Destructive fire incurred of wood is now enfettered in the water well," which reflects people's wishes for the peace and welfare of this little historic town (Fig. 47).

图 47 上里古镇街肆
Fig. 47 Street market in Shangli

图 48 江边的吊脚楼
Fig. 48 Pile dwellings near the river

牌坊，作为中国传统建筑的重要类型之一，是中国封建社会为表彰功勋、科第、德政、忠孝节义从而宣扬礼教而建的纪念性建筑物，最初由祭天祀孔的棂星门演变而来。就结构而言，牌坊的原始雏形名"衡门"，为两根柱子架一根横梁的简单造型。最早在《诗经·陈风·衡门》中有记载："衡门之下，可以栖迟。"牌坊滥觞于汉阙，成熟于唐、宋，至明、清时期，随以程朱理学为代表的封建意识的普及和深入而登峰造极。

Paifang (memorial archway), as one of the most important types of traditional Chinese architectures, is a memorial construction that was erected by the feudal society to honor feats, academic accomplishment, benevolent governance, and the social morals of loyalty, filial piety, chastity and righteousness. It was originally evolved from the Lingxing Gate that served the function of paying homage to the sky and honoring Confucius. As far as the building structure is concerned, the prototype of Paifang is simple with the two columns supporting a beam above, known as Heng Gate, which was initially recorded in Shi Jing: Chen Feng-Heng Men (The Book of Odes: The Song of Chen-Heng Gate). Paifang originated from the Han Dynasty, matured in the Tang-Song period, and reached its summit in the Ming-Qing period due to the prevalence of the feudal ethos and morals represented by the Cheng-Zhu school of Neo-Confucianism.

双节孝牌坊（图49）位于上里古镇南部的古道上，枋上横额阴文雕字镌刻"双节孝"三字，脊顶下正中精雕"圣旨"二字。该坊于清道光十九年（1839年）由清廷御赐旌表节孝，用以褒扬上里韩家六代杨母和七代范母姑媳二人守节尽孝之事迹。从建筑格局的角度考量，该坊为典型的三间四柱十二翼出檐多脊，规格属中等偏上（中国古代最高规格的牌坊是帝王陵寝的五间六柱式），其建造均取材于当地的石英红砂岩石。双节孝牌坊通高11.25米，进深3米，其主体基座宽7.8米，两侧出檐1.1米。坊前30米处左右竖立12米高六棱四方双斗石桅杆一对。坊上图饰以镂空石雕为主，施以石青、石绿、石红和金箔等彩绘，浮雕图饰精美、人物勾画细腻生动，所展现的历史故事与戏剧场面取材广泛且风格宏伟，反映了旧时上里人广博的知识造诣，以及当地匠人的精湛技艺。

图 49 上里双节孝牌坊
Fig. 49 Shuangjiexiao *Paifang* in Shangli

Shuangjiexiao *Paifang* (Memorial Archway for Chastity and Filial Piety) (Fig. 49) is located in the historic avenue of Shangli. Above on the banner is engraved with three characters cut in intaglio, "Shuang," "Jie," and "Xiao," meaning chastity and filial piety for two people. At the center of the top of the ridge are two elaborately engraved characters "Sheng Zhi," meaning royal decree. This *Paifang* was erected during the nineteenth year of Daoguang (1839 A.D.) under the order of the central government of Qing to honor the perseverance of chastity and abeyance of filial piety of two women from the Han family in Shangli. From the architectonic perspective, this *Paifang* belongs to the typical three-intervals-four-column frame, together with twelve wings, multiple ridges, and extending cornices. This format embodies a position slightly above the average with the five-interval-six-column frame for the imperial mausoleums being the highest. Construction materials were all drawn from the local quartz with red sandstone rocks. The *Paifang* has a building height of 11.25 meters and a depth of 3 meters. The major podium is as wide as 7.8 meters with the cornices extending 1.1 meters outside. 30 meters ahead from the *Paifang* stands a pair of 12-meter-high hexagonal stone masts with quartet double brackets. The decoration on it is primarily fretted relief sculpture with pigmented drawings of azurite, malachite, gold foil, etc. The sculpture was conducted with highly refined techniques and vividly rendered figures. The historical tales and histrionic scenes are presented in a grand manner with expansive materials and sources, which are strongly intuitive and reflective of the prosperity and diversity, as well as the superb skills inherited from old Shangli's architects and craftsmen.

街子 *Jiezi*

　　街子古镇（图50）位于成都市崇州城西北部，环抱于凤栖山和青城山的原始森林中，味江穿镇而过，得山灵水秀之惠，更是宋代王小波、李顺起义之处。从晋代（265年–420年）兴建的光严禅院开始，共有32座寺庙陆续兴建于此，街子独特的禅院建筑群落由此形成。街子镇北部与都江堰接壤，地势平缓。受岷江水系支流味江的影响，街子地下水丰富，流于石板路和房屋之间，有"川西水乡"之名。街子深受地方各级政府重视，为四川历史文化名镇和成都市"五大天府古镇"之一。

　　Jiezi (Fig. 50) is situated to the northwest of Chongzhou of the city of Chengdu. It is set at a location surrounded by the virgin forests of Fengqi Mountain and Qingcheng Mountain, with Weijiang River passing through. It is also where Wang Xiaobo and Li Shun started the uprising in Song Dynasty. Beginning at Guangyan Temple built in the Jin Dynasty (265 A.D.–420 A.D.), a total of 32 temples were erected in Jiezi, forming a unique architectural complex of temples. Jiezi connects with Dujiangyan Weir with a flat topography and is influenced by the Minjiang River system. Therefore, Jiezi has abundant underground water that flows around the stone walk and buildings, earning it the name of "Water-land in West Sichuan." Highly valued by various levels of local government, Jiezi is an important historic and cultural town of Sichuan province and one of the five "Tianfu Historic Towns" of the city of Chengdu.

图 50 街子古镇范围及主要建筑分布示意图
Fig. 50 Diagram of Jiezi Historic Town's scope and its major buildings

街子古镇的建置最早始于五代时期，最初因横于味江江畔而得名"横渠镇"。五代后蜀（907 年—960 年）改设为永康县，街子镇即成为其县治所在地，随后即逐渐衰落。至明朝万历四十二年（1614 年），百业凋敝，曾经繁华的街子镇只剩沿味江边的一条街，因而改叫"街子场"，1991 年重新建镇。在 2008 年 "5·12" 汶川特大地震中，街子古镇遭受重创，历经两年多才完成灾后重建。

Jiezi was initially established in the period of Five Dynasties and named as "Hengqu" since it was flying across Weijiang River. During the Later Shu Dynasty (907 A.D.–960 A.D.), it was changed to be a county called Yongkang County, and Jiezi was where the government sat. However, from then on, Jiezi had been gradually stepping into decline. Till the forty-second year of Wanli in the Ming Dynasty (1615 A.D.), due to the all-round decay industries, only one single and lonely street was left along the bank of Weijiang River in the place where the once prosperous Jiezi town lay. For this cause, it was renamed as "Jiezi Fair," until it was re-established as a town in 1991. In May 2008, Jiezi was severely stricken in the "5.12" Wenchuan Earthquake, which made it go through more than two years of post-disaster reconstruction.

　　街子古镇现以江城街为中心的六条街作为核心区域,古建筑总建筑面积约6.8万平方米。临街房屋大体遵照《清工部工程作法则例》营造，结构上多采用木制结构穿斗梁架方式，规格上多用单檐青瓦，辅以民居布局，前店后院式（图52-53），总体以清代中、晚期建筑为主，普遍体量不大，用材小巧，风格朴素，但局部的装饰性雕刻多工于精美。

　　字库塔（图51）建于清中后期道光年间，整个塔身综合利用了石条、石墩和青砖建成，其主体结构呈正六边形中心对称，塔高五层，其中上面四层刻有中国古典爱情传说《白蛇传》的壁画。唐朝"一瓢诗人"唐求曾在此读书吟诗。

Jiezi is centered at the Jiangcheng street and five other historic streets. The overall building area of the historic architecture reaches approximately 68,000 square meters. Constructions along streets were built primarily in accordance with *The Official Regulation of the Construction Department of the Qing Dynasty*. Structurally, wood frame with *Chuandou* structure was heavily utilized. From the perspective of format, single cornice with gray tales is the most popular form. The composition of the civil residence is laid out with the shops on the facade and courtyard at the back (Figs. 52-53). In general, the architecture of Jiezi reveals the style from the mid and late period of the Qing Dynasty, which usually implements small volume and exquisite material with simplistic styles, while the decorative engravings in the partial sense is more likely elaborate.

Ziku Tower (The Tower of Character Storage) (Fig. 51) was erected in the mid-late period of the Qing Dynasty during the years of Daoguang. The main body of the tower made a comprehensive use of stone sticks, stone blocks, and gray tiles during construction. The major structure is in the Centro-symmetric formation of the regular hexagon. The tower has five stores in total, with the above four engraved with the external fresco telling the classical Chinese love story, *Tale of the White Snake*. "*Yipiao* Poet" Tang Qiu of the Tang Dynasty once studied and wrote poems there.

图 51 街子字库塔
Fig. 51 *Ziku* Tower in Jiezi

图 52 当地的竹篾匠人
Fig. 52 Local bamboo craftsman

图 53 当地的铁匠铺
Fig. 53 Local smith house

　　字库塔的来历和中国古时特有的"敬惜字纸，惜字是福"的传统是密不可分的。受科举制度的影响，古人多认为文字是神圣和崇高的，是"古圣贤之心迹"，因而写在纸上的文字不能随意亵渎，即使是废字纸，也应诚心敬意地烧掉。明初凌濛初的拟话本小说集《二刻拍案惊奇》卷一《进香客莽看金刚经，出狱僧巧完法会分》开篇即有诗云："世间字纸藏经同，见者须当付火中。或置长流清净处，自然福禄永无穷。"而字库塔作为一种独立建筑形式更是源于古时人们对自然神灵的崇拜以及中国礼仪文化的传承和凝聚。相传黄帝史官仓颉造字时出现了"鬼夜哭""龙乃潜藏"等惊天动地的奇观，这些传说喻示着文字的出现和演变在中华文明发展过程中的深远意义。这种"敬天惜字"的独特习俗使得人们对焚烧字纸这一行为变得十分郑重，不但有专门的礼仪，还有特定的场所和设施，于是字库塔便应运而生，成为古人专门焚烧字纸的小型建筑，同时接受人们对字纸所承载的礼仪文化的顶礼膜拜。这样的尊崇一方面对中国文字和礼仪文化的发展起到了积极的推动作用，另一方面也掺杂了古人求取功名的功利主义思想。随着科举考试的盛行和"学而优则仕"观念的深入人心，字库塔后期逐渐演变为一种祈福德载体，多供有仓颉、文昌帝君、孔圣人等文神之位，学子们多在此祈求金榜题名，这既是一种思想的固化，又是一种对传统文化道德的尊崇。

The origin of *Ziku* Tower comes from the traditional Chinese morals of "Respect the papers with characters on." In old China, profoundly influenced by the imperial civil service examination system, people deemed that Chinese characters are noble and sacred, are the true feelings of ancient sages. Therefore, the characters on papers were not to be tainted. Even if the paper was no longer useful, it should only be incinerated wholeheartedly. In the storytelling style novel (*Amazing Tales: Second Series*), written by Ling Mengchu of the early Ming Dynasty, the first part describes people's homage to the characters in a poem saying that "all papers with characters on are as precious as Buddhism scripts; they all need to be incinerated if disposed and then put into a clean space or river; naturally, our younger generation will be blessed eternally." *Ziku* Tower, as an independent architectural format, could also originate to the people's worship to the prowess power of nature and the inheritance of the culture of politeness. It was said that when Cang Jie, the historian of Yellow Emperor, was creating words, some supernatural phenomena like ghosts crying and the appearance of dragons emerged, representing the significant role of the development of characters through the evolution of Chinese culture. This custom of respecting nature and cherishing characters makes the disposal of papers highly solemn. Therefore, not only certain etiquette but also particular place and facilities were established for this ritual. This was the inherent cause for the emergence of *Ziku* Tower, which then became the small-scale architecture solely utilized for the incineration of papers. It also received the ultimate reverence and admiration of the culture of decorum carried on by the written papers. On one hand, this distinctive homage positively propels the development of Chinese characters and etiquette culture. On the other hand, it also embodies the Benthamism for the pursuit of scholarly honors or ranks of scholars in old China. With the prevalence of the imperial civil service examination system and the decaying social morals of "good study can excel in the official career," *Ziku* Tower later gradually evolved into the carrier of people's prayers for blessings, with Cang Jie, Wen Chang Di Jun (God of Literature), and Confucius enshrined for the hope of success in examinations. This phenomenon is said to solidify the mind yet also uphold traditional virtues and culture.

古时人们对字纸以及字库塔这种崇敬的态度和心态在一定程度上影响了字库塔的规格和形式。明清时代的塔，其形制和建筑艺术大多沿袭了辽宋塔的形式，多为八角形或六角形，突破了唐塔端庄稳重、千篇一律的四边形。视觉上，古人在高大雄伟中多追求轻巧灵动之感，因此出现了如挑角飞檐等建筑部件，材料上多选用坚固耐久的砖石材料，但建筑技艺上则以砖石仿木结构居多，且塔檐等细节部位做工细致精巧。街子古镇的字库塔位于广场边缘，其本身高耸的造型在周围平坦地形低矮平房的映衬下更显威严，象征着字纸在封建礼仪文化和科举风潮中崇高的地位。塔身通体采用砖石材料，色调沉郁淡雅。

The respectful attitude towards the written words, to some extent, influenced the formality and construction of *Ziku* Tower. Towers in the Ming-Qing period, whose forms and building techniques mostly inherited the achievement of the Liao-Song period, were usually formed in octagonal and hexagonal shapes, which was a typical breakthrough of the stereotyped square shape of the Tang Dynasty. From the perspective of the visual and sensorial experience, they made an effort to pursue the exquisiteness and subtlety within the air of monumentality, which would be accomplished by architectural elements like jet-trajectory angles with flying cornices. Primary materials used were bricks and stones with considerable endurance, yet the building technique more likely revealed wood-imitation masonry. The architectural details, eaves and friezes in particular, were usually elaborately refined. The *Ziku* Tower in Jiezi is situated in the peripheral area of the open ground. Its own obelisk-like shape was further set off to be even more august by the surrounding flat topography and low architecture. This visual effect resembles the sublime status of written paper in the etiquette culture of the feudal times and frenzy of national examination. This entire tower body is constructed with bricks and tiles, with a gloomy tone and elegant hue.

光严禅院坐落于街子古镇的凤栖山，寺院占地面积 4.5 万平方米，建筑面积 8000 平方米。被大量珍稀古木如柏树、楠木、银杏等重重包围。古寺始建于西晋时期，晋文帝司马昭曾赐庙"青城三十六庵"，而光严禅院在其中规模最大，为三十六庵之首，原名"长乐庵"，隋朝开国皇帝隋文帝曾赐金匾书"光大严明"四字。唐武宗时期古寺被毁，后又于唐懿宗咸通五年（公元 864 年）由善思和尚重建，并改名为"常乐寺"。明朝永乐年间，为避"乐"字之讳，蜀献王朱椿奏请御赐寺名"光严禅院"，故又名"光严寺"。至此，古寺已规模宏大，僧众逾千，被赞为"佛及众生，鼎极一时"（图 54）。至清代，康熙皇帝为此寺御题"光严禅院"的匾额现在仍高悬于大门横额。

Guangyan Temple is located on the Fengqi Mountain of Jiezi, with an area of around 45,000 square meters and the building area of approximately 8,000 square meters. The temple was surrounded intensively by the forests composed of old rare trees including Cypress, Nanmu, Gingko and so on. This old temple was initially erected in the period of the West Jin Dynasty. Jin Wen Di (emperor of the West Jin Dynasty) Sima Zhao once bestowed the imperial blessings to build the "Thirty-six Temples around Qingcheng Mountain," amongst which Guangyan Temple has the largest building scale and enjoys the highest reputation and knowledge. The old name of the temple was Changle Temple. The founding emperor of Sui Dynasty Sui Wen Di vouchsafed a golden tablet with four characters, "Guang", "Da", "Yan", and "Ming", meaning everbrightness, impartiality, and strictness. During the period of Tang Wu Zong (emperor of the Tang Dynasty), the temple was destroyed. Later, during the fifth year of the years of Xiangtong (864 A.D.) of the Tang Dynasty, the temple was rebuilt under the leadership of Monk Shansi, and the temple was renamed as Changle Temple. During the years of Yongle of the Ming Dynasty, in order to avoid the literal confrontation against the character "Le," the king of the Shu vassal state Zhu Chun requested the emperor to officially confer the blessing to name the temple as Guangyan Temple. Till then, the temple had already occupied a monumental scale with over a thousand monks and disciples. It was then renowned as "Buddha blesses the entire mass at the height of power and splendor" (Fig. 54). During the Qing Dynasty, emperor Kangxi used the imperial brush to write the tablet with the temple name on it, which is still hung on the very front gate of the temple today.

蜀韵古镇

HISTORIC TOWNS IN SICHUAN:
THE CULTURAL HERITAGE PROTECTION AND UTILIZATION OF
HISTORIC TOWNS WITH DIFFERENT DIMENSIONS AND VISIONS
——多维视野下的古镇文化遗产保护与利用

图 54 凤栖山下的光严禅院 *
Fig. 54 Guangyan Temple at the foot of Fengqi Mountain

　　光严禅院在明朝时期深受皇恩，1344 年，17 岁的朱元璋迫于生计到洛阳皇觉寺投奔叔父法仁，并在此削发为僧。已经成为大明朝开国皇帝的朱元璋为报叔父七年的养育教诲之恩，下旨在全国各寺查访法仁和尚，最终由蜀王朱椿在常乐寺（光严禅院旧名）找到。然而法仁此时已为得道高僧，不为世俗所动，拒绝下山。朱元璋因此写下"纯正不屈"四字赠予叔父（此碑现仍嵌于古寺大雄宝殿前），后又下诏以"大明敕建"的规格重建常乐寺，赐皇锅一对，龙凤旗一对，銮驾半幅，琉璃瓦房殿堂五座（现存龙雕琉璃瓦数匹）。由于其悠久的历史和深厚的渊源，光严禅院历来为后世名流所青睐：古寺门口长联一副"芒鞋踏遍岭头云问者何在，锡杖遥挥天外路指月而忘"，相传为清朝四川总督所题；大雄宝殿二层檐下的"藏经阁"三字草书金匾为国民党元老、中华民国第一任监察院院长于右任所题；藏传佛教四大领袖之一的章嘉活佛也曾在此题下"严肃"二字。

During the Ming Dynasty, Guangyan Temple was considerably favored by the founding emperor Zhu Yuanzhang. In 1344, at the age of 17, he was short of alternatives of earning a living but to seek shelter from his uncle, monk Faren in the Huangjue Temple at Luoyang, and he ended up becoming a monk there himself. The founding emperor of the Ming Dynasty attempted to find his uncle, monk Faren in order to requite his help and teaching. Finally, Zhu Chun, the king of the Shu vassal state, found Faren in Guangyan Temple, who nonetheless refused to leave the temple for secularity's sake. Therefore, Zhu Yuangzhang wrote down four characters "Chun," "Zheng," "Bu," "Qu" on a stele for his uncle, to admire his characters of purity and fortitude. This stele is currently still well preserved in front of the main palace of the old temple. Later, Zhu Yuanzhang issued an imperial edict to rebuild his temple in accordance with the standards of national construction. In addition, countless treasures were bestowed to the temple. Thanks to its time-honored history and glorious past, Guangyan Temple has been highly favored by later gentries and celebrities. The long couplet was said written by the Governor of Sichuan of the Qing Dynasty. The golden tablet of Cang Jing Ge (Sutra Depository) on the second floor of the Mihavira Hall was inscribed by Yu Youren, the grand figure of Guomintang and the first chief of the Institute of Inspection of the Republic of China. In addition, one of the four great leaders of Tibetan Buddhism, Zhangjia Living Buddha, once inscribed "Yan Su" (meaning "solemnity") for the temple.

　　作为典型的佛教寺院，光严禅院从整体布局到局部规格都带有显著的佛教建筑特征。中国的佛教建筑在其初期虽受起源地天竺（今印度）的影响，但由于中国的建筑文化博大精深，中国佛教建筑很快就受到全面和深刻地本土化，多为严格对称的多进院落形式，光严禅院亦是如此：整个院落坐北朝南，呈轴对称分布，其主轴的最前方是山门。整个群落的主入口山门两侧各配有石狮一尊，看门守户，寓意吉祥平安。因"山""三"音近故山门又由平行的三道门组成，象征佛教的"三解脱门"——空门、无相门和无作门。山门后是接引殿（该殿在传统佛教建筑中应名为"天王殿"），用以供奉佛教护法四大天王、东来佛祖弥勒佛和四大天王座下三十二将之首——韦驮将军。随后是整个院落最为重要和核心的建筑——正殿，即"大雄宝殿"。正殿是整个佛寺建筑群落的中心建筑，无论在体量和空间上都远在其他单体建筑之上。不仅如此，正殿供奉佛祖释迦牟尼，因其德号为"大雄"，故获殿堂名"大雄宝殿"。从外观上来看，该殿气势宏大，面阔和通高均十分可观，采用中国古典殿式建筑的规格，配以重檐歇山顶，翼角高翘，整个建筑从平地直接拔高建于台面以上，凸显了它对周边建筑和景观的统领作用。殿内供奉佛祖三世身，正面即为现在佛释迦牟尼，东首为过去佛燃灯古佛，西首为未来佛弥勒佛。

As a typical Buddhism temple, Guangyan Temple is distinctly characterized by the features of the Buddhism architecture from the large-scale compound composition to the small-scale architectural elements. Buddhism architecture in China was initially under considerable influence from its origin, Tenjiku (current India). However, it was holistically and deeply localized; for instance, Guangyan Temple has a highly symmetrical multi-courtyard composition, since Chinese architecture is always so profound and grand. The entire compound, sitting at the north thus facing the south, is arranged along the symmetrical axis, whose very front lies on the Shan Men ("Mountain Gate") as the official entrance of the whole compound. This gate is accompanied bilaterally by a pair of stone sculpture of lions, with the meaning of guarding the temple for peace and welfare. Because "Shan" (meaning "mountain") and "San" (meaning "three") has close pronunciation, the Shan Men was built in a format of three parallel gates, which embodies "the Three Gates of Liberation" in Buddhism, Sunyata, Animitta, and Apranihita. After the Shan Men is the Jie Yin Palace (in traditional Buddhism architecture called "Tianwang Palace"), which houses and enshrines the Four Heavenly Kings of Buddhism, Maitreya, and Skanda, the most highly ranked general of thirty-two under the Four Heavenly Kings. Next is the most important and core component of the whole compound of Guangyan Temple, the main hall, also known as the Mahavira Hall. The main hall, as the semantic center of the whole Buddhism architectural world, considerably overwhelms all the other individual constructions in terms of volume and space. It always enshrines the greatest Buddha, Guatama Buddha, whose grand name is "Da Xiong" (Mahavira) that gives its name to the main hall. Looking externally, we may find that the main hall holds a magnificent air with huge building width and height. It incorporates the format of the conventional Chinese palatial architecture with a multi-cornice *Xieshan* roof and flange corners outstandingly raised. Built above a monumental podium, the whole building was directly set off from the ground, which reveals its overpowering and dominant role amongst the surrounding architecture and landscape. The main hall hosts the three lifetimes of the greatest Buddha, with the current Guatama Buddha in the middle, the past Dipamkara to the east, and the future Maitreya to the west.

李庄 Lizhuang

　　李庄古镇（图 55）位于宜宾东郊长江南岸，素有"万里长江第一古镇"之称，距今已有约 1460 年的建镇史。李庄地形平坦，水陆交通便捷，依长江繁衍生息，形成了"江导岷山，流通楚泽，峰排桂岭，秀流仙源"的自然景观。李庄还是抗日战争时期大后方的文化中心之一：1939 年，自"同大迁川、李庄欢迎，一切需要、地方供应"十六字电文发出起，国立同济大学、金陵大学、中央研究院、中央博物院、中国营造学社等十多家高等学府和科研院所，在抗战时期迁驻李庄。全国知名学者李济、傅斯年、陶孟和、吴定良、梁思成、林徽因、童第周、梁思永、劳干等云集李庄达六年之久，梁思成的《中国建筑史》这部扛鼎之作就诞生在李庄。

　　Lizhuang (Fig. 55) is situated on the east suburbs of Yibin, on the southern bank of the Yangtze River. With a history of around 1460 years, it has long been honored as the first historic town along the thousand-mile long Yangtze River. Lizhuang sits on flat land with convenient transportation both on ground and in water. Developed along Yangtze River, it has formed the natural scenery of "Yangtze River leading Minshan Mountain, winding towards the lakes in the Chu area, with mountains forming the Gui Mountain ridge, with creeks moistering this heavenly place." During the period of the Anti-Japanese War, Lizhuang became one of the most important cultural centers of the whole rear area of China. In 1939, Lizhuang published the open telegram to the entire nation that "Lizhuang welcomes Tongji University, with all needs provided locally." From then on, Tongji University, Jinling University, the Academia Sinica, the National Museum, the Society for the Study of Chinese Architecture, and other higher education agencies and research institutes moved to Lizhuang. Meanwhile, a large number of reputable professors and scholars stayed in Lizhuang for six years and resumed their research, including Li Ji, Fu Sinian, Tao Menghe, Wu Dingliang, Liang Sicheng, Lin Huiyin, Tong Dizhou, Liang Siyong, Lao Gan, etc. *The History of Chinese Architecture*, the greatest book written by Liang Sicheng, was finished in Lizhuang.

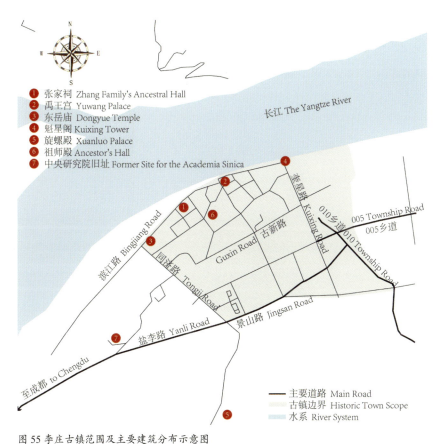

① 张家祠 Zhang Family's Ancestral Hall
② 禹王宫 Yuwang Palace
③ 东岳庙 Dongyue Temple
④ 魁星阁 Kuixing Tower
⑤ 旋螺殿 Xuanluo Palace
⑥ 祖师殿 Ancestor's Hall
⑦ 中央研究院旧址 Former Site for the Academia Sinica

长江 The Yangtze River

滨江路 Bingjiang Road
同济路 Tongji Road
古新路 Guxin Road
魁星路 Kuixing Road
010乡道 010 Township Road
005乡道 005 Township Road
盐李路 Yanli Road
景山路 Jingsan Road
至成都 to Chengdu

—— 主要道路 Main Road
古镇边界 Historic Town Scope
水系 River System

图 55 李庄古镇范围及主要建筑分布示意图
Fig. 55 Diagram of Lizhuang Historic Town's scope and its major building

作为历史文化名镇，李庄至今完整保存了 18 条明清古街巷和大量的古典民俗建筑，包括魁星阁、禹王宫、张家祠、东岳庙、旋螺殿、祖师殿、栗峰山庄和众多四合院以及老酒窖等。这些古典建筑既有宫殿祠堂的风格，又有川南民居的特点。

As a renowned town of history and culture, Lizhuang well preserves eighteen historic streets and a considerable amount of traditional civil architecture, for instance, Kuixing Tower, Yuwang Palace, the Zhang Family's Ancestral Hall, Dongyue Temple, Xuanluo Palace, Ancestor's Hall, Lifeng Villa, and a large number of quadrangle residences and old cellars. Some of these traditional architectures inherit styles from palaces and temples, while others reflect the characteristics of civil residence in southern Sichuan of the time.

蜀韵古镇
HISTORIC TOWNS IN SICHUAN:
THE CULTURAL HERITAGE PROTECTION AND UTILIZATION OF
HISTORIC TOWNS WITH DIFFERENT DIMENSIONS AND VISIONS
——多维视野下的古镇文化遗产保护与利用

　　李庄地区有人居住的历史可以追溯到3000前，春秋战国时期李庄亦为古僰人聚居地，后据传是因长江中打鱼为生的李姓兄弟聚居而得名。梁代大同六年（540年）李庄设南广县和六同郡，后因隋朝中期避隋炀帝杨广的名讳而改名为南溪县。唐代中期，戎州（今四川省宜宾市）府治曾迁于李庄直至北宋初年。从明代开始李庄正式设镇并成为长江上游的重要码头和物资集散地。抗日战争时期，李庄接纳了大量从东部沿海地区内迁的高校和科研机构，直至抗战胜利。

　　Lizhuang has a history of residence of more than three thousand years. In the Spring and Autumn period and the Warring States period, Lizhuang was the intensive residence of the ancient Bo people. Afterwards, Lizhuang was named in that it was a place largely inhabited by the large amounts of fishers with the surname "Li." In the sixth year of Datong of Liang Dynasty (540 A.D.), Lizhuang was set as part of Nanguang County in Liutong Prefecture. Later, it was renamed as Nanxi County to avoid the confrontation with the name of Yang Guang, King Yang of Sui Dynasty. In the mid Tang Dynasty, the center of the Rong Prefecture (present city of Yibin of Sichuan Province) was moved to Lizhuang until the early years of Northern Song Dynasty. Starting from the Ming Dynasty, Lizhuang was officially set as a town and became an important harbor and inventory distribution center on the upper reaches of the Yangtze River. During the period of the Anti-Japanese War, Lizhuang hosted a large number of higher education agencies and scientific research institutes that moved from the invaded eastern China until 1945.

李庄古镇位于川南地区，与成都平原地区有相当的距离，因而在其文化习俗、社会风貌和建筑风格方面均呈现出明显的不同。李庄的古建筑和古街古巷都带有明显的川南民俗风格。李庄汉代曾设驿站，由于濒临长江，在明清时期李庄成了水运商贸易的繁荣之地，因而这一时期的古建筑在此地大量出现，包括川南民居、各种庙宇、殿堂、沿街的酒肆茶楼等。李庄将明、清时期的这种古镇格局和风貌完好地保存了下来，整个古建筑群落规模宏大，布局严谨完整，石板街道脉络清晰。古建筑的元素和细节，尤其是封火山墙、木雕石刻、码头石阶等均保存良好，做工精细。一些有极高文化和历史价值的古建筑也保存完整，诸如禹王宫、东岳庙等"九宫十八庙"，被建筑大师梁思成称为"其梁柱结构之优，颇足傲于当世之作"的旋螺殿（图56），"李庄四绝"张家祠白鹤窗，文昌宫，"上海到宜宾两千多公里长江边建造得最好的亭阁"魁星阁和九龙碑，被誉为"川南民居的精品经典之作"的栗峰山庄，以及中国名酒"五粮液"的老酒窖等。

Lizhuang is in the south of Sichuan, with a considerable distance to the area of the Chengdu Plain. Therefore, fairly visible differences in culture customs, social features, and architectural styles reveal themselves in these two areas. The historic architecture, together with the historic alleys and streets, is characterized with South Sichuan traits. As such, Lizhuang was established as a posthouse in the Han Dynasty. Thanks to its closeness to the Yangtze River, Lizhuang became an intensive commercial trading point during the Ming and Qing Dynasties. By that token, architecture from that period was preserved in very good conditions, including the residence of South-Sichuan, multitudes of temples, palaces, halls, wine shops and teahouses on streets, etc. Lizhuang has been well preserved in the composition and appearances of historic towns of the time of Ming and Qing Dynasties. Therefore, the architecture complexes here have a fairly sizable scale with rigorous complete composition and arrangement, as well as distinct threads of flagstone pavement. The detailed architectural elements, in particular, fire-sealing gables, wood carvings, stone inscription, stairs, and harbors, are all kept in outstanding conditions that are still highly visible of the elaborate techniques and the vividness of the time. There still exists a large amount of historic architecture of highly cultural and historic value, for instance, the "Nine Palaces and Eighteen Temples" with Yuwang Palace and Dongyue Temple as representatives, Xuanluo Palace (Fig. 56), honored by architecture master Liang Sicheng who boasted that "the post and beam construction is matchlessly spectacular to any other in the world," the Fabulous Four of Lizhuang, a hundred-crane window in the the Zhang Family's Ancestral Hall, Wenchang Palace, Kuixing Tower ("the best shrine along the over-two-thousand-kilometer riverbank of the Yangtze River from Shanghai to Yibin"), and Nine-dragon stele, honored as Lifeng Villa of "the refined classic work of the southern Sichuan civil residence" and the old cellar of the best Chinese alcohol, Wuliangye Liquor.

图 56 旋螺殿外观
Fig. 56 Front appearance of Xuanluo Palace

旋螺殿，又名文昌宫，位于李庄古镇南部石牛山下的一块巨石上，始建于明万历二十四年（1596 年），清雍正、乾隆、嘉庆及道光朝均对其有一定规模的维护和修缮。

旋螺殿体量庞大，形如螺旋，采用三阶重檐攒尖顶，全高 25 米左右。屋面主体铺筒瓦兼小青瓦。殿平面呈正八边形，面阔、进深均为 8 米。殿内结构异于普通庙宇，由四井口柱直贯二层，井口柱间由抬梁、穿枋、角梁连接，形成梁架骨干。第一层抬梁结构承接殿内楞木楼板，东西两梁另下附梁枋，8 根采步梁上立中层檐柱 8 根，上承椽枋，下附檐椽；椽枋上为中檐斗拱。第二层抬梁结构承接顶层檐柱 8 根，檐柱平板枋上置拱，坐斗外侧为外檐斗拱，内侧构成网目状的藻井，殿的斗拱大致相同，因而层层而上，内承梁架，外挑檐枋。顶部藻井，八面均用斗拱，其左侧用如意斗拱，右侧斜翅和斗拱后卫向上重叠呈网目状，并向右旋转，形如旋螺，故有此名（图 57-59）。

Xuanluo Palace, also called Wenchang Palace, is set on a huge rock on the Shiniu Mountain south to Lizhuang. Xuanluo Palace was initially built during the twenty-fourth year of the years of Wanli (1596 A.D.). During the Qing Dynasty, in the years of Yongzheng to the years of Daoguang, there was continual maintenance and restoration for the temple.

Xuanluo Palace has a considerable volume with the typical shape of a helix. The palace incorporated the three-level cornice with the Zanjiang roof (pavilion roof). The overall height of the palace is approximately 25 meters. The primary construction material is pantiles with blue roofing tile as a supplement. Formally, the palace is in the standard shape of a regular octagon, with both building width and depth as eight meters. The internal structure of Xuanluo Palace varies from normal palatial architecture. The space of the first floor is penetrated through by four large columns arranged in the form of the Chinese character "Jing" (square form). Between neighboring beams is a connecting system composed of post and lintel frames, cutting pillars, and cantilevered corner beams, which cooperatively formulate the backbone of the structure. The first level of the post and lintel frames are further connected to the building floors made with arris wood. The east and west major beams are attached and supported by the girders. Above eight sleeper beams are eight mid-level peripheral columns, connected further to the rafters and beams on the above and attached further below to the entablatures. The bucket arches are installed above the beams. The second level of the post and lintel frames are connected to the eight top-level beams with another arches above the planes of the beam tops. Within the range of the bucket arches are the caisson realized by the coffering. The bucket arches throughout the palace are almost the same. Therefore, they are raised level by level with structural frames connected to the inside and wood cornice frames to the outside. The top caisson is constructed with eight bucket arches, with Ruyi bucket arch implemented on the left. The tilted wings and tail part of the bucket arches on the right are interweaving in the form of reticulation, which is whirling towards the right resembling the helix. This architectural phenomenon also provides the cause for the name of the palace (Figs. 57-59).

图 57 旋螺殿藻井
Fig. 57 Caisson of Xuanluo Palace

殿内槛墙上有五块清代碑刻，记述内容多为历代培修旋螺殿的详细情况。在殿内第一二层间抬梁上有"明万历二十四年丙申八月殿成"题记。据《李庄镇志》记载，旋螺殿修建之初曾有石刻："万历丙申岁，修建文昌宫。刻石留仙记，世代得兴隆。"文末属有"桂峰题"三字。旋螺殿供奉文昌帝君，"文昌"系道教神名，亦是中国古典神话中的"文曲星"，是主宰人间功名、禄位的神，从古至今多为读书人所祭祀。

图 58 旋螺殿斗拱细部
Fig. 58 Details of *Dougong* used in Xuanluo Palace

In the palace, there are five steles encrypted on the wall, describing the courses of restoration taken place in different periods. On the major post and lintel beam between the first and second level is the inscription saying "the palace was finished in August of the Bingshen year, the twenty-fourth year of Wanli of Ming Dynasty." According to *The Town Annals of Lizhuang*, this palace was initially accompanied with the stone inscription stating that "this palace for Wen Chang Di Jun (God of Literature) was erected in the Bingshen year of Wanli period. This inscription is created for the eternal prosperity of future generations." This inscription ended with the signature of "Gui Feng." Xuanluo Palace enshrines Wen Chang Di Jun. Wen Chang is the name of a Taoist god. He is also the Wen Qu Xing in the classic Chinese myths, a star in ultimate charge of the social rankings and wealth. He is unfailingly admired by intellectuals and scholars with their great homage.

旋螺殿这种独特的建筑样式吸取了周围环境的元素。殿宇所处的石牛山横亘于三条正冲的稻田之间，其山石地貌本身即形若旋螺。这种环境对建筑样式的影响在旋螺殿上体现得十分明显。旋螺殿内部结构精巧、严密，对建筑力学有着开创性的绝妙运用。不同于一般类型的古建筑所采用的层层爬梁叠砌而上的营造技法，它的梁架结构反复采用抬梁支柱法，并搭配了贯穿上、中、下三层的斗拱结构，分别承受屋面重量，然而其建筑技艺与历代传统的宫式建法并无雷同：为追求全殿总体造型、结构和装饰艺术的统一，其斗拱形制也根据其具体放置部位的不同而有相应的变化，而非拘于一格。这样的"妥协"反而使整个旋螺殿更加大方而新奇。此外，旋螺殿的顶部藻井同样新颖而奇特：上层檐下八朵角科斗拱的后尾与十六朵平身科斗拱右侧的斜翘层叠向上，这些平身科斗拱的左侧则雕作昂形，形成了八面都是由右侧转至顶的网格状花纹，类似如意斗拱。尤为值得一提的是，整个旋螺殿建筑采用纯木质结构耦合而成，没有用一根铁钉。

The unique spiral forms of the Xuanluo Palace take inspiration from the natural elements in the pre-conditions of the site. Shiniu Mountain, on which the palace lies, spans across the three large belts of crop fields squarely interlacing with each other. Its topography and landscape vividly resemble the granule's shape. This type of picturesque environment impacted the forms of the construction of the palace overwhelmingly. The internal structure of Xuanluo Palace is highly sophisticated and elaborate, standing for the path breaking application of the structural mechanic. Unlike the traditional constructions and technique of beams climbing layer by layer, its spar frame implements repetitive use of post and lintel system, with the bucket arches running through all levels of the building to bear the structure weight respectively. However, the architectural method is totally disparate from the conventional palace construction. To achieve the harmony of the entire forms, structures, and decorations of the palace, the detailed design of each individual bucket arch has also been carefully reshaped and reformed in accordance with the placement of the arch, rather than limited by the conventions. This compromise to the constraints in turn makes the entire palace even more handsome and novel. Furthermore, the design of the top caisson of Xuanluo Palace is also unique: the tails of the eight corner corbel-bracket set of bucket arches under the cornice of the top level are laminated in a crisscross manner upwards with the tilted wings on the right side of the sixteen levels of corbel-bracket set of bucket arches. The left side of these bucket arches is all engraved towards the shape of unwarp, formulating the latticed leatherwork that all the facets are whirled from the right side to the very top, like the Ruyi bucket arches. What is particularly noteworthy is that the entire construction of the Xuanluo Palace is accomplished with the coupling of purely wooden material, without even the slightest use of iron nails.

图 59 旋螺殿外墙板
Fig. 59 Exterior wall of Xuanluo Palace

蜀韵古镇
HISTORIC TOWNS IN SICHUAN:
THE CULTURAL HERITAGE PROTECTION AND UTILIZATION OF
HISTORIC TOWNS WITH DIFFERENT DIMENSIONS AND VISIONS
——多维视野下的古镇文化遗产保护与利用

图 60 中国营造学社李庄旧址
Fig. 60 Former site of Society for the Study of Chinese Architecture in Lizhuang

图 61 中国营造学社旧址匾额
Fig. 61 Horizontal inscribed board of Society for the Study of Chinese Architecture

图 62 中央研究院大厅
Fig. 62 Hall of the Academia Sinica

20 世纪 40 年代，随着中国营造学社（图 60-62）迁入李庄，其领军人物、中国现代建筑大师梁思成、莫宗江曾对该殿进行过细致的考察，并在《中国营造学社》第七卷第一期上撰文称该建筑"其梁柱结构之优，颇足傲于当世之作"。

During the 1940s, with the migration of the China's Society of Building Construction (Figs. 60-62), the leading figures and also the masters amongst contemporary Chinese architects Liang Sicheng and Mo Zongjiang conducted comprehensive survey and study of this palace and composed the article published in the periodical *Chinese Society of Architecture* (Vol. 7, Issue 1), stating that "the post and beam construction is matchlessly spectacular to any other in the world."

III 结论：
天府古镇的形成

Conclusion:
The Formation of Tianfu Historic Towns

　　千百年来，成都平原始终笼罩在一种备受眷顾的环境中。作为一个地道的成都人，常璩在《华阳国志》中骄傲地写道："从此水旱从人，不知饥馑，时无荒年，天下谓之天府也。""天府之国"的美名就这样代代相传，誉满天下，成了成都平原这片世外桃源的绝好写照。也许是生活实在富足，成都人用自己的勤劳、闲暇的岁月和大自然的恩赐，把自己的日日夜夜装扮得纷繁绚丽，留下了诸如"蓉城""锦官城"这样清丽的雅号。这点点滴滴的安逸悠闲和丝丝缕缕的静美姣好被成都人脚下的土地、身边的瓦片、头顶的窗檐和身前的院落一笔一画忠实地记录下来，从未湮灭，也从未被肢解，也许只是被淡淡地遗忘。

For thousands of years, the Chengdu Plain has hovered in a blessed environment. As a local person of Chengdu, historian Chang Qu wrote in *The Chronicles of Huayang*, "Nature is mastered by people who never have the vision of hunger and famine; the place, therefore, is flattered as the Land of Abundance." From then on, this reputation has been inherited for generations, as the best description of the Chengdu Plain reflecting its material richness. It is this gifted affluence, together with the diligence of the people there, that not only created the most relaxing lifestyle but also generated the profound and subtle culture recorded by the land, the tiles, the lacquers, and the buildings that never disappear but just may be monetarily forgotten.

在很长的一段时间内，以周庄、乌镇、西塘等为代表的江南水乡让人趋之若鹜、流连忘返，而成都平原上的古镇，孤芳自赏，偏安一隅。如果说江南水乡古镇是集万千宠爱于一身的大家闺秀，那么成都平原的古镇更像是犹抱琵琶半遮面的小家碧玉，芳华不让，却更多一分羞涩。就像成都如云的佳丽一样，旖旎的古镇在这片平原和周边成片出现，一样悠久的历史，不一样的味道，不一样的风韵，不一样的情感。

成都平原处在四川盆地的核心地区，背临巍峨的青藏高原，南守险要的横断山脉和奇峰兀立的云贵高原，东面有巫山与荆楚之地相隔，北方的秦岭在太史公的笔下更被描绘为"天下之大阻也"。这样的地理环境让遍览天下名山大川的诗仙李太白也发出了"危乎高哉！蜀道之难，难于上青天！"的感叹。同时，虽然西北部紧邻龙门山断裂带，但是以北川—汶川—康定—小金河为界向南，成都平原位于扬子地台上，地质平稳，至 2008 年以前已有 200 万年未有显著地质活动和造山运动。平稳的地理环境让这片沃土免遭大自然的蹂躏，而那些雄伟壮丽的山脉和高原阻断的不仅仅是寒流，更多的是让生灵涂炭的杀戮和战火。中国历史上几次大规模的战乱，包括战国时期的七国争雄、东汉末年的军阀混战、两朝十六国的粉墨登场，以及五代十国的争权夺利都没有对成都平原产生具有破坏性的冲击，而这些混战和人口流动伴随着文化融合甚至让"混一戎华"的现象罕有地发生在成都这片土地上。因而这里的文化和风情不仅完整地、未受毁坏地保存下来，更在独立地、自由地进化着。沉淀着这份厚重的历史文化财富的空间载体——古镇——也同样在保护中继续发展。

For quite a period of time, historic towns in the south of the lower reaches of the Yangtze River including Zhouzhuang, Wuzhen, and Xitang attracted the vast majority of attention, whereas the historic towns on the Chengdu Plain were obscured, as with other cultural figures of the same place. What has never been obscured is the beauty and elegance of these little towns, no inferior to their eastern counterparts with different charm and demeanor.

蜀韵古镇

HISTORIC TOWNS IN SICHUAN:
THE CULTURAL HERITAGE PROTECTION AND UTILIZATION OF
HISTORIC TOWNS WITH DIFFERENT DIMENSIONS AND VISIONS
——多维视野下的古镇文化遗产保护与利用

The Chengdu Plain, at the center of the Sichuan Basin, is backed by Qinghai-Tibet Plateau, guarded by the spectacular Hengduan Mountains and Yunnan-Guizhou Plateau to the south. On the east, it is separated from the Chu area by Wushan Mountains, and the Qin Mountains to the north are unfailingly described by historians as the most dangerous on the land of China. Furthermore, the roads entering the Chengdu Plain are literally compared as more difficult than ascending to the sky. Simultaneously, the plain is set on the Yangtze Platform, which has been free from severe geological activity and organic movement until 2008. This stable geological environment guarantees the Chengdu Plain from being hit hard by a natural disaster. The continuous series of mountains not only combat the cold wave during winter but also guard against warfare and the savagery of life. Therefore, the tumult throughout the Chinese history engenders significantly destructive influences on the Chengdu Plain. However, the chaotic mixture between Han people and other minority groups didn't separate people but brought all kinds of people to this land from different directions. The culture of Chengdu, thanks to all these factors, has been independently developing and freely evolving throughout its existence. The medium that inherits this historical and cultural treasure, historic towns, also continues to grow in the midst of preservation.

　　由于整个四川盆地远离海洋，中间又有崇山峻岭层层阻隔，其气候和风貌与同纬度地区有明显不同。与秦淮一线以南典型的亚热带季风气候有所不同的是，成都平原地区冬夏干湿差别较小，冷热差异也不是十分显著，同时季风风向转变也不明显。所以这里既有湿润季风带来的充沛降水，又没有换季温差之虞，且耕种期平均气温高于同纬度 5 至 8 摄氏度。不仅如此，成都平原地表松散，有厚达 300 米的地表沉积物，这些以粉砂和黏土为主要成分的紫土是最肥沃、最适合耕种的土壤。同时，平缓的地表相对高差（低于 20 米）和较小的平均坡度（低于 10‰）与都江堰水利工程这样的自流灌溉方式配合得天衣无缝，是成都平原成为中国千年大粮仓的优厚的先天条件。随着生产资料的丰富和生产力的进步，成都平原及其周边的盆地地区还发展出了先进的酿酒业、制盐业（主要是井盐）、桑蚕养殖业、轻纺手工业等初级制造业。这样的生产活动上游需要原材料和生产工具，下游需要运输和销售市场，因此平原上一个点一种行业的发达和繁荣很快就能带动整个行业链条和它们各自所在地区的发展，这种全面的经济发展为城镇化和城镇的稳定提供了基础和活力。而城镇除了为居民提供生活和居住的集中地，还为这些产业的运行和发展提供了稳定的平台。二者各取所需，相得益彰，像罗泉这样依靠井盐开采和制造业发展繁荣起来的古镇就是最好的例证。这样的成因特点必然对古镇自身的风貌和其居民的思想情感产生巨大的影响，这也正是盐神管仲在罗泉古镇得到筑庙封神、顶礼膜拜的重要原因。

The climate and appearance of the Sichuan Basin is considerably different from those of the regions along the same latitude, since it is far from the sea with multiple mountains blocking on the way. Differing from the typical sub-tropical monsoon climate which prevails in the south of Qin Mountains and the Huaihe River, the Chengdu Plain has humid subtropical climate with mild thermal and humidity difference between winter and summer. Meanwhile, the periodical change of the wind direction of monsoon winds is less obvious in this region, keeping the consistency of the rich precipitation. Accordingly, the average temperature during the yearly cultivation period is some five to eight degrees higher than that of the regions along the same latitude. Moreover, the Chengdu Plain has a loose and porous surface with more than 300 meters deep of surface sediments. This iconic purple soil primarily composed of silt and clay is normally regarded as the most fertile and farmable soil. Meanwhile, the surface, with relative altitude of less than 20 meters and average gradient of less than ten percent, is a perfect match with the method of gravity irrigation featured by Dujiangyan hydrological complex, which makes the Chengdu Plain a rich barn for China through thousands of years. With the fast advancement of the production tool and the enrichment of the production materials, the Chengdu Plain and its peripheral regions generated a highly developed wine industry, salt industry (primarily well salt), silkworm breeding industry, textile handicraft industry, and other similar preliminary manufacturing. Such production activities demand raw materials and production tools to the upstream, and to the downstream the transport channel and sales market. Thus, the development and prosperity of a single point or of a single industry triggers the leap of the entire production chain and the respective regions. This holistic economic improvement lays the foundation for the preliminary urbanization and its stabilization while consistently infilling it with dynamism. The town, more than a collective shelter for living and dwelling, was and is, in this way, able to provide a sturdy platform for industrial development. By this token, the town and the industry formulate a reciprocal relationship that is mutually beneficial. Luoquan would be a great demonstration of a town that rose to prominence due to the excavation and manufacturing of well salt. Such unique formulation undoubtedly exerts considerable influence on the thought and emotion of its dwellers, and that's why Guan Zhong, the God of Salt received such prominent homage and honors in Luoquan.

　　成都平原丰富的物产和资源不仅让当地的人民生活富足，还向贫瘠的藏区、天竺（今印度）、交趾（今越南）甚至波斯王国（今伊朗）等地源源不断地输送生活用品、茶叶、蜀锦蜀绣等。然而古代简陋的运输工具和四川盆地周围险要的自然环境无法提供当今这种四通八达的物流和交通。先人们用生命开辟出的一条条小路险径被后人忠实地保留下来，一次次重走。于是从成都平原发源并延伸出来的茶马古道、唐蕃古道、临邛古道、南方丝绸之路、盐道和多条水路成了连接川内和川外甚至国外的命脉，巨大的货物流量便压在这一条条货运道路上。随着时间的推移，这一条条漫漫长路上的驿馆客栈逐渐发展起来，形成了一定的气候。它们虽然位于险山恶水之中，然而这样的山水风景却恰恰是亚欧大陆秀丽雄奇之所在。因此，这些驿馆不仅会随着临时的客流而发展，而且大量长期往来于这条条道路上的商贾在积累足够的财富后，在其周边置家产建大宅，以永享山水天伦之乐。这两个方面推动了古镇的发展，并提供了源源不断的生机和活力。平乐古镇和上里古镇就是这类依托物流通道的区位优势而发达繁荣的优秀例证。

　　The abundance of materials and resources on the Chengdu Plain not only fed the local people but also made considerable exports to the barren Tibet, Tenjiku (current India), Cochin (current Vietnam), and even as far as Parthian Empire (current Iran), in terms of daily goods, tea, embroidery, etc. However, the rudimentary transports and the challenging natural environment could not provide such a demand as easily done by means of modern transportation and communications. Therefore, a multitude of slim and dangerous paths were pioneered through the sacrifice of lives and kept as the indispensable connectors between the Chengdu Plain and the world outside, such as the Ancient Tea-Horse Trading Route, the Tang-Tibet Ancient Trading Route, the Lin-Qiong Route, the South Silk Road, the Salt Route, etc. A gargantuan number of commodities with an equally large amount of people have been moving along these narrow paths, and, with the lapse of time, formulated clusters of inns, taverns, and relays. They are deeply trapped in the sinister surroundings of mountains and rivers; yet, it is such remarkable scenery that featured the quintessence of nature of in the heart of this continent. Hence, those who garnered tremendous fortune along the trading on these routes tend to squander their money to land and ground in such places of spectacles to enjoy their remaining life. This lavish hobby became a driver that triggered the development and formation of historic towns from mere clusters. Pingle and Shangli are the best examples of such towns that reap their prosperity along the channels of transportation.

　　成都平原古镇的发源和繁荣与成都这座千年古城有着千丝万缕的联系，它们的气质和涵养莫不与成都的气息契合，与成都人的性格相合。作为从古至今华夏文明里西南地区的中心，成都默默地吸收和包容着来自各地的人、思想与精神，还有他们的喜怒哀乐、旦夕祸福。这所有的一切都沉淀下来，凝聚在这一方水土上，也让包容性成了成都核心特性的一部分。这样的人文特性使得天府古镇在兴起和发展的过程当中能够较为完好地接纳和消化大规模人口迁移所带来的区域性影响。这样的影响具有很强的典型性：来自青藏高原的"昆仑文化"沿黄河流域和长江流域转移传播，在沿岷山地区和岷江流域向四川盆地迁徙的过程中留下了明显的痕迹；此后，在秦统一中国的过程当中又将其本身的关中文化和山东六国遗民代表的中原文化通过移民带到了四川盆地地区。类似区域性人口迁移还有明末清初的"湖广填四川"、客家大迁徙运动、抗战时期的全国战略大转移、中华人民共和国建设时期的干部南下运动和社会主义三线建设。这种人口迁移不断地为成都平原提供丰富的内涵和活力。洛带古镇就是这样一个深受岭南客家文化浸润的川西古镇。

This inception and evolution of historic towns on the Chengdu Plain have inextricable correlations with Chengdu, a city with thousands of years of history. What is hardly inconceivable is that their inherent characters are closely related to those of Chengdu, and of Chengdu people. As the consistent center in the south-west region of Chinese Civilization, Chengdu has been absorbing and taking into itself people, thoughts, and spirits from everywhere, together with their happiness and sadness, welfare and grievance. They all inherited into this place, condensed into the earth and water of Chengdu, and made tolerance and inclusiveness into the core characteristics of Chengdu. Such humanitarian quality equipped historic towns the capacity to admit and digest the regional cultural influence brought by massive demographic movements. Such influences are highly typical: Kunlun culture, which originated in Qinghai-Tibet Plateau, was transmitted along both ranges of the Yellow River and the Yangtze River and exerted very obvious traces across the area of Minshan Mountains and Minjiang River. Later, during the process of unifying whole China, Qin Empire translated its own Guanzhong culture and Zhongyuan culture represented by the adherents of the eliminated six countries to the Sichuan Basin area. Similarly enormous demographic movements include the Hu-guang Fills Sichuan movement, the great migration of Hakka people, the strategic shift during the Anti-Japanese War, the Southward Movement of Cadres during the construction period of P. R. China, and the Third Front Construction Movement of Socialism. Such continuous demographic migration unfailingly fuels the Chengdu Plain with continuous vitality. Luodai is a typical historic town on the Chengdu Plain that is profoundly trenched in Hakka culture from the Lingnan Areas.

HISTORIC TOWNS IN SICHUAN:
THE CULTURAL HERITAGE PROTECTION AND UTILIZATION OF
HISTORIC TOWNS WITH DIFFERENT DIMENSIONS AND VISIONS
——多维视野下的古镇文化遗产保护与利用

由此看来，天府古镇不仅仅源自四川，它们更是千百年来移民浪潮所裹挟的中华民族各种文化基因在这方水土间的汇聚、杂糅及演化，是多元共生的中华文明的缩影。

Based on the previously mentioned analyses, Tianfu historic towns were not only created within the Sichuan Province but were also cultivated by the convergence, mixture, and transformation of several sub-cultural genes brought by several immigrant movements in history. It is hence the epitome of the multiplex symbiosis of Chinese civilization.

中篇：
对比阅读
Part II :
Comparative Reading

　　本篇由两篇对比阅读研究文章组成：第一篇文章将天府古镇与江南水乡进行对比，第二篇文章则从保护与更新方式的角度将美国的历史小镇与中国的古镇进行更为系统的比较。本篇介绍了在不同地理文化区域背景下，在面对全球性文化旅游业和城市化冲击时，在面对历史文化遗产保护与文化旅游产业可能发生的利益冲突时，古镇地方政府和社会舆论等相关利益方是如何做出选择和应对的。

　　This part is composed of two comparative studies. One is a comparative study between historic towns of Sichuan and those of Jiangnan areas, and the other is a more systematic comparative study regarding protection and regeneration methods between historic towns in the US and those in China. This part introduces historic towns of different geographic location and cultural background. In addition, this part describes how stakeholders including local governments and social media had made their choices and responses when challenged by urbanization and cultural tourism in a global perspective, as well as by the different interests conflicts between cultural heritage protection and cultural tourist industry.

从小桥流水到山中人家：
江南水乡和四川古镇的对比

From the Bridge and River to the Mountain Village:
A Comparison of Jiangnan Water Towns and Sichuan Historic Towns

　　古镇，作为一种适应传统农耕社会的空间聚落形式，在中国的建置历史十分悠久。它是介于城市与村落之间的独特空间形态：一方面，古镇与传统农业经济有着千丝万缕的联系，但相对来说，它不如城市独立，也没有城市的坚壁厚垒，而是直接面向广大乡野农村；另一方面，古镇聚集了众多商人与手工业者，比乡村更具商业活力与文化影响力。在漫长的岁月长河中，这一独特的空间形态，伴随着中国古代农业经济的发展在大江南北遍地开花。数以万计的小城镇，因所处的地理环境不同，以及社会经济功能差异，孕育出了各自不同的地域文化和风俗民情，也形成了以地域划分的多个体系。其中最具特色的要数地处东部的江南水乡古镇与地处西部的四川古镇。

　　Historic Chinese towns, as a spatial form of settlement adjusted to traditional agricultural society, have a long standing history in Chinese culture, in primarily acting as a unique spatial typology between city and village. On one hand, the towns represent strong connections to traditional agricultural economies. They are neither as independent nor as strong as cities but instead embrace the rural countryside directly. On the other hand, these towns have historically gathered numerous merchants and craftsmen and thus encouraged commercial vitality and cultural influence. During the long history of China, such unique form of settlement had thrived all over the country, along with the development of agricultural economy. Meanwhile, tens of thousands of such historic towns have largely enriched local culture and ethnic customs based on specific geographical environments and economic conditions, in addition to forming multiple systems divided by regions. Among them, Jiangnan water towns in East China and Sichuan historic towns in West China are probably the most distinctive ones.

表1 中国古镇分布表
Table 1 Distribution Table of Chinese Historic Towns

省市（自治区） Province (province-level municipality/autonomous region)	数量 Number	比重 (%) Percentage	省市（自治区） Province (province-level municipality/autonomous region)	数量 Number	比重 (%) Percentage
浙江 Zhejiang	39	17.73	湖南 Hunan	5	2.27
四川 Sichuan	38	17.27	河北 Hebei	4	1.82
江苏 Jiangshu	23	10.45	山西 Shanxi	4	1.82
安徽 Anhui	15	6.82	陕西 Shaanxi	3	1.36
贵州 Guizhou	14	6.36	山东 Shandong	2	0.91
重庆 Chongqing	13	5.91	北京 Beijing	2	0.91
云南 Yunnan	11	5.00	湖北 Hubei	2	0.91
福建 Fujian	11	5.00	天津 Tianjin	1	0.45
上海 Shanghai	10	4.55	内蒙古 Inner Mongolia	1	0.45
广西 Guangxi	7	3.18	甘肃 Gansu	1	0.45
江西 Jiangxi	7	3.18	新疆 Xinjiang	1	0.45
广东 Guangdong	5	2.27	西藏 Tibet	1	0.45

数据来源：中国古镇网 劲游智库
Source: Chinese Historic Town website, Jinyou Think-tank

　　如果翻看中国古镇旅游的统计数据，不难发现浙江、四川和江苏所拥有的古镇数量分别是全中国的第一、二、三名。三省的古镇总数几乎占了全国的半壁江山，由此可见以浙江和江苏为代表的江南水乡古镇与四川古镇至今仍以它们无穷的魅力吸引着世人的目光。经过历史的演变，它们都展现出了丰富而深厚的内涵和有价值的人文传统。这两地古镇在空间、地理、环境以及当代保护方面具有很强的代表性，研究这两个类型的古镇体系，为人们理解中国古代小城镇的发展演变与风格特征，提供了最佳的切入点。

According to statistics, it is true that most of these historic towns are located in Zhejiang, Sichuan, and Jiangsu provinces. The number in these three provinces accounts for almost half of the total historic towns in China. Therefore, it is necessary and obvious to recognize the extraordinary value and vitality of Jiangnan water towns and Sichuan historic towns, respectively. In other words, they would represent Chinese historic towns in the best view and angle both generally in historical terms and holistically from a Chinese cultural viewpoint. Therefore, visiting such towns has become the best way to explore the evolutionary history, as well as their styles and features.

1. 共同的起源——发达的农业经济与繁荣的商业贸易

The Same Origins—Developed Agricultural Economy with Prosperous Commercial Trade

江南自古就有"鱼米之乡"的美誉，早在宋朝的《吴郡志》中即提到"天上天堂，地下苏杭"，而四川盆地从司马迁撰《史记》开始就被誉为"天府之国"。可见，这两个地方皆是气候温润，物产富饶，传统农业经济极其发达之地。两地因纬度相近，雨量充沛，自然条件优越，从来都是中华大地的大粮仓。

江南地区河道纵横交错，湖泊星罗棋布，加之历史上兵戈之争较少，政治环境较稳定，从东汉末年起便吸引了大批移民前来避祸开垦，形成了人口稠密、开发程度较高的区域。而四川盆地在都江堰水利工程的滋养下，"水旱从人，不知饥馑"，依靠丰富的水源、肥沃的土壤和适宜的气候，盛产稻谷、玉米等多种农作物，一直是中国西部地区农业水平最发达的地区。

Since ancient times, Jiangnan (the southern area of the Lower Yangtze River region) has been called "the land of fish and rice." Meanwhile, Sichuan Basin has been described as "The Land of Abundance" since Sima Qian wrote in *Shi Ji*. Located at similar latitudes, both regions are highly developed agricultural areas with superior climate conditions and rich production. Therefore, they have become the most valuable "granaries' of the entire nation."

With numerous intersecting rivers and lakes, the Jiangnan area is fit for agricultural activities. It has been always much more stable than North China in terms of political environment, thus attracting a large number of immigrants from the north since late years of the East Han Dynasty. These settlers brought population and new technology to reclaim such rich land. Concurrently, due to the help of Dujiangyan Water & Irrigation Project, Sichuan has developed into the agricultural center of West China. The prosperity of the ancient Sichuan area mostly relied on its abundant water, fertile soil, and mild climate.

发达的农业经济势必刺激商业发展，引发繁荣的贸易活动，从而使得手工业和商品经济在这两个地区格外活跃。交通也是催化商业发展的重要因素：江南地区河道纵横，水路运输网发达。特别是隋代建成的京杭大运河打通了中国南北交通的大动脉，使苏浙所产的米粮绸布可以供应北方的政治中心，也让江南一举成为名副其实的经济中心。与此相对应的是，成都平原位处联系少数民族地区的战略要津，北可达关中地区，南可至云南缅甸，东连荆楚，西达青藏，这里是茶马古道和南方丝绸之路的起点，拥有发达的商业网络。北宋时期，成都平原还出现了世界上第一种纸质货币——"交子"，其对外贸易之频繁，可见一斑。

In both places mentioned above, highly developed agricultural economies stimulated commercial activities and catalyzed new trade across these areas. Traffic conditions became another key in prompting the development of commerce. Water networks also played a crucial role in the Jiangnan area, especially after the construction of the Grand Canal connecting Beijing and Hangzhou. The Grand Canal allowed all kinds of products of Jiangsu and Zhejiang to be delivered towards the north easily, making the Jiangnan area the true economic and trade center of China. Meanwhile, the location of the Chengdu Plain was also quite important to the national trade network, as it was the node for connecting the Middle and Lower Yangtze River Region at the west, Shanxi Province at the north (the former political center of China), Yunnan and Burma at the south, Hubei Province at the east, and Tibet at the west. In addition, the South Silk Road and the Ancient Tea-Horse Trading Route started at Chengdu, connecting to Southeast Asia as a whole. Therefore, it is not difficult to understand that the first paper currency of the world, Jiaozi, was created in Chengdu during the Northern Song Dynasty.

由于商业与贸易的发达，众多古镇应运而生，也因此聚集了大量的人流和物资。江南水乡古镇与四川古镇多处在水陆贸易网络的枢纽，交通便利。在商业贸易的带动下，它们成为货物集散交易地，吸引了手工业者和商人前来定居。有着"中国第一水乡"之称的周庄（图63），即坐落在周边五个湖泊的中心。从元代起，周庄便随着水运的发展而兴盛繁荣起来，一时间商贾云集，人丁兴旺，明初富可敌国的大商人沈万三就诞生于此。浙江湖丝名镇——南浔，因所产湖丝质优而闻名。从明代开始南浔地区居民种蚕缫丝的技艺就声名鹊起，直到近代，南浔的辑里丝还多次在世界博览会上荣获大奖，受到海内外关注。南浔的蚕丝业辉煌了三百多年，也带动了地区蚕丝贸易。全盛时期的南浔镇客船往来不绝，沿河布满了店铺，码头停满船只，生成一派热闹而活跃的商贸景象。

Similarly, historic towns emerged from highly developed commercial and trade activities, and they gathered people and resources along the routes. Jiangnan water towns and Sichuan historic towns are often nodes of local trade networks, with easy access to adjacent rural areas. And thus, they became natural distribution centers of goods and resources, attracting numerous merchants and craftsmen to settle down. Zhouzhuang (Fig. 63), also known as "the Number One (or Best) Water Town in China," was developed from shipping and water-way trades back in the Yuan Dynasty because it was located at the border of four provinces (Jiangsu, Zhejiang, Anhui and Jiangxi) and in the middle of five lakes, in addition to having superior water traffic conditions. As it became the center of trade from adjacent areas, this small town embraced and welcomed a flourishing population and prosperity brought by commercial activities, including the wealthy businessman Shen Wansan during the early Ming Dynasty. Nanxun, another famous water town in Zhejiang, was well-known for its silk production. Since the Ming Dynasty, local residents have been recognized for their silk weaving skill, and today, Nanxun is so famous worldwide that it has been awarded many times in the World Expo. Nanxun had been the center of the silk industry for more than three hundred years, thus stimulating silk trading. In its heyday, Nanxun experienced ceaseless coming and going visitors and ships along the pier and stores.

图 63 "中国第一水乡"周庄，舟楫是主要交通工具
Fig. 63 In Zhouzhuang, "the Number One (or Best) Water Town in China," boats are the major transportation tool

图 64 黄龙溪古镇的水运码头，古代
这里往来船只络绎不绝
Fig. 64 At ferry of Huanglongxi,
numerous boats and ships stopped here
back from ancient times

　　天府之国中与其相似的是位于四川的黄龙溪古镇（图 64）。黄龙溪镇有着 2000 多年的历史，古代是拱卫
成都南门的军事要地。从成都出发约 40 分钟即可到达。据《仁寿县志》记载，该镇古称"赤水"，"赤水与
锦江汇流，溪水褐，江水清"，古人谓之"黄龙渡清江，真龙内中藏"，黄龙溪由此得名。该溪可通过府河（古
代称锦江）直达成都市区，在古代是连接成都与岷江下游地区的重要航道。府河在黄龙溪由宽变窄，因此过往
船只大多在此处停留换乘，众多商人也在此停泊与住宿。久而久之，来往与停泊黄龙溪的船只络绎不绝，人流
的汇集与停顿催生了市镇的繁荣。川西上里古镇自古地处要津，位于雅安、芦山、名山、邛崃四县交界处，是
四川地区著名的因商而兴的城镇。在明末清初的"湖广填四川"移民活动中，从风水学上来看此处恰好在两条
内河相交夹角处，是财源汇聚的宝地，上里古镇将汉、彝、羌、藏民族混居地区的经济活动紧密联系起来，为
多民族的经济发展与文化融合做出了贡献。

因农而兴，因商而隆，这是江南地区古镇与四川地区古镇显著的共同特征。当然还有一些因其他原因而闻名的历史名镇，诸如驻军戍边等因素，但总体来说，便利的交通与活跃的贸易是绝大多数古镇数百年不衰落的根本原因。古镇是中国传统农业经济在成长之路上当之无愧的见证者，它们随着小农经济社会的发展、辉煌和衰落而起起伏伏。

Huanglongxi (Fig. 64) in Sichuan Province shares several similarities with those water towns mentioned previously. It has a history of more than two thousand years and functioned as a military base protecting the southern Chengdu area. Located in the southern suburb of the Greater Chengdu Area, the town is only a forty-minute drive from downtown Chengdu. It is named from a belief that the river across the town looks like a yellow dragon. As the river gets narrower, ships with cargos always stop, waiting to change to smaller boats to enter the city of Chengdu. Therefore, it became a transfer station of water-way trade route connecting southern Sichuan and the Chengdu City. Another good example regarding trade and prosperity can be found at Shangli, a small town located at the border of Ya'an, Lushan, Mingshan and Qionglai. The town was close to those minority areas, so during the immigration event in the late Ming and early Qing period, most caravans coming from the Middle Kingdom went through this town. Shangli is also seen as a fortunate place, because it is located at the merging place of two rivers, which means that fortune from two directions gathers at this specific location. With the large scale immigration, Shangli promoted not only economic activities but also cross-cultural communications among Han, Yi, Qiang, and Zang ethnic groups.

Generally speaking, it is common to both the Jiangnan area and Sichuan province that commercial activities created these wonderful historic towns. Business and trade brought life to them with the flow of population and resources. Besides their military roles, most of the famous historic towns in these two areas benefited from excellent location and convenient traffic conditions on either land or water, ensuring their prosperity and flourish that continues into modern times. Upon observation of the development, glory and decline of the small peasant economy and society, historic towns are undoubtedly the witness of the growth of traditional Chinese agricultural economy.

2. 类似的空间形态——城镇尺度与布局

Similar Spatial Facts—Scale and Layout

正因为商业贸易构成了古镇发展的核心，江南水乡古镇与四川古镇在空间布局上都围绕这个行业建立。街道构成了两者在空间形态上最重要的因素，无论是水路还是旱路，古镇文化在空间方面的本质就是街道文化。临街而生、沿街而市是传统古镇在空间形态上的显著特征。

古镇居民的主要公共活动场所即为街道。从场地剖面上看，江南水乡古镇与四川古镇的街道在尺度上非常相似，主要街道宽度少则一米，多则四五米。老街以当地青石或卵石铺就，石材之间留有缝隙，雨水渗入其中，防止积水。老街同时注重街道的坡度，以达到快速排水的目的。两侧房屋以一层和两层为主，三层或三层以上的临街建筑较少（图65）。

As mentioned previously, commercial activity acts as a crucial role to generate a historic Chinese town's activity. Both in the Jiangnan area and Sichuan province, the spatial layout of these towns are mainly developed based on commercial function. In other words, street and waterway layouts constitute the core factor of the towns in terms of economy, traffic, and daily life and significantly shape the spatial morphology of the towns. This configuration became a typical architectural paradigm for historic Chinese towns.

Such streets as the above became the main public space of local residents. The scale of those towns in both the Jiangnan area and Sichuan province are relatively similar in terms of site sections, where the main street width is between one and five meters. Most of these old streets are paved with local bluestones or pebbles, generating a penetrated slope surface for rain infiltration to avoid floods. Buildings on both sides of the street are mostly one or two floors high, seldom having three floors or more (Fig. 65).

图 65 黄龙溪老街
Fig. 65 Old Street in Huanglongxi

蜀韵古镇

HISTORIC TOWNS IN SICHUAN:
THE CULTURAL HERITAGE PROTECTION AND UTILIZATION OF
HISTORIC TOWNS WITH DIFFERENT DIMENSIONS AND VISIONS
——多维视野下的古镇文化遗产保护与利用

图 66 江苏嘉善的西塘镇：长长的"雨廊"串
联起古镇的公共空间
Fig. 66 Xitang in Jiangsu, a long "rain gallery"
connects the public space of the town

　　临街而市的建筑也催生出许多临街檐廊。长长的街边廊道，一根根古香古色的柱子，构成了江南水乡古镇与四川古镇共有的风景。檐廊作为店铺的延伸和室内室外过渡的"灰空间"，为过往行人遮风避雨，也将街道划分出不同的活动层次。位于江苏省嘉善县的西塘镇便拥有长达 1.5 公里的檐廊，也被人称为"雨廊"，其出挑达两米多，形成廊棚（图 66）。中间局部地方还有木雕刻纹，十分精美。临水背屋的廊道串联起了西塘人的日常生活：不少商家把商品摊放在檐廊下，老人在檐廊下休息聊天，小孩则绕着古旧的柱子嬉戏玩耍，好一幅生动惬意的画面。

Traditional old streets create many eaves galleries with ancient style structures, an extraordinary spatial type shared by both Jiangnan water towns and Sichuan historic towns. As an extension of the front stores or "gray space" for the transition of interior and exterior spaces, an eaves gallery offers shelter for pedestrians and stratifies street activities in various hierarchies. Xitang, also known as "Rain Gallery," is one of the most famous water towns in China. It is located in Jiangsu Province and is famous for a one-and-a-half-kilometer-long eaves gallery (Fig. 66). It hangs out more than two meters to form a shelter corridor with exquisite wood carving. Such a corridor space connects the daily life of Xitang people with very traditional but vivid scenes: merchants putting their goods underneath the gallery, elder people chatting under the arches, and children playing around the old pillars erected in ancient times.

　　与此类似，四川乐山犍为县的罗城镇也因其独特的檐廊而出名。罗城镇老街东西长，南北短，很像一艘东西向行驶的大船，所以其城中老街又称为"船形街"。船形街的两侧都是出挑 3 米左右的檐廊，为来来往往的行人遮风避雨，罗城人形容这里是"风雨长廊"（图 67）。一百多根粗壮的圆木支撑起 200 米长的船形街檐廊。

　　檐廊作为一种重要的公共空间，串联起四川古镇与江南水乡古镇共有的市井生活。它不仅连接了各个空间，更如一条强有力的纽带联系起邻里乡亲的感情，赋予居民公共活动以安全感，为古镇带来和睦融洽的氛围。这是我们后世城市设计师应该学习借鉴的。

Similar to Xitang, Luocheng in Sichuan is also well known for its unique eaves galleries. In plain view, Luocheng's old town looks like a giant ship heading east with a longer distance in the east-west direction. Therefore, the old street in the center is called "Ship-shape Street," which extrudes a three-meter eaves gallery on both sides. Supported by more than one hundred thick root logs, it is regarded as "Wind and Rain Corridor," as it shelters any pedestrian in bad weather (Fig. 67). Ship-shape Street has become the public hub of the whole town, as it provides a space for local people to enjoy opera watching, tea chatting, and public gathering, cultivating local culture.

As a crucial public space, the eaves gallery catalyzes vernacular public activities for those traditional towns in both Sichuan and Jiangnan. It creates not only spatial connection but also strong social links among local folks, as it shelters people and fosters interaction and talking in close quarters. Such a method is also what current designers or planners should learn from as traditional methodologies carry on to today.

图 67 罗城古镇船形街檐廊下的日常生活
Fig. 67 Everyday life within the wide corridor along the ship-shaped street in Luocheng Historic Town

除了檐廊，还有一种建筑在两地古镇中占据重要地位，那就是寺庙。如果说老街与檐廊是古镇居民日常生活的核心场所，那么寺庙就是古镇居民的精神生活核心。在儒释道三位一体的宗教浸润之下，江南水乡古镇与四川古镇都有颇具影响的寺院或道观，供居民祈求个人福报或来年风调雨顺。江南很多古镇都有城隍庙，且居于城镇中央，如朱家角的城隍庙。同时，在这座距离上海市区仅四十多公里的江南小镇上，就有两座名刹：一个是始建于元代的圆津禅院，另一个是位于淀山湖边的报国寺。可见宗教对这座小镇影响深远。

俗话说，名镇必有名刹。川西名镇黄龙溪也有众多寺庙、宫观，可惜当年的不少寺院都毁于战火，如今只留存遗迹供后人想象。保存较好的三座寺庙分别是古龙寺、潮音寺和镇江寺，尤以位于古镇中心的古龙寺香火最为旺盛。古龙寺形制开阔，树荫葱葱，中央庭院种有几棵千年黄葛树。古龙寺多少年来一直是镇上居民的精神寄托之处，也诉说了古镇当年的繁华史。

In addition to the featured eaves, another architectural item, the temple, is also an important cultural pinpoint in both historic towns of Sichuan and Jiangnan provinces. The former, the eaves on the old street, can be seen as the core social space in everyday life, while the latter, the temple, is the spiritual center for local residents. Under the religious infiltration of Confucianism, Buddhism, and Taoism, people from both areas seek good fortune and pray for good weather, in these temples of great influence. There are many Chenghuang Temples in the center of Jiangnan water towns, such as the one in Zhujiajiao. This small town is only forty kilometers away from Shanghai and has two famous temples, the Yuanjin Temple built in the Yuan Dynasty and the Baoguo Temple next to the Dianshan Lake. Evidently, religion exerts quite significant influence over this small town.

According to an old Chinese proverb, a famous town always has a famous temple. Huanglongxi, one of the most significant traditional towns in Sichuan, has many palaces and temples. However, many of them were destroyed during war, leaving merely debris for people to imagine the original structure. Fortunately, three main temples in the town are still kept well: Gulong Temple, Chaoyin Temple, and Zhenjiang Temple. Among them, Gulong Temple is the most attractive one, as it has an orthodox plan layout and a grand courtyard. It has been the spiritual place for local folks for a long period, and it tells the prosperous history of the town.

3. 不同的文化符号——山水之异

Different Cultural Symbols—Mountain and Water

作为中国传统古镇的瑰宝，江南水乡古镇与四川古镇无疑在许多方面具有共同之处，但步入其间，却也能深刻地感受到两者的不同。两地相隔千里，地理、经济等条件相差较大，社会环境与历史背景也大相径庭，由此而产生的古镇文化当然也各有千秋。

As the real treasure of traditional Chinese towns, Jiangnan water towns and Sichuan historic towns share many similarities. However, at the same time, there are still apparent differences between them. Regarding the geological variety and economic differences, the old towns in both areas produce their own merits and cultures with different social environments and historical backgrounds.

　　水是江南水乡古镇的"魂"。江南水乡因水而生，依水而兴。因地处长江三角洲，古代居民依靠舟楫这一重要的交通工具往来于四里八乡，通达长江甚至大海。众多贯穿古镇的沟渠、湖泊、运河等成为将各地物资聚集于古镇的通路。可以说，江南的大多数古镇都是因水成街，因水成市，因水成镇（图68）。城镇的空间布局根据流经该地的河道形态而设置，或成"十"字形，或成"井"字形，水路串起了整个古镇的方方面面。如果说古镇是一个人的身体，那河流所形成的水路网无疑就是江南水乡古镇的骨骼与血脉，它成为居民生活、交通和贸易的中心，也是城镇与周边农村及城市的纽带。

　　江南水乡古镇的建筑布局强调"亲水"。建筑物大多背靠河流，面向前街，形成前街后河、临水筑屋的格局。不少楼宇都有水墙、水阁甚至穿过房屋的水巷。前街是居民做生意步行来往的场所，后河则是人们日常生活中洗衣、洗菜、聚集和出行的重要场所。水路和旱路两种流线空间在桥梁与河埠广场交汇，也成了居民主要的公共空间。

Water is the soul of Jiangnan water towns. They originate from water and are developed via water. Local residents use boats as their main transportation means because of the river network around the Yangzi River Delta. Thus, waterways became significant pathways for local areas by continuously conveying people and goods. Furthermore, the spatial layout of towns is based on the form of rivers, forming the shape of the Chinese character "十" ("ten") or "井" ("well"). It can be said that the waterway strung together the entire town in all aspects (Fig. 68). If those towns scattered around the delta area are seen as body organs, then rivers and waterways can be seen as arteries connecting different nodes, acting as centers of people's daily lives, transportation, trade, as well as the bond between urban and rural places.

In Jiangnan water towns, closeness to water is the main focus of a building's layout. Most architectural structures are near rivers, with their front towards the street, leading to the "front street back river" rule. Some buildings also have a water wall, water pavilion, or even a water alley that cuts through houses. The street was used for public space and commercial trading, while the back nearest river became more of a life-style space for local folks to do laundry, wash vegetables, and even commute. These two types of circulation spaces intersected with each other at the bridge and the plaza nearby, which was the major public space of the town.

图 68 前童古镇：家家尽枕河 *
Fig. 68 Qiantong: Houses with water around

* 来源：阮仪三，2010
  Source: Ruan Yisan, 2010

浙江宁海县的前童古镇是典型的"水镇"。全镇被大大小小几十条沟渠所环绕，因此前童大多数住宅临水而建。与大多数水乡古镇不同，前童是"前街前河"的空间形式。溪流从自家门前屋后流过，家家户户皆枕着流水而眠。古街狭长，很多地方宽度不足两米，每条街巷都有活水相伴，用现代设计语言来形容就是独特的街道亲水景观。人们通过架在溪流上的石板桥回家，小孩在门前的沟渠旁嬉戏，别有一番风味。

由"水"的文化符号所衍生出来的"桥"文化也是江南水乡古镇的特色。元代诗人马致远曾用"小桥流水人家"来形容江南水乡的美景。桥是古镇之间交通与交流的重要纽带，将水域与陆地完美结合在一起。同时，桥也是水路和旱路两种不同的流线交汇的地方，有桥的位置往往成为人流聚集的河埠和码头。这里类似于西方城市的广场，是居民交流议事的重要公共空间。如周庄著名的"双桥"就是由一横一竖呈90度的永安桥和世德桥组成，永安桥是平桥，世德桥是拱桥，一拱一平成为古镇颇具特色的地标。两个方向的人流汇聚于此，周围店铺阁楼鳞次栉比，来来往往的人流穿梭其间，使这里成为镇上热闹非凡的去处。

Qiantong, an old town in Zhejiang, is a typical water town surrounded by dozens of large and small ditches. Thus, most houses in Qiantong are built next to the river. Different from other water towns, the planning of this town follows the "front street, front river" rule. The river passes around houses, and residents go to bed hearing water sounds at night. The old street is relatively narrow with some places less than two meters wide, but each street has one river passing along with running water. It has a certain similarity with a waterscape in modern design, which creates a vivid and unique experience to go across the stream with a masonry bridge to get home. Children playing next to such ditches creates a particular flavor.

Derived from water culture, bridge culture is also a unique phenomenon of Jiangnan water towns. Ma Zhiyuan, famous poet in the Yuan Dynasty, used to describe the beauty of water towns with the phrases of "small bridges, flowing water and family cottages." Being the important bond between transportation and communication, bridges have unified water and land perfectly. Most bridges in water towns tend to be the major public space in a town with crowds of people and numerous commercial activities, which share almost the same function as plazas or markets in western cities. For instance, "Double Bridges" in Zhouzhuang is a landmark named after two bridges, Yong'an a beam bridge, and Shide an arch bridge. The bridges meet with one another perpendicularly, becoming quite a unique landmark of the old town. With the flow of people coming from both directions and the large number of stores attracting many people, it is definitely the busiest location of the whole town.

无论是轻盈圆润的拱桥、造型优美的折板桥，还是质朴厚重的平板桥，都为桥增添了水乡古镇独特而浓郁的文化气息。临水而生的建筑在桥的烘托之下与波光粼粼的河水相得益彰，一个转角，一个回眸，都是诗人吟唱寄托的对象。最具优雅与浓郁风情的江南水乡古镇就属乌镇了，在这百步一桥的地方，桥成为构成水乡独特魅力的重要因素。乌镇地方不大，却有桥梁 120 余座，大小各异，形态万千（图 70）。

其实，水也存在于天府之国的古镇中，在以陆路为基础的四川古镇里，水更多还是作为联系外界的运输线路和生活生产的水源。古代风水学讲求依山傍水，很多四川古镇便星罗棋布，在大河边发展并兴盛起来（图 69）。例如黄龙溪古镇就是从临水的码头发展起来的。河流是带动黄龙溪发展的交通动脉，为古镇带来络绎不绝的人流、商流与货流。

Whether an arch shape, folded plate shape, or flat shape, bridges produce a special oriental cultural prospect for the Jiangnan water town area specifically. This creates an elegant picture with buildings and bridges reflecting from the water, a scene that has always been admired or praised by Chinese poets for generations. Among all these water towns, Wuzhen may be the most attractive one in terms of its elegant cultural scenery. Although Wuzhen is not a big town, it owns more than one hundred and twenty bridges varied in shapes and sizes (Fig. 70).

In fact, water features also exist in Sichuan historic towns. However, instead of being a cultural symbol, waterways are mainly used as transportation paths and drinking water sources to counter mountainous terrain in Sichuan (Fig. 69). Many significant traditional towns in Sichuan are spread along big rivers with the convenience of waterways according to *Fengshui* rules, such as with Huanglongxi mentioned before. For example, it is the first waterway stop to the south of Chengdu City with the Huanglongxi River. The town is driven and developed by the river across, bringing a continuous flow of people, goods, and business.

图 69 望鱼古镇的街道，曾经是繁忙的茶马古道
Fig. 69 Main street of Wangyu Historic Town, used to the busiest Ancient Tea-Horse Trading Route

图 70 乌镇的水与桥之美
Fig. 70 The beauty of Wuzhen with water and bridges

蜀韵古镇

HISTORIC TOWNS IN SICHUAN:
THE CULTURAL HERITAGE PROTECTION AND UTILIZATION OF
HISTORIC TOWNS WITH DIFFERENT DIMENSIONS AND VISIONS
——多维视野下的古镇文化遗产保护与利用

图 71 福宝古镇 *
Fig. 71 Fubao Historic Town

图 72 远眺建在巨石上与山水交融的望鱼古镇
Fig. 72 Distant view of Wangyu Historic Town built upon a huge rock and
merged into the mountain and river

如果说江南古镇的特点是小桥流水，那么四川古镇的特点就是山中人家了。四川古镇更多地体现了"山"的意境。因四川地区多山，自古交通不便，很多道路需要盘山蜿蜒，众多的古镇就在商路的节点顺应山形地势而建。

应合风水理论，四川古镇的选址一般都依山傍水，顺应山势。位于川南的福宝古镇就是典型的依山而建之城（图71）。它坐落在蒲江之滨，整个镇几乎都在山上，镇即是山，山即是镇，城镇空间高差对比强烈，层次丰富。主街回龙古街顺应山势，由当地青石板铺就，宽的地方有六七米，窄的地方不到一米。两边为颇具四川特色的吊脚楼，依山就势，错落有致。拾石阶而上，立于山顶可见整个古镇被青山环抱，宽阔的青瓦屋顶高高低低，层层叠叠，袅袅炊烟不时从屋顶升起，一副充满生活气息的山地水墨画在眼前徐徐展开。

雅安地区位于成都平原边缘，也是连接古代茶马古道与成都平原的必经之路。位于雅安地区的上里古镇、望鱼乡以及荥河乡都是依山傍水的典型。望鱼古镇（图72）本身即坐落在山腰一块巨石之上，这块巨石因酷似望着河中之鱼的猫，而得名"望鱼"。上到场镇要登一百多级陡峭石阶，镇上只有一条依山而建的老街。老街两侧多为木质结构瓦房，轻巧简朴，与古朴的青石板老街融为一体。

If bridges and waterways are the most significant characteristics of Jiangnan water towns, then the mountain villages can be seen as the main feature of Sichuan historic towns. The mountainous Sichuan area embodies difficult traffic conditions; therefore, those towns at the nodes of trading routes get the largest chance of development. In another word, the mountain becomes the core concept to understanding Sichuan historic towns.

During ancient times, town site selection was based on *Fengshui* rule that it should face water with the mountain at the back, and it should comply with the landform naturally. An old Sichuan town called Fubao, located in southern Sichuan, is a typical one constructed under such a rule (Fig. 71). The town is built on a hill right next to Pujiang River, and it almost occupies the whole hill. In another word, the hill and the town are integrated with one another thoroughly, embodying rich landscape layers. The main street of Fubao follows the mountainous topography paved with local bluestone. With regard to local natural conditions, the widest part of the street(s) is about seven meters, while certain parts can be as narrow as one meter. One can easily find local stylish *Diaojiao* dwelling units with stilted columns along both sides of the street. Climbing up towards the hilltop, layers of *Diaojiao* with gray roof tiles and curls of smokes ascending from the rooftop can be viewed from time to time, resembling a traditional Chinese ink painting that vividly depicts local life and activities.

Ya'an area is located at the edge of the Chengdu Plain, and it is also the node connecting the Ancient Tea-Horse Trading Route and the Chengdu Plain area. Because of such commercial activities, several towns were developed, such as Shangli, Wangyu, and Yinghe. Wangyu (Fig. 72) itself is located on a huge rock next to the river, which looks like a hungry cat watching fish in the river, hence receiving its name "watching fish." One needs to climb around one hundred cliffy steps from the river bank to get to the town center, and there is only one old street, next to the hill. Buildings on both sides of the street are all light timber structures with tiled roofs integrated with the street paved by natural bluestone, all in a simple and easy manner.

图 73 荣河场古镇建在岩石上的吊脚楼
Fig. 73 *Diaojiao* Building built on the rock of Yinghe Historic Town

* 来源：何智亚，2009
  Source: He Zhiya, 2009

荥河场老街坐落在河边的小山峦上，有上街与下街之分。下街建在河岸堤坝之上，两侧都是具有浓厚川西色彩的吊脚楼（图 73），高于堤坝的吊脚楼在洪水上涨时还可以起到保护作用。上街位置较高，以木结构房屋为主，组成内街。上下两街的建筑遵循自然，与山水之势融为一体。

无论是小桥流水的"水"还是山中人家的"山"，都是古代先民出于对自然的理解与尊重而改造自身环境的典范，也是对"天人合一"传统思想的实践。鱼米之乡的居民利用水乡泽国的天时地利，发展临水而生的居住形态；天府之国的居民顺应山形地势，开发出独特的山地建筑形式。各自的实践都是对环境和自然的因势利导，当地居民得以生生不息，繁衍不止。这一理念在当今仍然值得我们后世的城市规划师与建筑师借鉴。

Also built on a small mountain next to the river, another old town called Yinghe has an upper and a lower street, respectively. The lower part is located on the river bank with Sichuan style *Diaojiao* buildings (Fig. 73) along both sides. Those *Diaojiao* columns function to protect the dwelling portion above during the floods. The upper town is built higher on the mountain, forming an inner street with wood-structured dwelling units. Both parts of the town follow the form or potential of nature, whether water or mountain, creating a very active but sustainable environment.

Generally speaking, when discussing water in the Jiangnan water towns or mountains in Sichuan historic towns, we are actually talking about ancient folks' respect to nature and to their own living environment. It is definitely the practice of traditional Chinese philosophy to keep in mind harmony between man and nature. In so doing, the residents in Jiangnan aim to make best use of local geographic conditions to develop unique housing typology close to the water, while the people in Sichuan Province follow the mountainous landform to create a stylish architectural form. All of these practice come from the same ideology that humans sustain themselves by sustaining a harmonious relationship with nature. The idea is still held worthy for architects and urban planners today.

4. 各具特色的文化精髓

Distinctive Cultural Essence

江南水乡古镇的独特地理环境孕育了独特的江南文化，由于良好的自然环境与相对稳定的社会环境，这里自古就吸引了众多文人雅士。江南文化在千百年的发展中已经成为中华文化的重要组成部分。江南水乡古镇的文化底蕴深厚、丰富多彩，许多吟诵江南水乡风光的诗作名篇也成了中国文学的重要组成部分。

Environment gives birth to culture. Because of its comfortable weather and relatively stable social and political environment, Jiangnan has attracted lots of scholars to settle there. With its rich and profound contents, Jiangnan culture has become an important portion of Chinese culture during its long history. Many famous works praising the beauty of Jiangnan also constitute a crucial part of Chinese literature.

周庄自古就是文人雅士寓居之处，最早便有晋朝的文学家张翰，因思念家乡周庄的莼菜和鲈鱼而拒绝出任官职，被传为佳话。近代著名作家茅盾先生出生在乌镇，在他的文学创作中，读者可以发现以乌镇为原型的故事场景，这些作品中乌镇的意象反映了茅盾先生对故乡深刻的记忆和深切的思念。有着 2500 年历史的甪直古镇不仅水乡景色秀美，人文景观也是星罗棋布。这里曾是近代著名教育家叶圣陶任教的地方，叶圣陶先生一直视甪直为培育自己成长的摇篮，并亲切地称其为"第二故乡"。他逝世后便安葬在甪直，叶圣陶纪念馆也建于此。

江南园林作为中国古典建筑文化中的一朵奇葩，体现着中国古代"文人造园""含而不露"等思想精髓。江南园林的实践也在江南水乡古镇中有突出表现，伴随着无数文人雅士寓居古镇，许多精美的园林也在古镇中诞生，其中不乏传世佳作。

Zhouzhuang used to be the best living place for ancient literati, where many important figures in Chinese history enjoyed their retreat life away from the political center. Uniquely, Zhang Han from the Jin Dynasty refused to leave Zhouzhuang, his hometown, for official position because he so loved the vegetables and bass fish there. Well known modern writer Mao Dun was born in Wuzhen, which also became a prototype of the background site in many of his famous novels. The artistic image of Wuzhen in his works greatly expresses his deep memories and love of his hometown. Another town called Luzhi has a history of 2,500 years with a beautiful landscape, as well as scattered cultural places. Ye Shengtao, a famous modern educator, used to teach in this town, and he regarded this place as his second hometown. Years later, he was buried here with a memorial adjacent to it.

The Jiangnan garden is unique in classical Chinese architecture, as it fully embodies traditional "literature garden" rules and a modest essence. Compared with those in big cities such as Suzhou and Hangzhou, Jiangnan's water towns own quite a lot of excellent Jiangnan gardens as well. These are the results of attracting famous scholars and literati throughout its history.

蜀韵古镇

HISTORIC TOWNS IN SICHUAN:
THE CULTURAL HERITAGE PROTECTION AND UTILIZATION OF
HISTORIC TOWNS WITH DIFFERENT DIMENSIONS AND VISIONS
——多维视野下的古镇文化遗产保护与利用

图 74 南浔小莲庄的荷花池 *
Fig. 74 Lotus pond in Xiaolian Garden, Nanxun

　　南浔古镇的小莲庄精妙非凡，即使同苏州城里的古典园林相比也可堪称精品。这座清代私家花园运用独特的造园手法，在不大的园林空间中创造出深藏不露的一番天地。园中央开阔碧绿的荷花池为人称道，不大的荷池画龙点睛，连接东西南北的亭台楼阁，一派宛如天作的自然景象（图 74）。另外值得一提的是毗邻太湖的木渎古镇，因其优美的自然景色而受到历代致仕官僚和退隐文人的青睐，也因此留下了大批园林宅邸，有着"园林古镇"的美誉。流传后世的佳作以榜眼府第、虹饮山房、羡园、古松园和灵岩山馆等几处最为出名。

　　Xiaolian Garden in the town of Nanxun is a high-quality landscape art piece as terrific as those well-known ones in Suzhou City. The garden was constructed during the Qing Dynasty, and it applied a unique landscape method to create an insightful space that looks much bigger than it is. There is an attractive lotus pond in the center. The pond becomes the focus of the entire garden, and it unifies the nearby pavilions and buildings into one system embodying a man-made but natural scenario (Fig. 74). Another small water town near Taihu Lake called Mudu also has many traditional gardens. It used to attract famous scholars and literati to settle there. Among those famous residences with beautiful landscape gardens, there are Bangyan Residence, Hongyin Residence, Xian Garden, Gusong Garden, and Lingyan Residence. Mudu has therefore been known as "Garden Town" for hundreds of years.

　　相比江南水乡古镇的江南文化，四川古镇的文化精髓则体现在"兼蓄并包，多元融合"上。四川地区在历史上多灾多难，经历了元末明初的战乱以及明末清初张献忠的屠杀之后，整个四川地区基本上十室九空，直到清代中叶这里还是人口稀少，可耕地多。为了发展经济，巩固边防，清朝政府制定了"插占为业"的人口吸引政策，引发了"湖广填四川"的移民浪潮。湖北、湖南、江西、广东、陕西等地的移民不远万里来到四川盆地艰苦创业，与当地文化融合，创造了兼蓄并包的新文化、新民俗。这种文化精髓也反映在古镇的发展上，其中最有代表性的要数有"中国西部客家第一镇"之称的洛带古镇。

　　位于成都龙泉驿区的洛带古镇由移民至此的客家人繁衍发展起来，这里是中国西部客家人非常集中的城镇。不少客家后裔直到今天仍能讲客家话。客家人的文化习俗在这里生根发芽，与当地蜀文化相融合，成为四川古镇兼蓄并包的典范。这一精神尤其体现在洛带古镇的四大会馆——广东会馆、湖广会馆、江西会馆和川北会馆的建筑风格上。这些会馆是各地移民聚会与纪念故土的场所。广东会馆在细节处理上体现着浓浓的岭南特色，大殿两旁的对联——"云水沧沧，异地久栖巴子国""乡关迢递，乘舟欲上粤土台"——生动形象地展现了广东客家移民的思乡之情。

Compared with Jiangnan culture in Jiangnan water towns, Sichuan styles exploit a tolerant spirit with multicultural integration. Unlike the stable political status of the Jiangnan area, the Sichuan province has suffered from war and disaster more frequently. Especially after the massacre during the chaos period between Yuan Dynasty and Ming Dynasty, Sichuan lost 90 percent of its population, leaving a vast unclaimed land. Therefore, the Qing government established a number of policies to encourage immigration from other crowded provinces including Hubei, Hunan, Jiangxi, Guangdong, and Shaanxi. Immigrants from these provinces moved to Sichuan thousands of kilometers away from their hometown and worked hard on establishing new homes; at the same time, they would bring their own culture, which was to be integrated with the local culture. After several hundred years, the integration gave birth to a new culture with merits combined from many other areas. Built by immigrants, Luodai, the so-called No.1 Hakka Town of West China, is the typical place embodying such new culture.

The town Luodai is located in Longquan District of Chengdu developed by Hakka immigrants, and it is the center of the Hakka community in West China. A lot of Hakka descendants there are still able to speak Hakka today. Their culture takes roots in Sichuan, and it is fully integrated with local culture, which makes Luodai a perfect example of multicultural spirit. Moreover, the important buildings in the town including Guangdong *Huiguan*, Huguang *Huiguan*, Jiangxi *Huiguan*, and North Sichuan *Huiguan* all apply this spirit on architectural design due to the fact that these buildings are meant to function as memorials to the home land of immigrants. For example, Guangdong *Huiguan* embodies intensive Guangdong style architectural detail, and the decorative antithetical couplets on both sides of the gate express the homesickness of local immigrants.

图 75 江西会馆的马头墙
Fig. 75 Horsehead Wall of the Jiangxi *Huiguan*

　　与本土的川西民居不同，洛带古镇的移民会馆大都反映了故土的建筑风格，在传统建筑群落中格外醒目。镇中心的广东会馆高 14 米左右，形制宏大，在古镇的建筑空间中居于中心地位。其歇山顶配以高高翘起的檐角，造型轻盈灵动；其山墙顶采用曲线造型，颇有岭南建筑的优雅动感，令人印象深刻。而另一处的江西会馆则运用马头墙这一地方特色浓郁的建筑形式，以表现会馆的地域属性（图 75）。

　　四川古镇在长期的历史发展中吸收了众多外来文化的建筑精髓，并与本土的建筑形式很好地结合起来。无论是广东会馆还是江西会馆，虽风格醒目，却都没有在古镇上显得格外突兀，而是在保持自身特色的同时很好地与周边建筑融为一体，创造出整体和谐的建筑氛围。同样的情况可以在大邑安仁古镇看到。这里曾是民国时期四川军阀刘湘、刘文辉与刘文彩的家乡，有不少传统街区和庄园建筑群。很多建筑因受民国时期西风东渐的影响采用了西洋风格，虽其形制和整体布局还是传统的中式庭院，但立面装饰运用欧洲古典风格。西洋的立面装饰配上中式院落的一进一间，造就了"中西合璧"的典范。

Unlike the native residence in Sichuan, those in Luodai Historic Town are basically community centers for local immigrants, and their architectural forms mostly follow the original styles of their hometown. Guangdong *Huiguan* in the middle of Luodai is a grand building with around 14-meter height, and it is definitely the center of the entire town. It is impressive that the roof of the hall has a high angle corner, while its apex uses many curved modeling techniques in order to show the lightness and elegance of Guangdong architecture. In another location of the town, Jiangxi *Huiguan* applies horsehead-shaped decoration on the apex, which expresses the unique architectural style of Jiangxi Province (Fig. 75).

Sichuan historic towns absorbed architectural essences from other cultures, and they are well-combined with local architectural forms. Both Guangdong *Huiguan* and Jiangxi *Huiguan* still preserve the harmonious relationship with the entire town, although their architectural style and form of language are distinctive from the vernacular ones. The same situation can also be seen in the old town of Anren, Dayi County, where there once were the home, for warlords Liu Xiang, Liu Wenhui and Liu Wencai with their luxury building compounds during the Republic of China period. A large number of these buildings were influenced by western culture at that time, when European classical style façades came into fashion. Therefore, a new hybrid articulation was generated in Sichuan, where traditional Chinese architecture layouts combined with neo-classical European façades and decoration. One can still find those unique but well-preserved compounds in the historic town Anren today, suggesting the combination history more than one hundred years ago.

HISTORIC TOWNS IN SICHUAN:
THE CULTURAL HERITAGE PROTECTION AND UTILIZATION OF
HISTORIC TOWNS WITH DIFFERENT DIMENSIONS AND VISIONS
——多维视野下的古镇文化遗产保护与利用

5. 建筑风格的差异

Variation of Architectural Styles

如前文所述，江南水乡古镇与四川古镇在文化精髓上有所不同，这种区域文化的不同实际上是建筑风格有所差异的重要原因。脱胎于本地地理气候等自然条件与历史经济等人文条件的文化，造就了古镇形态各异的建筑风格。建筑的形式反映当地居民的日常生活状况，建筑材料与构造的演变也反映了该地历史与经济活动的变迁。这些都是研究江南水乡古镇与四川古镇所必须考虑的。

江南民居造型轻巧灵活，多为木构穿斗式结构，外围护结构用砖墙（多数为空斗墙），一般上下两层楼。布局因地制宜，组合不拘一格，较为灵活，大多数建筑与水相结合，临水面开阔，有着前街后河的特点。同北方官式建筑相比，则显精巧更胜而气派不足。江南建筑在色彩上很明快，有着青瓦白墙的特色，为了反射过强的日光，墙面多粉刷白色，而屋顶也多建构得很轻薄，屋脊线轻盈舒展，屋檐宽阔，下面多为檐廊，为过往行人遮风避雨（图76）。

As mentioned before, the core cultures of Jiangnan and Sichuan are quite different, thus the difference is projected in local architectural styles. In fact, regional climates and economic conditions produce unique architectural features for both areas, as architecture is a mirror reflecting a citizen and user's daily life and environmental condition in the form of material, detail, construction, color and so on. Therefore, research about those architectural features helps us deeply understand both areas in a holistic view point.

The Jiangnan traditional dwelling is given a slim and graceful style, mostly constructed by timber *Chuandou* structure (a traditional Chinese building structure system in South China). These generally two-story buildings use brick walls as envelope and their layout usually keeps flexible adjusting to local topography. Many old Jiangnan buildings are integrated with water in various ways following the "front street, back water" rule. Compared with the royal architectural style in North China, Jiangnan buildings are more exquisite with small but attractive details. The color is light with white walls and black shingle roof. White walls help to reflect daylight during hot summer, while the shingle roof always keep thin with the ridge line stretching out gracefully. The space under the wide eave is often turned into an eaved corridor, which protects the passengers from wind and rain (Fig. 76).

图 76 阳光下的乌镇：层层青瓦屋顶与马头墙，典型的江南民居风格
Fig. 76 Wuzhen in the daylight: Conventional Jiangnan Style with layers of black shingle roof and Horsehead Wall

蜀韵古镇　HISTORIC TOWNS IN SICHUAN:
THE CULTURAL HERITAGE PROTECTION AND UTILIZATION OF
HISTORIC TOWNS WITH DIFFERENT DIMENSIONS AND VISIONS
——多维视野下的古镇文化遗产保护与利用

江南水乡建筑的山墙风格特征明显，一般作马头墙的形式，白墙上砌很薄的青瓦，有平整的脊线，也有起翘的脊线，风格多样。层层叠叠的马头墙配合高低错落的屋顶，形成了一幅鳞次栉比的生动画面。水乡古镇民居多使用色调素雅的砖雕与木雕来装饰，二层的外围护结构轻薄，多用木雕与花窗来装饰，高大的院墙上开有风格独特的透窗，使院内的园林景致含蓄而自然地流露出来。许多马头墙上还做有砖雕与彩绘，为水乡民居建筑增添秀美之色。

而四川古镇的民居建筑则相应要古朴得多，在四川这片多民族多文化的区域中，四川民居也是兼收南北东西文化的产物。它的形制和布局类似北方建筑，以庭院为空间组织因素，"一正两厢"的组合格局显得大气开敞。而在建筑构造上，川西民居又有着南方轻盈精巧的特点，其多为木质穿斗结构，结构构件断面较小，另有不少重要建筑如庙宇和会馆等受北方官式建筑的影响，为砖结构。还有许多靠近南部的古镇民居受潮湿环境及少数民族文化的影响，做有架空的吊脚楼。总之，四川民居博采众长，融合百家，吸收了各个地方的建筑精髓，这与四川古镇的文化特点密不可分。

The most distinguished characteristics of Jiangnan building style is the form of gables, which is called a horsehead wall style. The style has become the symbol of Jiangnan architecture with a thin layer of black shingles on the top of white wall and the roof ridge lines vary in forms and details. Multiple layers of roof and horsehead wall gables of buildings in different heights create a typical vivid image of Jiangnan. Local folks prefer brick and wood carvings to decorate their houses with light and simple color. Walls on the second floor are usually decorated by wooden windows and beautiful flower pattern carvings. Moreover, the high wall of courtyard is stylish with unique decorative windows on it, which bring the beauty of inner garden out smoothly. Numerous horsehead walls also have brick and color drawings on them adding color and elegance to local dwelling buildings.

On the other hand, Sichuan's local architectural style is more simple and natural. Located in a region with multiple ethnic groups, Sichuan's traditional buildings are the result of integration of different cultures. It is true that the proportion and layout of it are similar to those of the North China style: using courtyards to organize spaces in hierarchy. However, the style also embodies the slim and graceful style of Jiangnan architecture with a light *Chuandou* structure system and small size structural components. As for temples or *Huiguan*, brick structure influenced by North China becomes dominant. While those residential buildings located at the town near southern minority group region were deeply influenced by local climate and ethnic culture. They are basically stilted buildings called *Diaojiao* built to protect people during floods and to keep air ventilation efficiently underneath the living space. In general, local Sichuan architecture absorbed essences from different cultures, which closely connected with the fusion of traditional Sichuan culture.

四川民居保留了不少唐代以前的建筑风格，色彩浅淡，外墙多粉刷白色或灰砖色，在青瓦的映衬下显得格外素雅。建筑材料多因地制宜，就地取材，木材多用当地良材，木窗、木门及木雕皆作木材本色，朴素自然。除了砖墙和木板墙，川西民居的外墙还常采用土墙、石墙或编夹壁墙，经济节约，使古镇建筑富有浓郁的乡土气息，也符合古人"天人合一""与环境相融合"的思想（图77）。

Traditional Sichuan buildings inherit many traits from the ancient period before Tang Dynasty. The exterior wall is mostly painted white or gray color, keeping the simplicity and elegance in the sunlight. Building materials are extruded from local area, and wood is the prevailing material for construction and detail decoration. Those wooden components keep their original appearance to get closer to the nature. Other than brick walls and wooden panel walls, local people also installed economical and natural mud walls or stone walls, which fulfills traditional "Nature and Human Being Integration" of Chinese philosophy (Fig. 77).

图 77 上里古镇临水而建的本色木结构民居
Fig. 77 Wood-structured vernacular buildings built next to the water in Shangli Historic Town

蜀韵古镇

HISTORIC TOWNS IN SICHUAN:
THE CULTURAL HERITAGE PROTECTION AND UTILIZATION OF
HISTORIC TOWNS WITH DIFFERENT DIMENSIONS AND VISIONS
——多维视野下的古镇文化遗产保护与利用

6. 共同的未来——古镇保护与发展

The same future—Preservation and Development of Old Towns

　　随着传统农业经济的解体，无论是江南水乡古镇还是四川古镇，都丧失了赖以发展的经济基础，在近代工业化、城市化运动之后都不可避免地走向了衰落。如何才能保护古镇传统的建筑与人文环境，同时又使其得到现代化发展，改善古镇居民的生活条件，这是两地古镇所面临的问题。旅游业固然能够为古镇带来可观的经济利益，并为宣传保护古镇做出贡献，但大量的商业开发带来严重的问题，诸如破坏了原有的生态和人文环境，破坏了许多有价值的历史传统，大量粗制滥造的仿古建筑破坏了古镇原有风貌，等等。尤其是较早开发的江南水乡古镇，其商业化程度过高，反而使诸多历史传统被掩盖甚至消失。例如最早开发的周庄，蜕变成了商业活动的场所，无限制的游客与过多的商店，使这座"中国第一水乡"失去了"小桥流水人家"的意境，成为喧嚣嘈杂的旅游目的地（图78）。

As traditional agricultural economy collapses, old towns in both areas lose their foundation for development or even existence, which becomes the reason of their decline after modern industrialization. How does one protect traditional architecture and ethnic environment while local living conditions are improved simultaneously by promoting modernization? This is the same significant question the old towns in both areas have to answer. Of course, tourism is able to bring considerable economic benefits, and make contributions to promote public attention to old towns' preservation. However, too much commercial development also generates serious problems at the same time. It is obvious that over-commercialization damages original ecological and cultural environments, it destroys several valuable traditions and jeopardizes the original features of old towns by constructing low-quality fake antique buildings. The situation is especially critical in the development of Jiangnan water town in early years where over-commercialization has swept out lots of historic traditions. For example, Zhouzhuang, one of the earliest development in Jiangnan area, faces the problem that traditional town is becoming a highly commercial place without local residents. Unlimited tourists have turned this famous town which used to be the first in China to a crowed and noisy tourist destination (Fig. 78).

图 78 节假日人头攒动的周庄：过度商业开发的典型
Fig. 78 Crowded Zhouzhuang, an example of over-commercialization

159

蜀韵古镇
HISTORIC TOWNS IN SICHUAN:
THE CULTURAL HERITAGE PROTECTION AND UTILIZATION OF
HISTORIC TOWNS WITH DIFFERENT DIMENSIONS AND VISIONS
——多维视野下的古镇文化遗产保护与利用

这样的经验教训应该被后来者所吸取。受地理条件的限制，四川的很多古镇到如今依然保持着古朴的色彩与传统的生活，隐藏在大山深处的古镇人家仍然重复着几千年来相似的生活，这固然是一种落后，却也是发展与保护的机遇。红军长征路上的磨西古镇是一片尚未开发的处女地，却也因其淳朴无华的本色与良好的自然条件吸引了不少慕名而来的背包客，他们逃离城市喧嚣前来尽享纯净的阳光与空气。与此同时，有些四川古镇在近几年的旅游开发大潮中声名鹊起，却也引发了过度商业化的弊病，如成都的洛带古镇。如何在旅游开发的同时保护古镇的文化特色，这是每个关心四川古镇未来发展的人所要思考的问题。

Such a lesson as the above is supposed to be learned by the successor. Many Sichuan old towns still keep primitive simplicity with traditional life, restricted by geographical conditions. Those small towns hidden in mountainous regions still repeat the social and economic modes from thousands of years ago. Considering people's living standard, they need modern development for sure, but it is also an opportunity to protect these historic treasures wisely. Moxi in Sichuan, for example, is a virgin land without modern development, but the simplicity and natural features of it attract numerous backpackers escaping from the noisy and dusty city to enjoy bright sunlight and fresh air. Moxi is a case that shows that a well-preserved environment and traditions help economic development as well. On the other hand, some historic towns in Sichuan lost valuable features in the recent development wave with over-commercialization causing serious problems including the old town of Luodai. In conclusion, concerning development of Sichuan historic towns in the future, it may be wise to insist on the protection of traditional culture characteristics in the limited and well-planned tourism development.

文化旅游业发展中的历史保护问题：
以美国弗吉尼亚州亚历山德里亚市与中国江浙地区
苏州、乌镇、周庄的对比分析为例

Preservation through Cultural Tourism Development:
An Analysis of Alexandria, Virginia and Suzhou, Wuzhen, and
Zhouzhuang of the Jiangsu and Zhejiang Area of China

序言
Introduction

中国鼓励现代化以解决落后城镇和地区的问题。在江苏省，许多建筑过于老旧，已不适用于新的经济用途。随着人们从破旧倒塌的房屋中迁出，计件薪酬的工厂和临时宿舍遍布城市各地。核心基础设施的缺失导致了河道的污染，而与此同时，污染的水体却是当地居民的生活中心：人们在此打鱼、洗衣、炊饮与沐浴……新地区的发展、高速交通与核心基础设施的建设有助于缓解这些问题并提升市民的生活质量。

蜀韵古镇

HISTORIC TOWNS IN SICHUAN:
THE CULTURAL HERITAGE PROTECTION AND UTILIZATION OF
HISTORIC TOWNS WITH DIFFERENT DIMENSIONS AND VISIONS
——多维视野下的古镇文化遗产保护与利用

迅猛的发展在最大程度上挑战着传统建筑。皇家建造、知名庙宇和纪念性建筑被逐步保护起来，但乡村地区的乡土建筑却少有人过问。然而，正是这些本土的民居建筑组成了中国文化的丰富肌理，塑造着城市街道、市镇格局和人们的生活。如果没有适当的保护，这些深刻反映中国人民生活方式与文化遗产的古建筑将永远消失在历史的长河中。

China has encouraged modernization as a way to resolve problems in derelict cities and towns. In Jiangsu Province, many buildings are extremely old and no longer serve a distinct economic purpose. Piecework factories and makeshift homes littered the cityscape as families moved from crumbling structures. The lack of a central infrastructure resulted in contamination of the canals; yet, the polluted waterways were integral in the lifestyles of communities, serving as a place to fish, wash laundry, provide water for cooking and bathing, etc. The construction of new developments, highways, and a central infrastructure could alleviate these problems and raise the quality of life for citizens.

It is this rapid development that challenges traditional architecture most. Measures have been taken to protect imperial architecture, famous temples, and monuments, but little has been done to preserve the vernacular architecture of the country. It is vernacular architecture that constitutes the rich cultural fabric of China, shaping its streets, urban patterns, and people's daily lives. Without proper protection, this architecture that is most reflective of the Chinese people, their lifestyles, and heritage will be lost forever.

美国的文化遗产保护兴起于 1949 年国家信托组织成立后。这一联邦组织开始在全国范围内宣扬对文化遗产的保护，但时至今日，该组织也仍不具备影响大规模遗产保护与维护的法律权力。20 世纪 60 年代美国的"市区重建"运动正如今日中国的现代化建设运动一样：城市规划师与建筑师携手努力整建、重建、兴建着新的社区。需要指出的是，这样的"复兴"对美国历史老区和传统城市中心区带来了毁灭性冲击。

位于美国弗吉尼亚州的亚历山德里亚市地处波拖马可河，与首都华盛顿隔水相望，被美国国家历史名录列为历史保护区域。该地区采取了一系列政策措施以保护其建筑、考古、历史、工业和文化的整体性。通过保护再利用和精心的建筑规划设计，在维持城区多样性与人们现代化生活发展的同时，亚历山德里亚的老城区得到有效的保护。老厂房与集市被重新规划再利用为商业、餐饮、办公用地，有助于当地良性旅游经济的发展。

文化旅游是诸多历史街区以及世界文化遗产地的经济基础，它在保留遗产完整性的同时又创造了宜居的现代社区。文化旅游业在不破坏既有的遗产文脉的同时，也为当代技术的融入提供了可能性。但从另一个角度讲，仍有言论认为遗产旅游业会破坏历史区域，改变地区的交通与经济模式，以及整个区域的传统生活形态。或许在一些地区的确存在这个问题，但在中国江浙地区的水乡开发和亚历山德里亚市的案例中，文化旅游业成了在不隔断原有历史经济形态的前提下促进经济发展并保护文化遗产的催化剂。

江浙水乡和亚历山德里亚市的文化旅游业发展都离不开其原有的历史人文经济背景。苏州、周庄、乌镇和亚历山德里亚在旅游业兴盛的很早以前就已经有各自的经济与商业基础：中国江浙水乡自古以奢品贸易闻名，而亚历山德里亚自建立起就是一座贸易城市。文化旅游业恰恰反映了这些城市地区的经贸特性。

文化旅游业在江浙地区和亚历山德里亚的引入为遗产景区的保护、重建和维护提供了必要的资金支持。旅游业不仅复兴了当地经济，还创造了新型的宜居环境。通过文化旅游业，江浙地区水乡和弗吉尼亚州亚历山德里亚市的珍贵地方文化得以保存，从而保护了这些地区丰富的历史建筑遗产。

Preservation in the United States began in 1949 with the establishment of the National Trust. This federal organization began to create preservation awareness in the country, but even today, it does not have the legal power to protect and preserve on a large scale. Urban renewal movements of the 1960s in the United States mimic those modernization movements of China today, as planners and architects strove to jump-start communities with mass demolition and re-building. Notably, this "revitalization" had devastating effects on historic districts and traditional downtowns across America.

Alexandria, Virginia, located along the Potomac River across from the nation's capital, has been listed as a historic district by the National Register of Historic Places. The community has established tactics to protect the integrity of the architecture, archaeology, history, engineering, and culture of the district. Through adaptive reuse and careful architectural design and planning, the structures of Old Town Alexandria can be preserved while maintaining the vitality of the town and the modern lifestyles of the people within. Through adaptive reuse, warehouses and historic markets, have been made into places of retail, restaurants, and offices. These businesses generate a healthy tourism-based economy.

Cultural tourism serves as the economic basis of many historic districts and World Heritage Sites. It creates livable, modern communities while maintaining the integrity of heritage sites. Through cultural tourism, it is possible to integrate technology into a community without destroying its context. On the other hand, it has been argued that cultural tourism can harm a historic district, changing its traffic patterns, economy, and the pattern of life within the community. In some places, this may be true, but in the case of the water towns in the Jiangsu and Zhejiang area and in Alexandria, cultural tourism serves as a catalyst for economic strength and protection of heritage sites without disrupting the historic economic patterns of these places.

The towns of the Jiangsu and Zhejiang area and Alexandria can employ cultural tourism without deviating significantly from historically commercial economic patterns. Suzhou, Zhouzhuang, Wuzhen, and Alexandria all became market and business-driven commercial areas long before the introduction of tourism. Water towns of the Jiangsu and Zhejiang area were notorious for the trade of luxury goods, while Alexandria's own founding act declared it a city of trade. Cultural tourism reflects that same economic spirit.

Cultural tourism is currently employed in the Jiangsu and Zhejiang area and Alexandria and provides the necessary funding for the preservation, restoration, and maintenance of heritage sites. This tourism not only revitalizes the commercial economy of all these places but also creates livable communities. Through cultural tourism, it is possible to protect the valuable vernacular fabric of the Jiangsu and Zhejiang area and Alexandria, Virginia and thus preserve the rich, historic architecture of these places.

1. 中国江浙地区

Jiangsu and Zhejiang Area in China

本节将向读者简要介绍当今中国的建筑业发展与中国的江浙地区。第一部分将重点介绍明清的建筑形式与中国城市规划设计的基本哲学方法。第二部分将讲述苏州、乌镇和周庄的经济和交通发展历史与当今地区旅游业发展的合理联系。本节将以对中国新的建筑潮流的探讨作结。

省一级规划院和建筑设计院总体负责现代化发展中的大量规划设计任务。新建住宅区远离市中心的工作、商业、娱乐设施，与当地传统的社区建筑形式相背。新的开发区并不承继传统的历史文化环境，也不依从传统的建筑设计理念。在缺乏私有建筑事务所产业竞争的情况下，并无太多革新性的建筑设计诞生。

This section begins with a brief explanation of architecture in China today, then introduces the reader to the Jiangsu and Zhejiang area in China. The first part of the section focuses on Ming and Qing architectural forms, as well as the Chinese philosophies of urban planning and design that founded the construction of this architecture. In the second part of the section, economic history and transportation are discussed as relevant to the development of Suzhou, Wuzhen and Zhouzhuang, and as pertinent to tourism in the region. The section concludes with a look at new architectural movements in China.

State-owned planning and architecture institutions have responded to China's call for rapid modernization and great need for housing with economic, straightforward, and functional structures. Newly constructed housing is isolated from work, commerce, and recreation areas, thus hindering a sense of community that was once present through traditional design. New developments do not address the historical context in which they are placed and do not reflect traditional building styles or principles. Without the competition of private architectural industry, there have been few incentives to create innovative architectural design.

图 79 乌镇的风雨廊桥
Fig. 79 Covered bridge in Wuzhen

图 80 苏州古城典型的水街：两岸的人家、游船以及远处的拱桥
Fig. 80 Historic buildings next to the water street, with boats and an arched bridge in the distance, a typical scene in Suzhou Historic Town

今日受现代市场经济驱使的国有性质的建筑设计机构所负责的建筑营造方式，与中国传统的建筑营造方式反差极大。中国传统建筑业的发展几个世纪以来相对变化不大。在古代，中华文明的发展一直独立于外界的影响，地理条件在很大程度上造就了这个现象：山脉与海洋包围了东部、西部、南部，而北部又筑起了万里长城。工匠与手工艺人坚持着相对保守的建筑设计理念——匠人守则、师徒传艺，以及传统的形式与技术。正如许亦农在其书中所讲，中国城市自身稳固的经济模式为应对外界突然的变化冲击形成了缓冲。也正因为古代中国与外界沟通交流的局限，人们的生活习惯与城市建筑规划的发展变化都十分平缓。

在中国东南沿海的江浙地区，明清两朝的建筑和城市规划仍依稀可见。苏州是长三角地区主要的经济城市之一，而周庄和乌镇则位于流经苏州的运河水系上。江浙地区的城市肌理受运河水系影响。在小规模的河道两旁各家有自己的小码头，城镇道路依地势发展。在小型的乡镇村落里，水路优先于陆路，道路绕河道延伸，并不相通。这些蜿蜒狭窄的乡村小路十分安静，并不承担繁重的交通运输任务（图 79-81）。

The modern, economically-derived architecture designed today by municipal architectural firms particularly contrasts with traditional architecture because China's architecture has remained relatively unchanged for centuries. From the earliest times, Chinese civilization developed independently of outside influences. Geographic features largely caused this isolation: the mountains and ocean to the east, south, and west, and the Great Wall to the north. Artisans and craftsmen adhered to relatively conservative architectural design trends based on manuals, apprenticeships, craft traditions, and traditional forms and techniques. As Xu Yinong explains in his book, the stable economies of Chinese cities also provided a buffer against sudden change. As a result of China's isolation and limited interaction with other countries, lifestyle changes, in addition to architectural and urban planning changes, were very gradual.

In the Jiangsu and Zhejiang area along the southeast coast of China, Ming and Qing architecture and urban patterns still exist today. Suzhou, one of the main economic centers of the region, is located at the center of the Yangtse River Delta. The water towns of Zhouzhuang and Wuzhen formed along rivers and canal systems outside of Suzhou. The urban fabric of the towns in the Jiangsu and Zhejiang area was dictated by these water systems. On minor water streets, every house had a private dock. Major roadways were laid as straight as the terrain would allow. In smaller villages and towns, streets were secondary to the waterways, winding around them, often leading to dead ends. Traffic was quiet and infrequent in the smaller, twisting lanes of the villages and towns (Figs. 79-81).

理想模式下，中国传统城市用地一般依南北主轴线进行布局，呈方形展开，四周城墙环绕，每面城墙上各开三座城门。建筑空间无论是实体还是形象上都充分反映出中国人对天人合一这一理想的实践。城市中的建筑依照封建礼制等级建立。灰色是常见民居的颜色，而红墙金顶则是皇室专用。施漆、彩绘和繁复的支架结构都不允许出现在民居建筑上。但在民宅和商业建筑中并不存在明显的等级制度，每一种结构都被视为整体建筑的组成部分。

公私之间、世俗与宗教之间、民居与商铺之间的界限并非那么清晰。建筑本身并不与居住者及其家庭或者从事的职业直接相关，各类活动都在那里发生着。对于建筑的怀旧之情也因此屈居次位，尽管楼宇结构本身可以唤起人们的特殊记忆。建筑结构可以被无限重复延续，因为中国人的生活方式、理念、宗教和哲学都是亘古不变的。中国的古城呈现出一种"超时空"的状态，因为其并不服务于某个特定的历史时代。正如许亦农所说，文字才是中华民族传承历史的最重要形式，对历史人物和事件的记忆往往存在于文学作品中。而建筑只是被视作一种庇护结构，它们可以在时间的长河中基于不同的目的和功能被反复重建和使用。

Ideally, an urban area was laid out according to a dominating north-south axis. Designed in the layout of a square, cities were surrounded by walls with three gates on either side. Architectural space was defined figuratively as well as physically in order to demonstrate man's ability to maintain order on earth as it is in heaven. Buildings in cities and towns were constructed according to the hierarchy established through the imperial system. Gray was traditionally the color allotted to the common villagers, whereas red and gold were reserved as colors of the royalty. Lacquer, color painting and corbel bracket supporting were prohibited in the construction of vernacular dwellings. Within village houses and businesses there did not exist a ranking system, as each structure was viewed as part of a greater whole.

Distinctions between public and private, secular and non-secular, and residential and business were blurred. Buildings themselves did not embody the spirit of a family or business, but rather the activities that occurred there. Nostalgia for buildings, bridges, and monuments is secondary to Chinese people, as these physical objects serve as symbolic reminders of the stories and importance of past events. Structures can be built and rebuilt as often as desired because the concepts, rituals, and philosophy of the Chinese lifestyle are permanent. Chinese cities represent a "continuum in time" because they are not based on time or historic periods. As Xu Yinong writes, "For the Chinese, the past is one of words, not stones...." The memory of specific historic or important people or events is kept alive most often through literature, which proved to be the greatest commemoration. Since buildings were viewed merely as structural shelters, it was common for them to be used over time for several different purposes and functions.

现存传统的明清时期建筑充分反映出中国人对自然环境的敏感。各类民居建筑强调自然性，旨在为房主人提供一个精神自由的空间。如南方中国的宅院，大多为正南或东南朝向。高耸的屋脊和适当的房顶高度，据说可以保证良好的通风与隔热，以抵御夏天的炎热。相较单层住宅设计而言，二三层的房屋和小窗设计更适合当地湿热的环境。灰、白、黑等简单、自然的颜色谱系营造出令人印象深刻的静谧和简约感。白墙黑瓦、不施油漆的原木色门窗，常用的颜色只有灰、白，以及灰黑色。

得益于原材料的可获得性和可标准化，木结构早在公元前5000年就被广泛使用。基于其复杂而巧妙的半刚性榫卯节点构造特点，木结构建筑可以有效抗震。谚语"墙倒屋不塌"就是对这一木结构坚实耐久特点的形象刻画。木结构屋宇由三部分组成：底基、立柱和支撑屋顶的梁架。屋顶表达着建筑的整体情感，墙体作为非支撑结构仅为分割空间服务。

Existing traditional structures of the Ming and Qing Dynasties accurately demonstrate the Chinese sensitivity to the environment. Various vernacular dwellings emphasize naturalness, providing a framework conducive to greater personal spiritual freedom. Houses in southern China are built mostly facing the south or southeast. These well-ventilated dwellings are also well insulated against the heat of summer due to the high ridges and generous depth of the roof. Compared to single-floor homes, the design of smaller windows of two-to-three story houses protects against the warmth and humidity. The simple, natural color scheme such as gray, white and black creates an impressive overall composition that reflects a quiet simplicity. Wall surfaces are plastered with lime and the top of walls are covered with convex and concave tiles. Doors and windows are mostly unpainted. The colors most often used are gray and white, with dark gray highlights.

Wood frames date back to 5000 B.C. and were historically used because wood was readily available and easily standardized. Due to the intricate, semi-rigid joint construction of buildings, such structures were able to withstand the forces of earthquakes. The proverb "the house does not collapse when the walls fall down" is a reflection of the durability and resilience of wood-frame construction. Wooden pavilions were of tripartite construction, consisting of a base, columns, and corbels supporting the roof. The roof conveyed the overall feeling of shelter, since walls were non-structural and served as screens used to divide space.

图 81 周庄背靠背民居之间的河道与游船
Fig. 81 Back-to-back dwellings next to the river with tourist boats in Zhouzhuang

最常见的建筑当属大殿或厅堂、两层及多层楼阁、亭子、外廊或独立的连廊。通常，北、东、西向的木柱之间会有坚实的砖墙填充，而南面墙体上多安排有半透明窗纸装饰的门窗等。

古代中国的城市和乡村按照儒家礼教原则兴建。首都被认为是国土的焦点，并被认为是沟通人世与天庭的媒介。严格的对称和轴线等结构性秩序在儒家思想的指导下应运而生。对大自然的深刻崇敬也在中国古代城市规划中表现出来。园林建设的首要理念是让人们在保持居家空间私密性的同时，尽可能地感受到自然美。自然地势地貌在很大程度上决定了很多中国城镇乡村房屋和道路的选址布局。

事实上，正是特殊的地形地貌影响了江浙地区的历史发展。这里水土丰饶，气候湿润，是中国种植水稻最好的洼地。这里除了是其他地区农产品的主要提供者，其渔业和畜牧业也十分兴盛发达。许多诸如捕鱼、早市和汰洗的习俗延续至今，但农业已不是该地区发展的重心。

The structures most frequently constructed were main halls, halls of two or more stories, pavilions, and galleries or freestanding corridors. Typically, the north, east, and west walls of a structure consisted of solid mud or gray-painted bricks formed between or partially around the wooden columns. On the south side of structures, doors and windows of translucent paper were built.

Historic Chinese cities and villages were designed according to Confucian principles. The capital city was viewed as the focal point of the land and was regarded as the responsible mediator between the moral patterns of earth and heaven. A strict order of symmetry and reliance on an axis derives from the basic pragmatism of Confucianism. A deep respect for nature also dictated the planning of Chinese cities. The principle objective of the garden was to allow participants to enjoy the natural aesthetics without leaving the privacy of a high-walled structure. Natural terrain features dictated the placement of buildings and roadways in many Chinese towns and villages.

It was, in fact, the unique qualities of the terrain that determined the development of the Jiangsu and Zhejiang area historically. With its fertile land and warm, humid climate, the region is the richest rice-growing bottomland in all of China. In addition to serving as the primary agricultural provider for the broader region, fishing, and stock raising are also prominent activities and provide daily necessities. Many of the daily activities of fishing, bringing products to the early morning markets, and washing laundry in the canals still persist, but agriculture no longer plays such an important role in the region.

苏州原有的独立水乡格局使其保持原始的生活方式成为可能，但在历史发展的长河中，当地乡村却很早就开始从农渔经济转向商业化经济发展。早在北朝时期，苏州持续的粮食积累就为农民的生活提供了良好的保障。至唐代（618 年—907 年），苏州因先进工具的发明迎来了经济的大繁荣。到了明朝，物质的极大丰富使得越来越多的人可能从事工商业。奢侈品交易和纺织业开始逐渐兴盛，而发达的水路交通也让原材料和产品的运输方便快捷（图 82）。16 世纪，苏州就已经成为中国知名的经济和文化中心之一，其在经济上的首要地位一直保持到 19 世纪中叶，直到被新兴的近代工商业化城市上海超越。

尽管苏州城及其周边的郊区和乡村都建立在儒家礼教所倡导的农渔传统产业基础之上，但其商业化的转向是无法避免的。不断增加的奢侈品贸易、过剩的服务性商业和传统儒家思想所倡导的节俭等道德形成了巨大反差。当生活方式越来越奢侈浪费，那么更多的奢侈品会被不断生产和分配。

The former isolation and inaccessibility of the water towns around Suzhou made it possible for them to maintain a traditional lifestyle; however, historically, the economies of these rural villages moved away from agricultural and fishing backgrounds long ago to embrace commercialism. In Suzhou, from as early as the Northern Dynasty, the increased production of rice freed farmers from the necessity of retaining crops for subsistence. Economic growth blossomed in the Tang Dynasty (618 A.D.–907 A.D.), when new tools for tilling and irrigating the soil were invented and implemented. By the Ming Dynasty, it became possible for the growing population to engage in secondary production and distribution. Production of luxury goods and the construction of textile industries tailored to the increasing public demand for specialty goods and services, and the added convenience and economy of water transportation made it possible to distribute raw and finished products with ease (Fig. 82). By the sixteenth century, Suzhou was known as the economic and cultural center of China. In fact, the economic centrality of Suzhou became so great, that it was only surpassed in the second half of the nineteenth century by the rise of Shanghai, when the modern era of mechanized transport and industry started.

The city of Suzhou and its surrounding suburban areas were founded on the humble Confucian principles of an honest agricultural and fishing based community, but the economic shift to commercialism was inevitable. The increase in the production of luxury goods and the extravagant services and habits were contrary to those morals advocated by Confucians. The more extravagant lifestyles became, the more the communities continued to produce and distribute luxury goods.

图 82 延续至今的高档旗袍作坊透露出苏州昔日的奢侈与繁华
Fig. 82 Continued *Qipao* (cheongsam) craftsmanship in Suzhou, reflecting its old charm and luxury commercial city life

HISTORIC TOWNS IN SICHUAN:
THE CULTURAL HERITAGE PROTECTION AND UTILIZATION OF
HISTORIC TOWNS WITH DIFFERENT DIMENSIONS AND VISIONS

图 83 同里排队的游船
Fig. 83 Tongli's tourist boats waiting in line

蜀韵古镇

——多维视野下的古镇文化遗产保护与利用

尽管人们的生活方式从农渔业转向了工商业，江浙人民为了在精神上追求儒家的高尚境界，开始投入文化、教育与艺术的怀抱。文学、音乐、绘画、书法、手工艺、装饰艺术、园艺和收藏得到了极大的繁荣发展。教育更多是为有钱、有闲暇且不用发愁生计的上等阶层服务的。苏州变成了清朝中国学历水平最高的城市。江浙地区的繁荣不仅仅表现在当地居民的生活方式、服饰方面，还表现在村落的建筑风格上。城市的繁荣更是在其建筑、饮食、礼数、交通、习俗各个方面均有所体现。

随着苏州城市经济的发展，其城市人口不断增长，城市范围不断扩张，周边卫星城镇也不断产生并发展繁荣。在明代，大城市昆山、常熟、太仓、嘉定、吴江、无锡和江阴就已纷纷建立。这些商业城市围绕并依靠苏州发展起各具特色的丝绸、贸易、交通经济，而苏州也在周边商业市镇的簇拥下更好地发展了自身特有的以奢侈品及服务业为主导的城市经济。

Although lifestyles had been irreversibly converted from farming and fishing backgrounds to those of businesses and industries, the people of the Jiangsu and Zhejiang area began to use their increased wealth to embrace education and the arts in an effort to return to the valued principles of Confucius. Literary arts, music, painting, calligraphy, craft arts, decorative arts, gardens, and collections were embraced. Education during this period of time was reserved for those of the wealthiest classes in society. They were the only ones capable of devoting the time and energy to studies, as they did not have to be concerned with earning, producing, or receiving daily provisions. Suzhou became the city with the highest number of degree-holding scholars in all of China during the Qing Dynasty. The wealth of the region was reflected not only in the extravagant lifestyles and dress of the Jiangsu and Zhejiang people but also in the design and architectural style of the villages. The overwhelming wealth of the city was visible in its architecture, food, gifts, transportation, and lifestyle.

As the population and wealth of Suzhou grew, its boundaries expanded, and its surrounding lands were inhabited and divided to create suburban counties. In the Ming Dynasty alone, Kunshan, Changshu, Taicang, Jiading, Wujiang, Wuxi, and Jiangyin were formed. These market towns became specialized in silk, trade, or transportation, relying on Suzhou to provide them with basic necessities. In return, Suzhou relied on these smaller towns for the specialty luxury goods and services that now characterize the city.

蜀韵古镇

HISTORIC TOWNS IN SICHUAN:
THE CULTURAL HERITAGE PROTECTION AND UTILIZATION OF
HISTORIC TOWNS WITH DIFFERENT DIMENSIONS AND VISIONS
——多维视野下的古镇文化遗产保护与利用

至 20 世纪末，旅游业已成为当地最大的收入来源。苏州是中国继京、沪之后的第三大旅游城市，并且是周边地区最大的旅游目的地。与苏州周边的小型水乡周庄、乌镇一样，苏州市中心（老城区）的宾馆数量很有限，面对旅游业的快速发展，外来游客数量一直攀升，面临住宿的问题和挑战。

随着旅游业的增长，交通也在不断变化。连通苏州和上海的大运河曾是主要的货运和客运交通载体，而现在苏沪间高速公路车程仅为一小时。曾经，京杭大运河的开凿成功带动了苏州及其周边的发展；今日，陆路高速公路网的建立让中国人能够更方便快捷地到达并开发偏远地区。交通的进步也给江浙地区曾经少人问津、与世隔绝的水乡带来了发展（图 83-84）。

By the end of the 20th century, tourism had become the largest source of income. Suzhou is among the top three tourist cities in China after Beijing and Shanghai, and is the No.1 tourist destination in the region. The number of hotels in the old city center of Suzhou is very limited. In the face of the rapid development of tourism, the number of tourists has been climbing and the challenges of accommodation are huge. Smaller water towns around Suzhou, such as Zhouzhuang and Wuzhen, have experienced similar surges in tourism, resulting in similar challenges.

With the increase of tourism, transportation is evolving. The Grand Canal from Shanghai to Suzhou used to be the major source of transportation for both material goods and people; now it merely takes one hour to drive the same distance on the highway. The construction of the Grand Canal led to the initial formation of the suburbs around Suzhou; today, newly constructed highways introduce Chinese people to undeveloped outerlying rural areas, making them accessible to all. These transportation advances have made it easy to access the formerly isolated water towns of the Jiangsu and Zhejiang area and have caused much of the growth in the area (Figs. 83-84).

图 84 西塘的水边酒家
Fig. 84 Restaurants next to the river in Xitang

蜀韵古镇 HISTORIC TOWNS IN SICHUAN:
THE CULTURAL HERITAGE PROTECTION AND UTILIZATION OF
HISTORIC TOWNS WITH DIFFERENT DIMENSIONS AND VISIONS
——多维视野下的古镇文化遗产保护与利用

根据传统儒家观念，今日大多数中国建筑师仍然崇尚以人为本同时兼顾与环境和谐的原则。可持续的设计理念在专业人群中也日渐流行。追求与自然的和谐一直是传统中国建筑的最重要原则，回归这一原则对今日中国的当代建筑发展将有极大帮助。此外，人们对重新认识传统建筑作为古典传统艺术和文化遗产的重要价值的认识程度也与日俱增。事实上，因为建筑师们的主张，很多历史建筑得以在大拆大建的过程中保存下来。与此同时，对于公共空间如城市绿地和步行街需求的规划共识也在不断增长。

中国建筑师们在探寻传统建筑和现代建筑的平衡中仍然面临诸多问题。而如何在保持地方传统的建筑特色的同时跟上全球化步伐，则是所有问题中最棘手的。在城市建设中人们很难做到对新建建筑的设计既有合理的限制又不减少其创意。对于环境的考量也让可持续建设成为热点。在这些理念不断兴起的同时，如何在鼓励通过公共交通出行的同时又兼顾私人车辆的可达性等问题也不容小觑。如何在有限土地资源条件下为13亿人创造良好的就业和生活环境依然是个巨大的挑战。综上，最严峻的问题还在于如何应对各个领域过于快速的发展和变化。

Following traditional Confucian principles, most Chinese architects today agree that design should place man at the center while simultaneously seeking harmony with the environment. This idea of sustainable design is growing among professionals. The importance of the relationship between natural landscape and built form has always been important in traditional Chinese architecture; a return to this environmental awareness could only improve current architectural design. In addition, the importance of preserving ancient traditional architecture is gaining momentum as appreciation grows for these buildings, which serve as reminders of a rich heritage. It is, in fact, due to the concern and initiative of architects that much of the traditional architecture has been saved from destruction. There is also an increased awareness of the need for public spaces, including green areas and pedestrian streets.

Several issues still puzzle architects who strive to reach a balance between traditional architecture and modern design in China. The maintenance of cultural and regional characteristics of Chinese architecture in the face of globalization remains the first and foremost problem. It has been difficult to establish proper restrictions on urban architecture without compromising the creativity of design. Environmental concerns have sparked new interest in the creation of sustainable design. As these concerns have risen, so has the problem of how to encourage mass transit amidst the mass production and accessibility of private vehicles. Providing good working and living conditions for 1.3 billion people with limiting land resources also remains a challenge. Above all, the most perplexing problem remains confronting overly rapid change.

2. 弗吉尼亚州亚历山德里亚市

Alexandria, Virginia

美国弗吉尼亚州亚历山德里亚市通过保持原有经济形态的方法来保持传统的建筑形态：基督教堂和长老会客厅仍保持其宗教用途，约翰·加兹比酒馆仍然是一个小酒馆，历史民居仍然被保留作为联排住宅。老城区的氛围并没有改变，历史建筑被复原重建；老的海港仓库和市民中心被改造成了进出口商店、图书馆、博物馆和会议厅。尽管拥有现代化的商业经济，历史建筑仍保存完好。这些建筑的功能随时间变化而变化，反映出现代商业经济的诉求，但建筑的品质和美感被保留了下来，维护了古城的完整性（图85）。

图 85 约翰·加兹比酒馆
Fig. 85 John Gadsby's Tavern

The citizens of Alexandria, Virginia have managed to preserve much of its architectural integrity while maintaining the original economic use of its historic buildings: the Christ Church and the Old Presbyterian Meeting House remain churches; John Gadsby's Tavern is still a tavern; historic homes remain historic townhouses. The atmosphere of Old Town is not contrived, but has been restored to reflect the layout of the original town: old seaport warehouses and former town centers have been adapted into import shops, libraries, museums, and meeting halls. Despite a modern commercial economy, the historic architecture has been preserved. The function of these buildings has changed over time to reflect a modern commercial economy, but the aesthetic quality of the structure has been preserved in order to maintain the historic integrity of the town (Fig. 85).

HISTORIC TOWNS IN SICHUAN:
THE CULTURAL HERITAGE PROTECTION AND UTILIZATION OF
HISTORIC TOWNS WITH DIFFERENT DIMENSIONS AND VISIONS
——多维视野下的古镇文化遗产保护与利用

本节将结合建筑、经济和交通讨论亚历山德里亚市的历史。通过讲述其丰富的历史，说明保护原有城市形态与格局的必要性。作为促进宜居社区发展的有效恰当的手段，亚历山德里亚市初期的规划导则仍沿用至今。本节的第二部分将介绍各个历史保护组织在地区保护中的法律或协助作用。总之，亚历山德里亚市的开发已成为文化旅游和保护的一个典范。

亚历山德里亚市 60 英亩的土地由木桩定界，城市规划呈网格状。该市曾有十条老街，每条 66 英尺宽。东西走向的七条道路中有六条以英格兰皇室命名，分别为国王（图 86）、王后、王子、公主、公爵、公爵夫人大街；第七条则命名为卡梅伦大街，用以纪念卡梅隆家族的男爵——费尔法克斯勋爵。历史上，流经城市的波托马克河两岸的土地被拍卖私有化，土地的所有者严格依照亚历山德里亚市的规划和标准建造房屋。

This section discusses the history of Alexandria as it relates to the development of the city's architecture, economy, and transportation modes. Through discussion of the town's rich history, it becomes evident that there is a need to protect this carefully conceived and laid out city. The guidelines used at Alexandria's inception are still perceived as pertinent methods for promoting a livable community today. The second part of this section introduces organizations dedicated to the preservation of historic districts and explains what these groups can do legally and practically to assist derelict historic communities. In short, Alexandria has become a model of cultural tourism and preservation.

Alexandria was founded on a gridiron plan, demarcated with wooden stakes on sixty-acre tracts of land. There were ten original streets, each sixty-six feet wide. Six of the seven roads running from East to West were named after the royalty of England—King (Fig. 86), Queen, Prince, Princess, Duke, and Duchess Streets; the seventh named Cameron, honoring Lord Fairfax, Baron of Cameron. The land along the Potomac River was auctioned, and every owner built upon the land in adherence to rigid building standards mandated by the city of Alexandria.

图 86 主要商业街国王大街的街景
Fig. 86 View of King's Street, the main shopping area

图 87 小镇市政厅
Fig. 87 The municipal hall of Alexandria

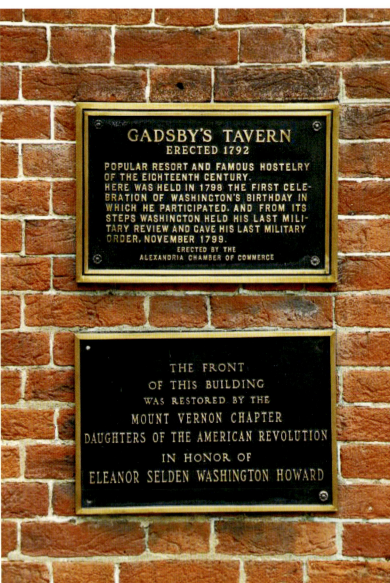

图 88 乔治亚风格的红砖
Fig. 88 Red bricks in Georgia style

自 1752 年城市建立之初，受托人就立下了以下施工规范和规定："购买土地两年之内，所有者必须以 20 英尺见方的面积建造完成一栋砖、石或木结构的房屋……如果不能按规定时间和要求完成，这块土地将被受托人重新投资并卖给能够按照规定完成建造的人。"

建筑细则不仅仅明确了高度、材料、风格和用地边界，还严格规定了居住用地的布局和朝向。规定还包括："所有居住房屋从今往后必须以其主立面朝向街道，房屋山墙面等只能在两条街道相交呈现一定角度时面朝街道，否则将予以拆除。"

受托人因此按照一个严格的总体规划设计了新的亚历山德里亚市。街道整齐有序，小型商业街区密集并有人行道环绕通达，住宅和商业用地都有各具特色的建筑风格。这种严格统一的规划布局创造了一种安全宜居的社区环境（图 87-91）。这些品质在今日社区建设中依然受到人们的重视。

The trustees established the following construction specifications and regulations in the Founding Act of 1752: "Within two years of purchase, the owner of every lot was to 'erect, build, and finish one house of brick, stone, or wood well framed with the dimensions of twenty square feet...' if this was not done, the lot would be reinvested in the trustees to be sold to others who could comply with the requirements."

Architectural specifications not only dictated the height, material, style, and square footage of buildings but also created restrictions regarding the layout and directionality of residences. The founding act continued, "All dwelling houses from this day not begun or to be built hereafter shall be built in the front and be in line with the street as chief of the houses are now, and that no gable or end of such house be on or next to the street, except an angle or where two streets cross, otherwise to be pulled down."

The trustees, therefore, designed the new city of Alexandria according to a strict comprehensive plan. The streets formed small, regular blocks within which houses and businesses were built flush with the sidewalks at a high density, and residences and businesses alike adhered to a specified architectural style. This solid, consistent layout created a secure and livable community (Figs. 87-91). These qualities are still desirable in communities today.

蜀韵古镇

HISTORIC TOWNS IN SICHUAN:
THE CULTURAL HERITAGE PROTECTION AND UTILIZATION OF
HISTORIC TOWNS WITH DIFFERENT DIMENSIONS AND VISIONS
——多维视野下的古镇文化遗产保护与利用

在 1749 年被议会授予立法权之前，沃尔特·雷利爵士领导下的 18 世纪中叶的亚历山德里亚市并不是一个商业城市。而为了取得发展波托马克河沿岸城市的法律支持，向位于威廉斯堡的议会提供一个关于亚历山德里亚城市发展的规划就变得十分必要。一旦城市被授予立法权，在土地进行公开拍卖前，要迅速选举市长并建立市议会。

在 18、19、20 世纪，有着三种主要的建筑师群体：绅士型建筑师、匠人型建筑师和职业型建筑师。绅士型建筑师主要指当时多才多艺并具备创新精神的人，这些人知识面广，建筑设计只是他们涉足的领域之一。匠人型建筑师则指擅长通过木工和手工艺技术进行建筑和规划设计的优秀技术人才。在这三类建筑师中，只有职业型建筑师接受过专业的法国巴黎国立高等美术学院派建筑设计训练。法国美术学院是位于巴黎的建筑设计学院，强调采用传统的制图和模型开展设计。方案化的设计模式，或者说，两周出方案图的设计模式便起源于此。迅速出图的模式有助于促进快速设计解决方案的诞生。直到 18 世纪中叶后，英国才开始有体系化的建筑设计教育。职业化的建筑师开始被训练为方案起草者并任职于建筑师事务所。

Officially surveyed in the mid 18th century under the direction of Sir Walter Raleigh, Alexandria did not become a commercial town until it was granted legislative rights under the General Assembly in 1749. It was necessary to petition and present a projected urban plan for the land of Alexandria to the General Assembly in Williamsburg to receive legal support for a new city along the Potomac River. Once rights were granted, a mayor and city council were elected prior to the public auctioning of the land.

There were three main types of architects in the 18th, 19th, and 20th centuries: the gentleman architect, the master builder or carpenter, and the architect by profession. Gentleman architects were versatile, innovative men of the time—affluent men knowledgeable of a great many things, the design of buildings being one of their many specialties. Master builders were men adept at the building and planning of woodworking and carpentry. Out of the three types, only professional architects were educated in the formal process of design as products of the école national supérieure des Beaux-arts de Paris architectural training. The école national supérieure des Beaux-arts de Paris was a Paris-based architecture school that emphasized creativity through extensive drawings and modeling. Charrette design, or the design of an architectural project within a two-week span, originated in this school. Charrettes were created to encourage exhaustive and rapid production of design solutions. It wasn't until the second half of the 19th century that it became possible for men to receive architectural training in England. Professional architects were trained as draftsmen and served apprenticeships in architectural offices.

无论是绅士型、匠人型还是职业型的建筑师都根据既有的图样手册来进行英格兰式的建筑布局和设计。受英国政治统治的美国殖民者将这些在英格兰十分流行的图样手册作为主要的建筑导则。18 世纪 50 年代，威廉·亚当的《苏格兰式建筑图册》和巴蒂·兰利的《建筑师助手大全》都是当时十分畅销的指南式书籍。1842 年以后，安德鲁·杰克逊·唐宁的《小别墅》和 阿舍·本杰明的《建造师指南》被广泛运用。1857 年，美国建筑师学会在纽约成立，为"建筑师"一词正名，明确了其与木作匠人和营造商的区别。1865 年，麻省理工学院以法国巴黎国立高等美术学院为原型创办了第一所建筑学校。"建筑师"因其接受了更为专业、更加侧重于设计的教育而成为受人尊敬的职业化人才。

Gentlemen architects, master builders, and professional architects alike strove to imitate established, dignified English architecture through the use of pattern books of architectural layouts and designs. These pattern books, popular in England, became guides for American colonists yet under the political rule of Britain. In the 1750s, William Adam's *Vitruvius Scoticus* and Batty Langley's *The Builder's Complete* Assistant were especially popular guidebooks. After 1842, A. J. Downing's *Cottage Residences* and *Asher* Benjamin's *The Builder's Companion* gained usage. Finally, in 1857, the American Institute of Architects was founded in New York City to protect the title "architect" from misuse and to finally distinguish architects from carpenter-builders and contractors. In 1865, the first school of architecture was established at the Massachusetts Institute of Technology, modeled after the école national supérieure des Beaux-arts de Paris. "Architects," because of their specialized education, were better qualified to design and were recognized as distinguished professionals.

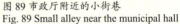

图 89 市政厅附近的小街巷
Fig. 89 Small alley near the municipal hall

图 90 市政厅附近街景
Fig. 90 Street scene near the municipal hall

　　约翰·卡莱尔和坎普顿·康威是亚历山德里亚市建立之初有名的两位绅士型建筑师。他们深刻影响了这座新城的建筑设计。他们两人都熟悉基本的经典建筑设计原理，并利用英国的图样手册在亚历山德里亚建立了自己的居所。建于 1766 年，位于卡梅隆和皇室街交汇处的约翰·盖茨比酒馆就是按照当时的乔治亚式风格建造的：有水台和石阶，拥有五开间的由弗拉芒砖砌成的建筑立面，以及有着显眼拱心石的石拱窗。基督教堂和长老会会客厅均设计有阶梯形的庑殿顶、带山墙的入口、外角构建、帕拉第奥式的窗户、飞檐托饰，以及相同的 60 英尺×40 英尺的建筑平面。源自图样手册的维多利亚式和意大利式风格在当时也十分流行。

　　John Carlyle and Captain Conway were gentleman architects at the inception of Alexandria and greatly influenced the architectural styles of the new town. Both were knowledgeable of the basic principles of classical architecture and built their homes in Alexandria using British pattern books. John Gadsby's Tavern, built in 1766 at the intersection of Cameron and Royal streets, was built according to Georgian models of the time, complete with water table and stone string course, a five-bay Flemish bond brick facade, and flat stone arches with pronounced keystones over the windows. Christ Church and the Old Presbyterian Meeting house were designed with steep hipped roofs, pediment doorways, quailing, Palladian windows, modillion cornices, and the same 60×40 square footage. Victorian and Italianate styles were also popular styles to imitate from pattern books.

图 91 老城外面的新高层住宅
Fig. 91 New high-rise residential buildings outside the historic town

　　1838 年，风格化的精美建筑对于住在亚历山德里亚市的人们来说仍然十分重要。当年 11 月出版的《亚历山德里亚公报》这样记述道："对于一个小镇或者城市的建筑展陈而言，没有比拥有优美潇洒的建筑而非廉价丑陋的房屋更令人开心的了。对建筑的品味是值得被培养的，尤其是在这个国家的这个区域……凡是去过北部各州的人大都会驻足观赏那里优雅的公共和私人建筑，到处都是那么赏心悦目……那里有柱子、门廊、穹顶和类似的形式，而非简单的四面墙、门窗和屋顶组成的房子。我们应该感到十分欣慰，至少我们知道这种时尚的存在，因为我们还有很大的空间来进行变革和改善。"

　　In 1838, stylish and distinguished architecture was still important to those living in the town of Alexandria. *The Alexandria Gazette* in November of that year writes: "Architectural display...nothing adorns a town or city as handsome buildings, and these can generally be built as cheaply as common ugly ones. Architectural taste ought to be cultivated, in this section of the country more than it is...who that has traveled in the northern states has failed to pause and admire the handsome public and private buildings...that everywhere greet the eye?...They have columns, porticos, domes, or something of the kind—something besides four walls, doors, windows, and a roof. We should be glad, indeed, to have at least this fashion introduced among us, for there is room for great reform and improvement in regard to the whole subject."

图 92 游船码头
Fig. 92 Dock for the tourist boats

亚历山德里亚市是作为一个商业交流中心而建立的，其城市设计也是在风格化的总体规划指导下进行的。印第安原住民将词语"Patowmeck"和商业活动联系起来，并把波托马克河称为"贸易之河"。下议院通过立法确立了把谷物和烟草贸易作为亚历山德里亚的经济重心，并由此确立了该市的殖民属性。烟草仓库、磨坊、烘焙工坊和造船港口构成了最初的河岸景观（图92）。随着仓库和磨坊的发展，波托马克河沿岸开始涌现出商铺、酒馆和客栈等以满足来往水手们的需求。19世纪80年代，鲱鱼和高级鲟鱼鱼子酱成为波托马克河的新兴渔业产品。但随着污染的增加，渔获越来越少。亚历山德里亚港的便捷优势也随着贸易船只吨位的增加而日渐减小。港口河道的水深难以满足新型船舶的吃水量，而城市内部也缺少足够庞大的贸易水道网络。局限的用地、混杂的住区肌理和落后的交通设施最终使它在沿河两岸的名气和热度降低。

Alexandria was to be a thriving commercial center designed with the guidance of a stylish comprehensive urban plan. The Indians associated the word "Patowmeck" with trade, and the Potomac River came to be identified as the "trading river." The House of Burgess mandated through early practical legislation that economic factors—namely the trade of grain and tobacco—be present to give the city of Alexandria permanence as a colony. Tobacco warehouses, mills, bakeries, and shipbuilding docks made up much of the original waterfront (Fig. 92). With the development of these warehouses and mills along the Potomac came a building boom of shops, taverns, and inns to accommodate and entertain visiting sailors. In the 1880s, herring and caviar-bearing sturgeon from the Potomac founded new fishing operations; however, as pollution increased, catches became more and more rare. The convenience and feasibility of using Alexandria ports decreased as trade-bearing vessels increased in size. Channel depths were no longer able to comfortably withstand water traffic, and there was a lack of transportation networking in town. The limited area, interwoven residential fabric of the community, and poor transportation facilities decreased the popularity of the waterfront.

从经济层面上看，今日的河岸地区已不再如昔日一般是城市的重心。居住区、公园和娱乐设施以及道路用地为当今城市土地功能的主要构成。商业用地已屈居其次，工业用地的比例则更是直线下降。

总体来说，亚历山德里亚今日的城市发展仍然以 18 世纪建城初期的规划与设计导则为基础。沿河居住区由狭窄的地块紧密开发而成。商业和办公用地主要沿华盛顿大街发展，并接管占用了不少沿河的老旧仓库。古董店、礼品店、手工艺画廊和其他特色小店沿河岸的步行街发展起来，吸引了大批观光购物的人群（图 93-95）。

从历史上看，商业主导了亚历山德里亚市的城市和交通发展格局。河岸地区为烟草贸易提供了商业便利。19世纪，将切萨皮克－俄亥俄运河从乔治城延伸至俄亥俄河的计划在很大程度上依赖于亚历山德里亚老城区的支持。不幸的是，受火车线路竞争的影响，运河最终没能连接到俄亥俄河，此项工程在马里兰州坎伯兰终止。随着铁路运输日益便捷，亚历山德里亚开始进行铁路建设。1846 年，铁路建设正式开始，但内战的爆发中断了工程和资金，迫使亚历山德里亚市将其权益卖给 B&O 铁路公司。此时的亚历山德里亚市成了一座贸易净输入城市而非净输出城市。最终，煤矿运输无法再支撑运河的发展，运河于 1886 年停止了运营。随着 20 世纪六七十年代输油管道建设进程的加快，水路运输的需求量彻底跌至谷底。

今日亚历山德里亚市的交通主要依靠私家车、公共汽车和公共轨道。殖民时代的方格状城市道路系统并非是针对新兴的城市交通需求而建成的，因此有必要重新规划老城区的街道。老城区的华盛顿大街是一条四车道街道，同时也被小型街区、交通指示灯、沿街停车位和人行道分割着。通向哥伦比亚特区的庞大交通人流主要由 1 号公路和帕特里克亨利走廊分流。地铁也为人们出入哥伦比亚特区和进入周边地区提供了便捷的公共交通方式。

Economically, the waterfront today is no longer the focal point that it was in the past. Residential zones, parks and recreation, and streets account for the greatest percentage of the land usage today. Commercial usage is the second most prominent usage of land, and industrial usage has plummeted.

Largely, urban development today continues to follow the design guidelines for Alexandria from the18th century. Residential areas adjacent to the water tend to be tightly developed on narrow lots. Commercial businesses and offices have gained prominence along Washington Street and have taken over many of the old warehouses along the river. Antique shops, gift shops, artisan's galleries, and other specialty shops have been developed along water walkways and generally require a concentration of similar uses to encourage window shopping and browsing (Figs. 93-95).

Historically, commercial motives guided the urban development of Alexandria as well as transportation patterns. The waterfront provided trade and communication access necessary for the trade of tobacco. In the 19th century, the Chesapeake and Ohio Canal, which was to have extended to the Ohio River from Georgetown, was a heavily relied upon feature in Old Town. Unfortunately, due to railroad competition, the canal never made it all the way to the Ohio River, as construction ceased in Cumberland, Maryland. As railroads became more efficient than water transportation and made travel over land convenient, Alexandria attempted to build rails throughout the city. Construction for railways began in 1846, but the civil war halted construction, and debts forced the city to sell its interest to the B&O Railroad Company. At this time, Alexandria became a net importer rather than a net exporter. Finally, the shipping of coal could not justify the continued operations of the canal, and it ceased operations in 1886. With the construction of pipelines for the transport of oil products in the 1960s and 1970s, the demand for water transport fell entirely.

Traffic in Alexandria today is limited to private automobiles, public buses, and mass transit on metro railways. The colonial grid system was not geared towards modern day traffic needs, and it was necessary to redirect thoroughfares around the Old Town district of Alexandria. Washington Street in Old Town is a four-lane road through the main streets, broken up by small blocks, traffic lights, street parking, and crosswalks. Heavy commuter traffic to the District of Columbia has been directed to Route 1 or the Patrick Henry Corridor. The Metro provides mass transit in and out of the District of Columbia and into surrounding neighborhoods.

亚历山德里亚市因地处哥伦比亚特区和华盛顿故居芒特弗农之间，成为游客理想的中转站。20世纪60年代，文化遗产保护成为促进经济和商业健康发展的重要手段，使得特产商店、旅馆、餐馆和其他服务设施因公共交通的便捷而变得有人问津。正是这种将充足的旅游设施与反映城市殖民史的河岸地区发展相结合的模式吸引了大量的游客，从而满足了该地区文化历史和当今社区发展的需求。由于对美国殖民历史的日益重视，人们对文化遗产的保护意识也逐渐觉醒。

文化遗产保护者们不仅力求保护历史建筑，还要力争保护历史街区的整体性。本土建筑不仅直接反映了美国东岸的政治、战争、大灾难或重大事件，也是对人们日常生活经历和体验的记录。美国国家历史保护信托组织非常强调人与本土建筑的直接联系："社区记忆的缺失大多与他们熟悉的地标性建筑或景观的破坏直接相关，而这些是关于我们是谁、我们信仰什么以及是什么在塑造我们的最真实的表达。"

Alexandria's position halfway between the District of Columbia and Washington's home, Mount Vernon, makes it a logical stop for tourists. In the 1960s, historic preservation became a method to improve the economy and health of businesses in the area with specialty shops, hotels, restaurants, and additional services to be available by mass transit. It was this combination of adequate tourist facilities with attractive waterfront developments reflective of Alexandria's colonial past that would draw tourists to the area to boost the historic and current needs of the community. The growing importance of America's colonial past led to the subsequent development of preservation awareness.

Preservationists seek to preserve more than just buildings; they strive to save historic communities. Vernacular architecture is not only a direct reflection of our past politics, war, the cataclysmic or the spectacular but also the everyday commonplace human experience. The National Trust for Historic Preservation emphasizes the direct connection we have to vernacular architecture: "The loss of community memory happens most dramatically in the destruction of familiar landmarks and landscapes, which are tangible manifestations of who we were, what we believed, and what shaped us."

图 93 滨河的港口仓库变身文创休闲中心
Fig. 93 Warehouses along the riverfront, being transformed into creative industry and leisure center

图 94 主商业街一角
Fig. 94 A street corner of the main shopping street

图 95 商业街招牌
Fig. 95 Road sign for the shopping area

　　对一个地区的历史、建筑、考古、文化和工程资源等进行普查为该社区的文化遗产保护提供了基础资料。国家重点保护的景点、建筑、物品和区域则由国家历史地标项目确定。这些保护对象由专家团评定是否符合反映美国文化遗产的标准，并最终由内政部长批准进入保护名单。美国历史建筑普查（简称 HABS）和美国历史工程纪录（简称 HAER）是两个由联邦政府创立的为记录历史遗产提供帮助和支持的项目。

　　美国保护历史文化遗产最有力的法律文书是"106 条款"。1966 年《国家历史保护法案》的第 106 条款（法案第 89-665 页）表明，凡进入美国国家史迹名录的地产由联邦政府给予一定的保护。这一法规为联邦政府介入该地区的开发提供了依据，但对于各州以及地方或者私有的土地并不起到约束作用。为了让联邦政府更加重视在开发过程中对历史建筑形态和样式的保护，文化遗产保护类法规也适用于推动经济与社会变化。

A survey or study of an area's history, architecture, archaeology, culture, and engineering resources provides the basis for an effective community preservation program. National sites, buildings, objects, and districts are recognized by the National Historic Landmark program. These sites are qualified for registration by the Secretary of the Interior after evaluation by an advisory board if it is deemed that they possess exceptional value in illustrating or interpreting the heritage of the United States. The Historic American Building Survey, or HABS, and the Historic American Engineering Record, HAER, are two federal programs that were created to provide assistance with the documentation of historic places.

One of the strongest federal laws that protects historic sites in the United States is "Section 106." Section 106 of the National Historic Preservation Act of 1966 (P.L. 89-665) states that properties eligible for inclusion in the National Register of Historic Places are afforded some protection from the adverse effects of projects undertaken by federal agencies. This law may prove effective when the federal government is involved in the development of an area, but it holds no legal power over private ownership of land, or land held by state or local governments. In addition to requiring the federal government to respect traditional building forms and patterns with any new construction, preservation laws can be used to promote an improved economy and social change.

历史保护理念常常被地区用于保护文化遗产的同时重建经济影响力。人类聚居点的空间格局，如人口密度和用地规划，对一个地区的经济发展起决定性作用。统计数据显示，历史保护有助于促进地区商业的发展。每年弗吉尼亚州的游客花在历史文化景点上的资金高达 91 亿，而这些景点也是该州最著名的旅游目的地。每 100 万用于重建历史建筑的资金投入将创造 15.6 个施工岗位和 14.2 个相关经济岗位。历史保护工程每年还会带来 779 800 美元的家庭收入增加值。除了能为地区创造一个更广阔的商业经济基础领域、增加收入来源，仅与历史保护直接相关的项目本身就能提高地区居民的生活质量。在亚历山德里亚的老城区，每年能带来有将近 800 万美元因住宿和餐饮带来的税收收入，而这些收入都来自参观历史保护区的游客（图 96）。亚历山德里亚、威廉斯堡和弗吉尼亚海滩是弗吉尼亚州最有吸引力的三个旅游景点。

Preservation is oftentimes used by communities to regain economic power, while at the same time protecting the cultural heritage of an area. Human settlement patterns, such as the density and land use, have a profound impact on the economic prosperity of a community. Statistics show that historic preservation is good for a community's business. Every year in Virginia, tourists spend approximately 9.1 billion dollars on the historic and cultural sites that are the No.1 attraction sites in the state. For every one million dollars spent on the rehabilitation of an historic building, 15.6 construction jobs are created, in addition to 14.2 jobs elsewhere in the economy. Preservation also adds over 779,800 dollars to household incomes. The activities directly related to the process of historic preservation alone increases the quality of life for residents of a community, in addition to creating a broader commercial economic base for the area and increased source of revenue. In Old Town, approximately 8 million dollars a year are generated in lodging and restaurant taxes by visitors drawn to the historic district (Fig. 96). Alexandria, Williamsburg, and Virginia Beach are the top tourist destinations in Virginia.

文化旅游业致力于对某种特定文化发展理念的解释与推广。其目标人群是受过一定教育的、对环境和政策都有一定考量的、思想开放的人群，他们经常旅游并且能够欣赏差异性。

文化旅游业和世界文化遗产地的保护是携手并进的，它们总体上都是建立在历史保护先于旅游业发展这一理念上。结合保护规划，文化遗产地的保护可以创造吸引游客的氛围与环境。1972 年，联合国教科文组织主持签署公约，为世界文化和自然遗产地的保护提供法律、行政和财政援助。世界文化遗产名录正是在寻求、确立并保护具有"突出世界价值"的遗产地这一全球性公约下诞生的。遗产地主要分为两类：文化遗产（人为的并与文化相关的）和自然遗产。文化遗产必须包含杰出人类创造或重要历史事件的客观证据。"世界遗产"是超越政治与地理界限的。

Cultural tourism is dedicated to the explanation and promotion of a specific cultural idea. The target group for cultural tourism is generally a group of educated, environmentally and politically conscious, and open-minded people who appreciate differences and travel frequently.

Cultural tourism and world heritage site protection go hand in hand. It is generally assumed that preservation precedes tourism. Together with conservation planning, preservation of heritage sites creates an atmosphere that appeals to tourists. In 1972, UNESCO hosted a convention to provide legal, administrative, and financial assistance to the protection of world cultural and natural heritage sites. The world heritage list results from a global treaty that seeks to identify, recognize, and protect places that are of "outstanding universal value." The two main categories of heritage sites are historic (man-made and cultural) and natural sites. Man-made sites must contain physical evidence of outstanding human creativity or important historic events. "World heritage" recognition transcends all political and geographic boundaries.

蜀韵古镇

HISTORIC TOWNS IN SICHUAN:
THE CULTURAL HERITAGE PROTECTION AND UTILIZATION OF
HISTORIC TOWNS WITH DIFFERENT DIMENSIONS AND VISIONS
——多维视野下的古镇文化遗产保护与利用

图 96 主商业街店铺
Fig. 96 Shops along the main shopping street

　　签约的成员国承认维护、保留并保护文化遗产地首先是本国的责任与义务。城市历史保护区的管理应该是其中一项最艰巨的任务："它们就像生命体一样，通常聚集了庞大的人口，基础设施不断恶化，面临巨大的发展压力。"必须建立一项能够架起沟通文化遗产和社区发展桥梁的总揽性政策。对于文化遗产的保护必须纳入城市总体规划中。同时，也必须完善针对居民与游客的保护和统领文化遗产和社区的配套服务设施。为有效防范恶劣天气、繁忙交通和自然损耗对遗产地的影响，加强相关学习与研究十分必要。成员国必须采取适当的法律、科学、技术、管理和财政手段对文化遗产地进行保护和展示。

Member countries recognize that it is primarily their responsibility to maintain, preserve, and protect cultural heritage sites. The management of urban historic sites is arguably the most difficult task: "They are like living organisms, often densely populated, with deteriorating infrastructures and enormous developmental pressures." A general policy must be established to bridge preservation of heritage sites with living communities. Protection of heritage sites must be integrated into comprehensive plans. Services must also be created to conserve and interpret sites for community members and visitors alike. Studies and research are necessary to effectively protect heritage sites against inclement weather, heavy traffic, and natural wear and tear. Member countries must be aware of the appropriate legal, scientific, technical, administrative, and financial measures they must take to preserve and present heritage sites.

全面的保护计划对于想获得联合国教科文组织世界文化遗产提名的地区来说十分必要。这些地区通常是在国家层面上进行整体维护。边界普查与描述、用地规划与历史保护研究也是监管计划中必不可少的组成部分。对于当地设施和服务的特殊考量也很重要，要考虑好如何在不打扰原有民俗习惯的情况下将文化旅游业合理地嵌入社区。旅游规划是地区整体规划中的重要环节。游客服务诸如住宿、餐饮、卫生、游览、向导、信息、博物馆建设、道路和交通等问题都必须整合入景区的总体规划中。往来文化遗产地的交通本身就能够构成一个专门的课题。应严格建立市镇的旅游限制条件，比如应该要详细分析这一地区对每季度、每个周末、每晚甚至长期停留的游客的承载量。公共汽车可以作为城区与邻近旅游地之间的直达往返交通工具，从而避免过度的交通荷载、停车压力和道路局限等问题。旅游商业和交通可以被限定在历史景点周边的特定范围内，以保护当地居民免遭不必要的交通影响。

Comprehensive preservation plans are necessary for nomination of world heritage sites to UNESCO. Sites are generally maintained on the national level. Boundary surveys and descriptions, land use plans, and conservation studies are necessary components of regulatory plans. Special consideration must be given to the utilities and services of a community and how these functions fit with the preservation of an area without disrupting the lifestyles of the community. A tourism plan is an important part of the comprehensive plan for an area. The guest services—accommodations, food, toilets, tours, guides, information, museum installations, paths, and transportation—must be incorporated into the urban fabric of the existing site. The transportation to and from a heritage site alone may necessitate a separate study. It is important to firmly establish the limitations of a town—how much tourism the community is willing and able to handle—seasonal tourism, weekend visits, overnight stays, or extended visits. Buses may be used to shuttle tourists from a satellite location into the town to protect the town from excessive vehicle usage, parking problems, and road limitations. Commercialism and traffic may be restricted to specific zones within a historic district in order to protect residence from unwanted traffic.

HISTORIC TOWNS IN SICHUAN:
THE CULTURAL HERITAGE PROTECTION AND UTILIZATION OF
HISTORIC TOWNS WITH DIFFERENT DIMENSIONS AND VISIONS
——多维视野下的古镇文化遗产保护与利用

汽车使用和公共厕所是世界文化遗产地需要提供给游客的服务中最容易产生问题的地方。旅游景区的重中之重在于，尽可能不让游客打扰到遗产地居民的正常生活。这就意味着旅游的时间和空间都有可能受到约束。特殊形式的交通，特别是那些景区本土特色交通方式，被鼓励用于景点游览，这有助于对该地区原有的用地、规划和生活方式的维护。马车、缆车、船或小型有轨电车等都可以减少尾气排放，既能合理控制人群，又比汽车交通更具观赏性。世界文化遗产成员国也被鼓励用最环保和最小影响的理念推进解决景区的交通和卫生问题。

正如世界文化遗产地景区管理者手册所述，尽其所能保护遗产地景区并引起公众的重视是世界文化遗产成员国应尽的义务："世界性文化遗产保护组织的目的在于应对日益加速的变化所带来的挑战，也是在全球范围内建立共识和推进文化遗产保护科学发展的需要。"

Automobile usage and public restrooms are among the most visually disruptive services that world heritage sites must provide for visitors. It is of the utmost importance that visitors do not interfere with the natural lifestyles of the residents of the heritage community. This may mean that tourist hours or zones of the site are restricted for visitors. Special forms of transportation, especially those indigenous to the cultural site, are encouraged to promote tourism without hindering the conservation of the land, site, or lifestyles of the community. Horse-drawn carts, funiculars, boats or small trams may reduce fumes, as well as reduce or control crowds, and they can be more picturesque than automobile traffic. World heritage members are encouraged to solve traffic and restroom problems in the most environmentally conscious and inconspicuous way possible.

As stated in the site manager's handbook to world heritage cultural sites, it is the responsibility of world heritage members to protect sites to the best of their ability and to create public awareness: "The purpose of such an association of the world's conservators was to meet the challenges posed by the accelerating pace of change, the need to create an awareness on a global scale, and to forge the advancements in the science of conservation."

3. 文化遗产保护与文化旅游

Preservation and Cultural Tourism

20 世纪 60 年代，美国突然爆发的现代技术带动了保护历史建筑和遗址的潮流。当今的中国正面临同样的考验，中国政府正在借鉴西方应对现代化大潮的经验。美国国家历史信托组织和地方政府已通过立法和建立指导方针促进传统城市中心的恢复和重建，防止出现对环境保护的忽视和蔓延式的开发。更重要的是，诸如亚历山德里亚这样的美国历史城市，需要通过保护传统的城市规划和建筑来维护其历史文化环境。为确保这类文化遗产保护运动的成功，作为对现代经济和商业发展的保证，文化旅游被引入进来。

周庄、乌镇、苏州等在现代化建设中，尽力保护那些影响了他们世代生活的古典建筑和城市肌理。这样的城镇保护行动中不乏对美国历史保护经验的借鉴。

The sudden surge of modern technology into the United States triggered a movement for preservation of buildings and land in the 1960s. As China now experiences similar confrontations with development, the country has looked to the West to evaluate how Americans coped with the problems of rapid modernization. The National Historic Trust and local governments in the United States have enacted legislation and have established guidelines to facilitate the restoration and rehabilitation of traditional downtowns to guard against environmental neglect and developmental sprawl. Most importantly, cities in the United States, like Alexandria, desire the preservation of a historic culture through the protection of traditional urban planning and architecture. To ensure the success of these preservation movements, cultural tourism was introduced as insurance of a commercial, modern-day economy.

As towns such as Zhouzhuang, Wuzhen, and Suzhou struggle to protect the ancient architecture and urban patterns that have shaped the lifestyles of these communities, they have looked at the preservation experiments of the United States.

HISTORIC TOWNS IN SICHUAN:
THE CULTURAL HERITAGE PROTECTION AND UTILIZATION OF
HISTORIC TOWNS WITH DIFFERENT DIMENSIONS AND VISIONS
——多维视野下的古镇文化遗产保护与利用

蜀韵古镇

本节首先探讨美国针对土地、建筑和社区的文化遗产保护战略。其中几个法律条款和保护激励机制与亚历山德里亚市直接相关，其他则主要围绕遗产保护和文化旅游的建立。然后，本节研究了中国文化遗产保护背后的理念和哲学。最后，对文化旅游业作为今日中国文化遗产保护的一个策略进行评估。

作为第一个被成功殖民的州，弗吉尼亚拥有美国最悠久和最丰富的历史文化遗产。麦克马洪等多位学者在他们共同完成的一份研究里这样描述弗吉尼亚州重要的历史文化景区："历史文化景区就如同殖民时期的州府威廉斯堡一样丰富和多元，包括位于罗阿诺克的老市场、位于里士满的纪念物大道、位于亚历山德里亚的滨水区域、众多总统和爱国者们的故居、内战战场，以及诸多位于英联邦区域内的历史性村镇。"在该州近 60 个地区都有旨在保护和保存文化遗产、建筑、考古、工程和文化景区的历史街区，亚历山德里亚、米德尔堡、诺福克、里士满、罗阿诺克、史密斯菲尔德等都在这些地区之中。

The following section discusses the preservation tactics developed in the United States to protect land, buildings, and communities. Several of these laws and preservation incentives are related directly to Alexandria; others are part of the broader formation of preservation and cultural tourism. The section then moves on to focus on the ideals and philosophies behind preservation in China. Lastly, cultural tourism is evaluated as a preservation tactic in China today.

As the first state to have successful colonies, Virginia shares a heritage that is among the oldest and richest in America. McMahon and his colleagues identify a few outstanding historic sites in Virginia in their co-finished research: "Historic sites are as diverse as the colonial capital of Williamsburg, the historic market in Roanoke, Monument Avenue in Richmond, the waterfront of Alexandria, the homes of presidents and patriots, battlefields from the Civil War, as well as historic villages and towns across the commonwealth." Approximately sixty localities in the state have historic district ordinances designed to protect and preserve heritage, architecture, archaeology, engineering, and cultural sites—Alexandria, Middleburg, Norfolk, Richmond, Roanoke, and Smithfield are a few of these districts.

由于开发商希望开发最省事却又最赚钱的地产，弗吉尼亚州有意识地鼓励开发商改造老的历史街区和经济衰落区而非农村地区。弗吉尼亚州的地方政府被授权可以用州资金配套计划、税收优惠和保护地役权来促进现有社区的保护工作。老区复兴最重要的方面当属现有土地和建筑的再利用和开发。在老区建设基础上的填充式发展并不需要建设新的道路或额外的公共设施，并能够与城镇发展模式相一致，不仅使居民生活更加方便，长远来说，也在实际上为开发人员和社区居民节省了投入。

税收优惠是促进"填充式"开发的手段之一。通过不同的评估和税收，建筑物及资产的税率为修缮重建再利用前的税率。税收抵免可被用于抵销住宅和商业物业的修缮再利用费。达标税收抵免的地产必须有至少20年的历史，并由联邦、州或地方政府认定。在历史保护区内并对历史保护区有贡献作用（依据环境法第25条）的地产也可能符合该项税收福利。税收减免对于促进商业和企业在历史地段和历史建筑上的投资起到巨大的鼓励作用，有助于让其重现当年的辉煌。

As developers tend to build where easiest and most cost efficient, Virginia has attempted to create incentives to build in older communities and economically distressed areas rather than undeveloped rural lands. Virginia localities are authorized to give certain incentives such as state fund matching programs, tax incentives, and conservation easements in order to encourage the preservation of existing communities. One of the most important aspects of revitalization is the reuse and development of existing land and buildings. Infill development does not require the construction of new roads or additional utility services, is consistent with development patterns of the town, oftentimes is more convenient for residents, and can actually save money in the long term for developers and members of the community.

Tax incentives are one way to promote infill development. Through differential assessment and taxation, buildings and properties are taxed at rates established prior to restoration or rehabilitation. Tax credits can be used to offset the cost of the rehabilitation of a residential or commercial property. To be eligible for tax credits, property must be at least twenty years old and designated by the federal, state, or local government. Properties may also qualify if they are located in and contribute to a historic district (Environmental Law Institute 25). Tax cuts may be enough to encourage businesses and companies to invest in the building or land and restore it to its previous historic glory.

除了税收优惠激励政策，通过历史保护地役权捐赠土地或建立特殊地带也可以保护某个历史区域。把可保护历史地产捐赠给州政府将有利于保障地产的环境质量并确保它能成为开放的公共空间。例如，亚历山德里亚城外的弗农山庄（乔治·华盛顿的故居和坟墓所在地）就受到了历史保护地役权的保护监管。这些特辖区域可以在不与其他基础设施建设产生冲突的情况下取得服务和建设的资金支持。此类区划可通过市议会或地方组织对其指定区域进行法律保护。

中美的发展有很多的相似之处。尽管中美政体、经济体制和文化传统不同，但现代化给这两个国家带来的是同样疯狂的城市扩张。西方人刚刚才认识到交通膨胀带来的一系列问题——空气污染、道路拓宽、停车用地紧张和噪声等。在相对传统的美国城市，人们的居住地大都离工作地点比较近，新城市的人们基本都选择自驾车上下班。尽管中国有 2 亿自行车，或者说每五个中国人就拥有一辆自行车，但汽车仍然是城市复兴的关键。

In addition to tax incentives, donations of land through conservation land easements and the establishment of special districts or zones can protect a historic area. Land donated to the state as conservable property can protect the environmental qualities of that property or ensure that it will remain open space. For example, conservation easements are responsible for the protection of the view shed of Mount Vernon (the old house and grave of George Washington), just outside of Alexandria. Designated special districts can finance services and facilities directly without having to compete with other infrastructures needs. Zoning gives legal protection to areas designated by a city council or local organization.

There are many similarities between the development trends in China and the United States. Despite strikingly different political, economic, and cultural systems, rapid modernization in the United States and in China has resulted in the development of sprawl and edge cities. In the west, we have only just realized the consequences of increased traffic—air pollution, the widening of streets, the demand for parking, and noise. People in the United States spend more time driving to and from work than they did when living in the older traditional American cities because they worked closer to where they lived. Although there are approximately 200 million bicycles, or one bicycle for every five persons, in China today, the car still remains the basic key to revitalization.

要完全理解中国建筑发展的走向，首先需要回顾传统中国建筑的哲学理念。古代中国建立了天人合一的世界观。宇宙规律对于中国这个农业社会来讲尤为重要，因为农业需要紧紧追随大自然的周期与节奏。江浙地区的水乡规划也处处反映出对大自然的回应。街巷与建筑以人们的步行生活为尺度而和谐展开。城镇的品质受人们生活状态品质的影响，而人们的生活又受制于城镇街巷和建筑的布局走向以及它们如何回应社区发展的诉求。

至今，江浙地区仍有少数地方还大量保持着明清时期的生活状态。近六成的当地房屋仍然是明清时期的遗存。据乌镇旅游发展公司的负责人周平介绍："除了电话、电视、电灯等现代化生活用品外，当地人仍然保持着南宋（1127-1279）以来的基本生活状态。"对年轻一代的教育同样有助于促进对古建筑的保护和修缮。一个城镇的经济活力决定了文化遗产保护的起点。全世界越来越多的国家意识到，迅猛的扩张式发展将在很大程度上改变历史文化城镇的面貌。

To fully understand the parameters for development and architecture in China, it is necessary to review the philosophies and values that structured these guidelines. Ancient China established a worldview that placed them at the center of the world, second only to the cosmos. Cosmic order was especially important for this agriculturally founded society because this order dictated the cycles and inherent rhythm of nature. Nature is reflected in the urban planning of the towns of the Jiangsu and Zhejiang area. Streets and buildings were originally laid out according to human dimensions to create comfortable, walkable space. The quality of a town depended on the quality of life of its citizens, which in turn was influenced by the layout and structure of its buildings and streets and how well they responded to the needs and demands of the community.

Today, there are still communities within the Jiangsu and Zhejiang area that remain remarkably the same as they did in the Ming and Qing Dynasties. Almost sixty percent of the buildings in the area date from the Ming and Qing Dynasties. According to Zhou Ping, the manager of the Wuzhen Tourism Development Company, "Aside from the telephones, TV, and electrical lights, people here basically live as they did in the Southern Song (1127-1279)." The education of younger generations is necessary to encourage the preservation and protection of this ancient architecture. A town's economy and vitality as a livable community becomes the starting point for preservation. There is a growing concern amongst countries around the world, that rapid development and sprawl will begin to mask the history and culture of historic towns.

费孝通指出现代化扩张将破坏乡村环境：随着人口密度的不断增加，城市土地和人员工资的成本也随之增加，再加上日益严重的环境污染问题，不少城市工业被迫向乡村转移。这不仅是中国目前面临的趋势，也是全世界目前面临的趋势。除了扩张到城市近郊和本国内的其他乡村地区，大型资本企业还将在第三世界国家寻找可以扩张的区域。

尽管人们表达出对发展会破坏历史建筑格局的担忧，但人们也越来越清楚地意识到现代化的不可阻挡性。正如学者赫莱茵·普伦蒂斯所说："你无法将社区变成一座博物馆，你也无法将一个大城市全部变成一座博物馆。"古镇保护中最重要的一环是如何在新的城镇建筑格局中保护社区的社会结构。

20 世纪 90 年代中期，苏州市市长章新胜联系了贝聿铭和他的儿子贝庭中，一起探讨关于如何在保证经济发展的同时促进古城保护、提高美学品质的课题。他们重点挖掘出三个问题：建立健康有效的城市基础设施，强调城市绿地、景观等环境建设的重要性，以及以古迹旅游为工具，在保护城市历史核心区的同时改善当地居民的生活。

Fei Xiaotong explains that "sprawl" development will destroy rural environments: As population density increases, the rising cost of land and urban salaries, as well as serious pollution problems, have pushed the development of certain urban industries to the limits; the expansion of large urban factories into the rural areas has become a general trend not only in China but also throughout the world. Besides expanding into the suburbs and rural areas of their own countries, big capitalist urban enterprises have begun to find their way into third world countries, expanding industries into the countryside—new "sprawl."

As much as there is concern that new development will destroy traditional building patterns, there comes a realization that one cannot stop modernization. According to Helaine Prentice, "You can't make it [a community] a museum. You can't make a whole big city a museum." It is important to preserve the social structure of a community within a new typology.

In the mid-1990s, the Mayor of Suzhou, Zhang Xinsheng, contacted Bei Yuming and his son, Bei Tingzhong, to discuss ways to preserve the history of the town and improve its aesthetic quality without depleting its economic development. Three main aspects of the town were evaluated in the study: the construction of an effective and healthy town infrastructure, the landscape and green space of the town and its environmental importance, and lastly, the use of heritage tourism as an economic tool to promote the livelihood of the townspeople while protecting the historic core of the city.

按照普伦蒂斯的理论："历史保护工作所创造的强大认同感一定会因其形象本身散发出强大的吸引力。"历史城镇内的遗址景区保护工作将衍生并带动旅游业，促进商业的繁荣。为了使苏州园林的美和自然风光得到最大限度的呈现，将绿地、人行道和街心公园等复合景观有机联系起来，发挥了景观的双重价值：一要营造城市花园氛围，二要提供更有趣的人流交通方式。将各种运河水道进行再连接，让水上的士和观光船成为可能，为城市提供更多休闲娱乐和交通出行的选择；林荫道路和花园空间的建设能够为游客提供更好的户外空间步行游览体验。城市景观和环境品质的提升将极大影响游客的感受。

苏州的河道水质以及整个城市的基础设施从一开始就急需整治。在地下安置新型的排水管道、电缆和通信系统将有助于改善水质，同时减少地面明线数量，从而美化城市的天际线。这也将有助于将城市水质级别提升到三级，以达到开设观光船的标准。此外，在现有建筑外墙和构筑物上加设照明设施也将有助于减少路边电线杆、路灯的建设量。

According to Helaine Prentice, "Preservation creates a powerful identity that attracts growth on the strength of image alone." The preservation of historic sites within a town can generate tourism and increase commercialism. To maximize the beauty and naturalness of Suzhou's famous gardens, it was important to carefully connect green spaces, create pedestrian walkways, and recognize the dual purpose of the landscape—as an instrument in the development of a park-like atmosphere and as a circulation tool. Linking the canals together to create water taxi and pleasure boating access would improve the recreation and transportation features of the town. Tree lined streets and garden spaces would encourage tourists to linger in outdoor spaces and to have a more enjoyable walking experience. The landscape and environmental quality of a town greatly affects the experience of the visitor.

The condition of the water in the canal systems and the overall infrastructure of the city of Suzhou were initially very poor. Placing sewage, plumbing, electrical, and telephone systems underground ameliorated the pollution of the water and removed wire clutter from the skyline. This would also upgrade the quality of the water to a grade III, suitable for boating. In addition, mounting outdoor lighting onto existing buildings and structures would remove poles from the sidewalks and streets.

诸多旨在保护苏州历史核心品质的措施都在陆续得到实施，如设立近 14 个历史保护景点，对古建筑和结构修缮再利用进行荣誉提名，以及在历史街区内设置明显的互动性旅游线路标识等。与此同时，作为具体的城市保护规划细则也被整合到城市总体规划中，明确了包括建筑材料、色彩、屋顶高度、屋顶风格、屋檐尺度、建筑细节如窗框和空调装架等在内的设计细节。围绕历史街区的新开发必须遵循特定的建筑和设计原则，但不必像现存的建筑形式那样严格遵照上述规定。

在苏州，文化遗产保护计划的实施创造了一种灵活的兼顾保护与开发的新规划和发展理念。苏州也因此成为一个能吸引游客在此停留多日的旅游目的地。

为了满足旅游业发展的需要，应该建立更多的相关设施。酒店、餐馆和交通枢纽的纷纷建立是苏州能成为一个多日停留的旅游城市的支撑条件。大多数旅游服务设施都建立在远离景区和居民区的区域，为的是尽量不破坏苏州原有的日常生活节奏。

Several steps were taken to improve the quality of Suzhou's historic core, including the designation of approximately fourteen landmarks on which to focus preservation efforts, the nomination of other buildings and structures for renovation and adaptive reuse, and the creation of well-marked interpretive routes through the historic zone. A preservation plan was incorporated into the city comprehensive plan in which design materials and colors, roof height-lines, roof styles and overhangs, and architectural details such as window trims and the usage of air-conditioning units were specified. New development around historic districts should reflect specified architectural and design principles, but need not adhere as strictly to these guidelines as existing buildings must.

The implementation of the preservation and conservation plan in Suzhou created a new appreciation for the dexterity and compromise that contextual planning can require while protecting the historic integrity of a place. Suzhou is now a multiple-night tourist attraction.

To adequately provide for tourists, the construction of additional amenities was necessary. Hotels, restaurants, and transportation to historic sites were created so that Suzhou could become a multiple-night tourist town. Most tourist facilities were constructed away from the historic and residential districts so as not to disrupt the daily activities of these sections.

苏州对于文化旅游业的引入几乎是毫不犹豫的。但对于像周庄、乌镇这样的小型水乡来说，尽管已经有了世界文化遗产的头衔，但它们正面对更多的争议。"作为一个 4A 级景区，周庄的旅游业迅猛发展。"周庄的宣传册这样记述：周庄"在迪拜举办的'改善生活博览会'上获评最佳示范奖"，获得了世界对其文化、历史和城镇发展的肯定，赢得了声誉。

设计方案中包括临水茶室、餐馆、小店、画廊、开放景观和供摇桨观光船停泊的码头。方案将工业发展区和高速公路与古镇分离开，以创造一个无污染的步行旅游环境。汽车不允许在狭窄的石板街巷上行驶，而高高低低的小桥流水也不具备自行车的骑行条件。

与苏州不同的是，周庄并没有排水系统。其电力由上海的发电厂供应。这里的人们仍常常使用传统的便携式木质"马桶"。

Suzhou developed a cultural tourism economy with little resistance; however, smaller water towns such as Zhouzhuang and Wuzhen, though listed as world heritage sites, have encountered more controversy. "As a 4-A grade scenic zone of tourist attraction in China, Zhouzhuang has witnessed rapid development in tourist industry." Promotional, information books about the town of Zhouzhuang present the water village as "winner of best demonstration award at the 'Exhibition of Improved Living' at Dubai," gaining cultural, historic, and urban development fame and recognition from the rest of the world.

Design schemes have created waterfront teahouses and restaurants, small shops, art galleries, landscaped open spaces, and docks for oarsmen-operated pleasure boats. Design regulations separate developing industries and highways from the historic core of the village to create a relatively pollution-free and pedestrian-only environment. Cars are not allowed in the narrow, stone-slab streets, and the stepped bridges over canal-ways are not practical for bicyclists.

Unlike the city of Suzhou, Zhouzhuang does not have running water or central sewage systems. Electricity is provided to the town through electricity plants in Shanghai. The *Matong*, a portable wooden lavatory, is still largely in use.

HISTORIC TOWNS IN SICHUAN: THE CULTURAL HERITAGE PROTECTION AND UTILIZATION OF HISTORIC TOWNS WITH DIFFERENT DIMENSIONS AND VISIONS ——多维视野下的古镇文化遗产保护与利用

周庄目前并没有实行客流量限制。这引起了当地居民对于游客过多而影响生活的担忧。部分游客甚至因其过度接待而导致的拥堵放弃到周庄旅游。越来越多的人开始担忧那些慕名而来的投资商和中国当代某些媚俗文化有可能毁掉这个古镇的声誉。

乌镇是过去 10 年里江南地区 6 个开放古镇中最后一个被开发的。乌镇鼓励游客在这里进行一日游：白天沿河道观光、购物、光顾餐厅和茶馆等，感受古镇如公园般的景观风貌。但小镇并没有建设太多支持在此过夜和多日游览的基础设施。

文化旅游的开展让更多的关注投入到服务高端游客的基础设施上。访卢阁已经被改造成高档餐饮场所。因历史街区发生的经济变化，近 400 户人家选择离开了他们在乌镇的传统居所，选择在城外的西式风格的房屋中生活，以远离众多的游客。这些居民住宅被改造成商业住宅，出租给那些来镇上捞金的投资客们。

Regulations restricting the number of tourists in Zhouzhuang do not currently exist. This has raised concern among residents that there will be too many visitors in the small village and that daily activity will be disrupted or halted. Some tourists have even stopped going to the village altogether because it has become so crowded. There is serious concern that migrant vendors and Chinese kitsch will soon sully the reputation of the town.

Wuzhen is the latest of six old water towns in the Jiangnan region to be restored and opened to tourists over the last decade. Tourists in the town of Wuzhen are encouraged to visit for the day, shop, patronize the restaurants and teahouses along the canals, and enjoy the park-like landscape; however, the town is not structured to support the strain and necessary construction for overnight or multiple-night tourism.

The implementation of cultural tourism has caused concern that facilities that used to serve the needs of residents will now cater to wealthy tourists. Already, the Fanglu Pavilion has been converted from a comfortable restaurant and meeting place for the people of the village to a ritzy, high-class tourist teahouse. In response to these economic changes within the historic district, nearly four hundred families have abandoned their traditional homes, opting to live in western-style homes on the outskirts of town and away from tourists. These traditional homes have been converted into businesses, where thay are rented out to entrepreneurs who aspire to invest in the new circulation of money in the village.

蜀韵古镇

如今，乌镇在诸如建筑材料、新结构和古建修复等方面有了更加明确的施工规范。规范指出，所有朝街的装有空调的窗户都必须采用传统木格珊形式。曾经被用来增强建筑防潮效果的钢筋混凝土和金属外墙饰面也被要求换成更符合传统审美的雕花木质装饰板。许多街巷都重新铺设了地板，屋顶也铺上了新瓦以创建更加干净舒适的旅游环境。部分区域安装了西式的下水系统和卫生间设备以应对蜂拥而至的游客。

尽管有新的城市基础设施，以及在建筑细则、保护组织等方面的改进，有关文化旅游业的终极问题仍然无法回避：文化旅游创造的效益是否比社区遭到破坏的代价更重要？文化旅游业在带来巨大经济利益和提高居民收入的同时，也带来了交通膨胀和游客过载等问题。小型市镇往往仅能通过文化旅游来积累资金以促进现代化设施建设，但面向游客的商业观光游船、高档餐饮和特色店铺却越来越背离当地居民的生活。游客的入侵改变了当地居民生活的品质，因为游客已经成为古镇的一部分。

Building codes in Wuzhen now dictate the appropriate construction materials, new structures, and the repair of the old. Regulations specify that outside air conditioning window units must be screened through traditional-style lattices. Concrete and metal siding—initially added to buildings for better insulation and protection against the rainy weather—must be replaced with more aesthetically pleasing wooden panels and carvings. Many roofs and streets have been re-tiled and re-paved in an effort to create a clean and comfortable place for visitors. In some areas, plumbing and western-style toilets have been installed to aid with the steady influx of visitors.

Despite new town infrastructure, building codes, and protection organizations, the ultimate question remains: do the benefits of cultural tourism outweigh costs to the community? Cultural tourism, while generating a steady economy and increasing the income of residents, also causes traffic to increase and can bring overwhelming numbers of visitors to a town. Modern amenities are oftentimes available to small communities only through the increased wealth perpetuated by cultural tourism, but commercial pleasure boating, expensive restaurants, and specialty shops geared towards tourists exclude residents. The quality of life has changed for residents because tourists have become a part of their towns.

文化遗产保护规划必须确保文化旅游业不会严重影响当地居民的生活质量。文化旅游业必须以当地居民的需求和愿望为本。历史保护的策略必须在尊重历史原有文脉和保持对现状的足够敏感性的基础上指导发展。虽然今日江浙地区还未真正实现保护与发展间的平衡，但相信随着时间的推移，这样的平衡一定指日可待。

Preservation plans must ensure that cultural tourism does not adversely affect residents' quality of life. Cultural tourism must be adjusted to adequately fit the needs and desires of residents. Preservation tactics must be used to guide development to respond more sensitively to the existing context. A balance may not yet be realized in the Jiangsu and Zhejiang area today, but over time, it is possible for the achievement of such a balance.

4. 结语

Conclusion

    中国正在不断完善社会主义市场经济的建设，对于新技术、新发展和现代化的需求正在迅猛增长。来自商业和零售业的国际竞争压力助推了古建更新与重建的势头。

    当代的中国建筑师和规划师都有将古建筑风格融入新设计的潜在意识。他们正面临着新技术与新设计在不打扰传统生活习俗的条件下又融入城市景观中的挑战。尽管大部分皇家建筑可以在不影响居民生活的情况下被改造为文化遗产景点，但地方建筑的修缮改建却仍是一项更为严峻的任务。理想情况下，修缮后的古建筑将为现代化提供便利，古典形式有助于公民传统的社会互动，而传统风格与审美亦能反映中国丰富而悠久的历史。

As China moves from a formerly social economy to a new market economy, the demand for new technology, development, and modernization has sharply increased. Pressure from businesses and retail to compete internationally fuels the momentum to renew and rebuild.

Modern-day architects and planners have an underlying desire to combine traditional Chinese form with new design and construction. They face the challenge of incorporating new technology into existing cityscapes without significantly altering the traditional lifestyles of the people within. Whereas imperial buildings are no longer in residential use and can be promoted as heritage sites with little risk of disrupting the privacy and daily lifestyles of towns and people, the restoration and rehabilitation of vernacular architecture proves to be more challenging. Ideally, restored buildings would offer modern conveniences, with an ancient format conducive to traditional social interaction of citizens and an aesthetic style reflective of the rich Chinese past.

早年在中国高等院校间兴起的古今结合的建筑思潮如今已影响到了官方设计院。建筑师们或许能够认识到古建筑及其形式的价值，但仍有很强大的呼声认为，在满足经济需求的建设中保全古建风格是不可能的。这并不是因为人们对古建筑的审美疲劳，而是因为人们还没找到古建形式与现代化发展之间的平衡点。

在苏州、周庄、乌镇这样的水乡，这一新旧平衡是可以通过文化旅游业实现的。对于同时满足居民和游客需求的规划，其实施后的评价与分析需要一定的时间。然而，该体系一经建立就将极大地促进经济发展。一份强有力的文化遗产保护计划可以有效控制某一景区每日、每季度、每年的游客流量和时间。周庄作为一个新的旅游景点吸引了过盛的游客，但只需稍加管理就可以让每日人流量得到控制，并把原有的生活归还给当地人。规划除了为保护工作提供基本指导外，还可以被不断完善改进以进一步解决新出现的问题。

The movement to resolve the conflict between traditional architectural form and technology began in universities in China and has now infused government architectural forms. Designers may recognize the value of traditional architectural forms, but there remains a prevailing attitude that it is impossible to respect these forms while constructing economically viable housing. The problem is not a lack of appreciation for ancient architectural forms and buildings but instead a lack of balance between these old forms and modern-day demands.

Cultural tourism can be used to achieve this balance of new and old in the city of Suzhou and the smaller water towns of Zhouzhuang and Wuzhen. It takes time, evaluation, and analysis before a plan can be developed that addresses the needs of residents, as well as accommodates the demands of tourism. But once established, it is possible for a thriving commercial economy to exist. A strong preservation plan can regulate the number of tourists that visits a town a day, a season, or a year, as well as how long and where these visitors stay. Zhouzhuang may be overcrowded due to the popularity of the town as a new tourist destination, but with a few simple regulations, the number of people can be controlled, and the daily lives of the residents can resume. Plans provide initial guidelines or projections, but they are designed with the knowledge that they will be altered and re-worked to reflect additional needs or to solve newly arisen problems.

　　文化旅游业保持了苏州、乌镇、周庄原有的商业经济文化的稳定。这些中国水乡起源于特产贸易，沿着这一经济模式，文化旅游业将继续促进手工艺品、地方特产和教育的发展。商业奠定了水乡的经济基础并确保了它的活力。

　　保护文化遗产并不意味着要阻碍发展，而是要促进负责任的发展。负责任的开发指通过经济和环境的设计解决方案来维护原有的城市肌理和场所感。被列为历史建筑和历史街区的场地的电线铺设、下水管道、供暖和空调等的设计施工方案需要更为谨慎，而不是将这些现代化的设施排除在外。

　　乌镇、周庄和亚历山德里亚的保护组织以及权力机构尽管不尽相同，但都运用了文化旅游业这个促进文化遗产地保护、修复和重建的手段。在美国，由各州州长任命的历史保护办公室工作人员统管州内的保护工作。世界遗产组织也会委任负责人确保各个文化遗产地保护工作的顺利开展。对周庄这种新进入文化遗产名录的水乡来说，形成完善的审查委员会和负责人管理体系将有助于它们在今天乃至未来建立有力的社区发展与历史保护规划。

Cultural tourism maintains the commercial economies of the Suzhou, Wuzhen, and Zhouzhuang. The towns in China were founded on trade and production of specialty items; continuing this economic pattern, cultural tourism promotes the production of handcrafted goods, regional specialties, and educational items. Commercialism grounds the economy of a town and ensures its livability.

Preservation is not meant to hinder development but rather to encourage responsible development. Responsible development references context, provides an economical and environmental design solution, and maintains the urban fabric of its place. Sites that have been designated as historic buildings or districts require sensitive incorporation of electrical wiring, plumbing, and heating, and air conditioning, but these amenities are not excluded from preserved places.

The preservation of towns like Wuzhen, Zhouzhuang, and Alexandria differs in organization and legal power; however, both use cultural tourism to promote the restoration, preservation, and protection of historic heritage sites. In the United States, State Historic Preservation Officers, appointed by the governor of each respective state, oversee the preservation affairs of the state. World heritage sites designate a manager to verify that sites within the country are well-protected. With Zhouzhuang and the other water towns recently designated as world heritage sites, the formation of a review committee and general world heritage site manager would help these water towns establish a firm community and preservation plan for the present as well as the future.

HISTORIC TOWNS IN SICHUAN:
THE CULTURAL HERITAGE PROTECTION AND UTILIZATION OF
HISTORIC TOWNS WITH DIFFERENT DIMENSIONS AND VISIONS
——多维视野下的古镇文化遗产保护与利用

这代人需要在面向未来的前提下实现现代化与历史保护之间的平衡。相信通过严谨的规划和设计，中国一定可以找寻到更好的兼顾发展与历史保护的方案。

This generation must work towards the future generation to create an appropriate balance between historic preservation and modernization. With careful planning and design, it is possible to attain an architectural solution for better development and preservation in China.

下篇：
关于文化遗产的公众教育

Part III :
On the Public Education
of Cultural Heritage

本篇是四川大学附属中学高中生对四个古镇进行独立探访后形成的考察报告。尽管分析的深度和专业性有限，文笔也还显稚嫩，但在编者看来仍然是十分难能可贵的。作为尚未接受专业训练的中学生，这种观察是更为接近常人的，感受也多是自发的。古镇的文化传承需要年轻人参与，他们的关注和认知正是古镇文化遗产保护事业新的力量和希望之所在。

In this part, there are four investigation reports drafted by high school students from the Affiliated High School of Sichuan University. Although their descriptive and analytical tools are limited, and their writing styles are somewhat immature, in the eyes of editors, they are still rare and commendable. Because for them who have not received professional training, their observations are closer to ordinary people, and their feelings are often spontaneous. The cultural transmission of historic towns always needs the participation of young people, and their attention and care are the new forces and hopes in the cultural protection cause of historic towns.

古镇考察报告之一：

黄龙溪 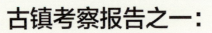 印象

Historic Town Investigation Report No. 1:
Huanglongxi

1. 历史背景

Historical Background

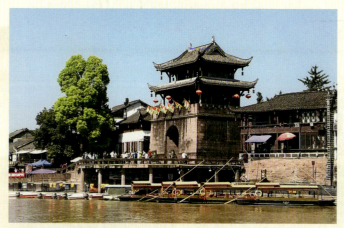

图 97 黄龙溪古镇码头
Fig. 97 The old dock of Huanglongxi

图 98 黄龙溪古镇导览图
Fig. 98 Travel Map of Huanglongxi

这里，曾是开明王朝最后的军事据点，金戈铁马，一个王朝在此陨落；这里，曾是刘备登基的舆论策源地，壮士沉鼎，一个时代就此开始；这里，还是大宋水码头重镇，舟楫如梭，商家云集，文人荟萃；这里，镌刻有原始农耕文明的印记；这里，保存有最古老的遗址、民俗；这里，自古便是成都商贸往来的黄金口岸，自古便占平原沃野之优势，自古独享军马衔接之要冲，自古就有"日游千人拱手，夜来万盛明灯"的繁华盛景（图97-98）。

Huanglongxi, a well-known town, used to be a vital position of dynasties. A lot of historic events occurred here. It was not only the last stronghold in the Enlightened Dynasty but also the symbol of Han Dynasty's emergence. Huanglongxi shows the trace of primitive agriculture and the evidence of ancient cultural relic and custom. Since the ancient time, Huanglongxi has chosen to be the essential center of trades and military hub in China, and it thrived at that time (Figs. 97-98).

图 99 黄龙溪古镇的街道
Fig. 99 Street in Huanglongxi

黄龙溪古镇一直流传着一个传说：东汉末年，黄龙溪与东站门之间出现一条龙，九日方离去，因而得名黄龙。到如今已有 1800 年历史的黄龙溪，最为著名的便是当地的古街，一街有三庙，即龙头镇江寺、龙身潮英寺和龙尾古龙寺。整条街全长一百米，由石板铺成（图 99）。整个黄龙溪的建筑也独具特色，大多为木结构，门也大多为传统的护板门。

黄龙溪镇历来就是成都南面的军事重镇。蜀汉时，诸葛亮南征，曾派重兵把守于此，结果战败，加速了大蜀国的灭亡。黄龙溪原名"永兴场"，原址毁于一场大火，故又名"火烧场"。

According to an ancient myth, a huge dragon stayed between the Huanglong River and the Dongzhan Gate for nine days in the Eastern Han Dynasty, which brought this place its name—Huanglongxi (Yellow Dragon River). Through the entire 1800 years of its recorded history, the most famous landscape of Huanglongxi is its old street, about 100 meters long, paved with stone slabs (Fig. 99). Walking along this old street, people may find three temples—the Zhenjiang Temple, the Chaoying Temple and the Gulong Temple—which represent the dragon head, dragon body, and dragon tail respectively. In Huanglongxi, the traditional houses are also ingenious masterpieces. They are wooden huts erected without a single nail, reflecting the wisdom of ancient Chinese people.

Huanglongxi used to be a significant military town in south Chengdu. Over the period of Kingdom of Shu, Zhuge Liang used to troop here, spreading the war to the south; yet, he failed, and this accelerated the extinction of Shu Kingdom. The original name of Huanglongxi is "Yongxing Chang" (forever prosperous place). As the old site was destroyed by a big fire, it was later called "Huoshao Chang" (fire burnt place).

蜀韵古镇
HISTORIC TOWNS IN SICHUAN:
THE CULTURAL HERITAGE PROTECTION AND UTILIZATION OF
HISTORIC TOWNS WITH DIFFERENT DIMENSIONS AND VISIONS
——多维视野下的古镇文化遗产保护与利用

图 100 廊柱下方的柱础
Fig. 100 Column base along the street corridor

图 101 空斗墙
Fig. 101 Vacant brick wall

　　两千多年前，古蜀先民在此繁衍生息；汉代古墓群留下了前辈的足迹；唐宋时期日渐繁荣，黄金水道成了南方丝绸之路的集散地；明清时代的木板民舍、青石小径流传着历史的故事；已有三百余年历史的全木结构古戏台保存完好；六株千年古榕树掩映着古镇魅影；古老的唐家大院演绎着客家文化的风云；古朴的民风民俗增添了小镇无穷的魅力；兵家必争、商贾云集从而孕育了丰富的码头文化；独具特色的川西田园古镇风貌使这里成为西南的天然影视基地（图 100-104）。古镇名扬中外，游客慕名而至。

　　More than 2000 years ago, the ancestor of Shu had arrived here; the tombs of Han had left the footprints of the ancestors; the regime of the Shu Han had risen here; it had once being flourishing during the period of the Tang and Song dynasties, since its golden waterway became the distributing center of the South Silk Road; the wood house made by blanks as well as the alley made by the bluestones have both shown the history of this area. The 300-year-old wooden stage has been well preserved; six millennial banyans show the beauty of the old town; the old compound of Tang's Family showed the history of the Hakka; the austere folk custom has added a lot of glamour to the small town; the concentration of the business had formed its abundant wharf culture; the special structure of the town has made it become the film base (Figs. 100-104). This historic town has its international fame and attracts thousands of tourists from all over the world.

图 102 黄龙溪的穿斗式民居
Fig. 102 *Chuandou*-styled vernacular building in Huanglongxi

图 103 黄龙溪主要建筑常采用的歇山屋顶
Fig. 103 *Xieshan* roof commonly seen in some key buildings in Huanglongxi

图 104 黄龙溪的建筑色彩
Fig. 104 Architectural colors in Huanglongxi

　　古镇不大，很有"水城"的味道，一水划镇而过，两岸都是用青石铺成的石板路。水面有数座铁吊桥，河畔有一株古榕树，盘根错节，据说有近千年的历史，是古镇的标志，游人每到此总要在树下留影。有些地方还存有昔日的容貌。

　　This waterside town seems a little bit small; you can see the bluestone road on either side. There are some suspension bridges built up on the waterways as well. Near the bridge, you can see an old banyan, which had lived for about a thousand years. This old banyan has been considered as the sign of the town which attracts countless tourists to visit here.

2. 建筑外形简析

Brief Analysis of Its Architectural Forms

　　黄龙溪古镇位于成都市双流区西南部，因其旁流过的黄龙溪而得名。黄龙溪古名为"赤水"，与穿越成都城区的锦江在此合流。溪水褐，江水清，颜色交织，汇合成为黄色。另一说是龙纹鼎沉入水中，故名黄龙溪（图105）。

　　全镇现有明清时代街坊七条，完好的寺庙三座，分别为古龙寺、镇江寺和潮音寺，明清民居七十六套，具有四川特色的吊脚楼依山傍水，建筑风格与罗泉古镇极其相似（图107-109）。整体形成带状，如同一条黄龙，起于龙头，终于龙尾，整个小镇的所有建筑围绕带状中心扩散开来。

Huanglongxi is situated at the southwest of Shuangliu, Chengdu and is named after the local river passing next to it. The river's ancient name is Chishui (Red Water), which joined with another, Jinjiang (Brocade River), a wider and clearer river that passes through the downtown of Chengdu. Because of the meeting of the two rivers, the brown water turns into yellow water. In addition, once there was a dragon pattern tripod dropping into the river; therefore, this place is called Huanglongxi, the Yellow Dragon River (Fig. 105).

There are seven Ming and Qing dynasty style streets, seventy-six Ming and Qing dynasty residences that include the Sichuan characteristic *Diaojiao* buildings established in accordance with the location and nature of the place, and three intact temples, including the Gulong Temple, the Zhenjiang Temple, and the Chaoyin Temple (Figs. 107-109). The town is a ribbon-like configuration and similar to a dragon whose head and tail are the start and the end of the town. Besides, major constructions all surround the ribbon.

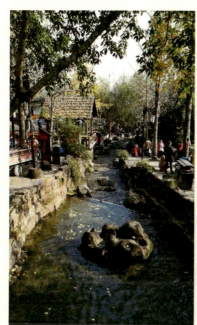

图 105 水城黄龙溪
Fig. 105 Huanglongxi as a water town

蜀韵古镇

HISTORIC TOWNS IN SICHUAN:
THE CULTURAL HERITAGE PROTECTION AND UTILIZATION OF
HISTORIC TOWNS WITH DIFFERENT DIMENSIONS AND VISIONS
——多维视野下的古镇文化遗产保护与利用

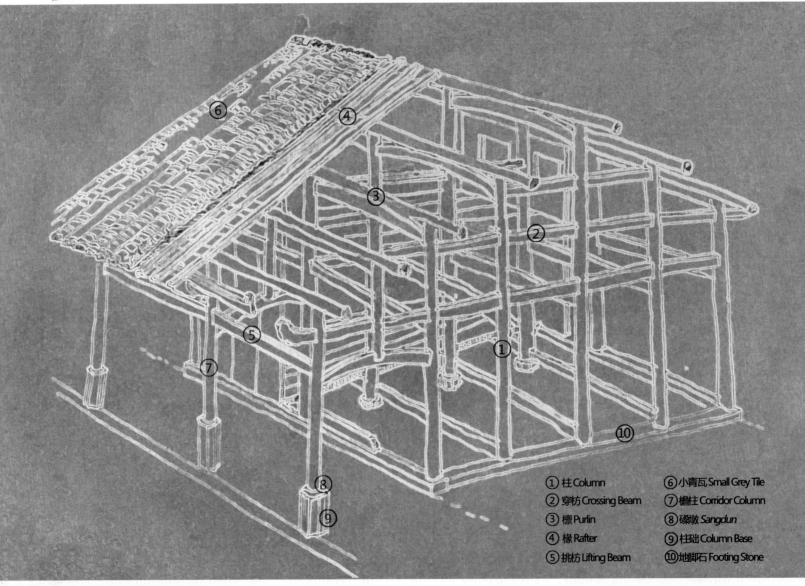

① 柱 Column	⑥ 小青瓦 Small Grey Tile
② 穿枋 Crossing Beam	⑦ 檐柱 Corridor Column
③ 檩 Purlin	⑧ 磉墩 *Sangdun*
④ 椽 Rafter	⑨ 柱础 Column Base
⑤ 挑枋 Lifting Beam	⑩ 地脚石 Footing Stone

图 106 穿斗式结构示意图
Fig. 106 Diagram of the *Chuandou* structure

　　古镇整体由黄龙正街、上下河街等主要街道构成。古时街道由石板铺就，贴合了当地的地形，根据依山傍水的原则修成，地形有起有伏，街道按照这一特点，踏步与平路结合。建筑为穿斗式结构，沿街或沿河而建，当建于坡度较大的地方时，会利用坡屋面让整个房屋与地形完美贴合。

　　黄龙溪地处全年潮湿多雨的四川盆地，另外又由于四川地区的传统古代建筑是易受害虫和霉菌损害的木质结构，房屋容易腐烂。湿气大多数都集中在靠近地面的地方，所以在设计的时候建筑的底层就必须与地面保持一定的距离。因此，我们经常会看到房屋底层的柱子下端都有高出地面的柱础，柱础与柱子间还有礤墩，帮助将木结构的柱子与潮湿的地面隔离开。

　　黄龙溪建筑的另一个特点就是采用了中国南方常见的穿斗式结构。房屋通过布置檩，再在檩上布椽，省去梁的结构，直接由檩把力传给柱，柱子再用枋穿起来，构成榀（图 106）。

The ancient town is made up of the main streets, such as Huanglong Street and Upper and Lower Rivers Street. The streets are paved with stone from the ancient times and fit the local terrain, but also in accordance with the principle of into terrain, there are ups and downs, the streets according to the characteristics of cross combination of stairs and roads. The building is a bucket house with the characteristics of Tianfu, all along the street or along the river, and sometimes built-in the slope of the place. There is sometimes sloping roof, so that the whole house perfectly fits the terrain.

Huanglongxi is located within the Sichuan basin, which is featured in its humid and rainy weather. As ancient traditional buildings are often built in wood structure, they are prone to be eroded by humidity, pests, and molds. Because moisturized air is often accumulated near the ground, ancient designers and builders needed to invent a structure to avoid or delay such a natural process. Hence, one may easily find frequent use of stone column bases together with a small layer of *Sangdun* that isolate the wooden columns from humid ground.

Another representative construction feature of Huanglongxi's vernacular buildings is the *Chuandou* structure commonly seen in southern China. By placing rafters above purlins, the latter transfer forces to columns directly without load-bearing beams. Columns are then connected with small beams to form the roof trusses (Fig. 106).

蜀韵古镇

HISTORIC TOWNS IN SICHUAN:
THE CULTURAL HERITAGE PROTECTION AND UTILIZATION OF
HISTORIC TOWNS WITH DIFFERENT DIMENSIONS AND VISIONS
——多维视野下的古镇文化遗产保护与利用

木结构之间的空隙用黏土和壁板来填充，屋顶用茅草和其他废渣来铺垫，当然对于某些富贵人家来说，瓦是更好的选择，布置简单，但相对耐用。受亚热带季风气候影响，四川盆地的森林非常茂盛，因此四川地区可以建造比茅草结构房屋更稳定的穿斗式木结构房屋。简单材料的稳定性和广泛性确保了穿斗式结构在四川地区无法撼动的地位。

用稻草废渣和黏土填充而成的空心砖砌成的墙，具有隔音性好、用料省、重量轻等特点，广泛用于四川地区。但是由于年久失修，黄龙溪的大多数空斗墙已经倒塌。

The space between the wooden structures is filled with clay and siding, and the roofs are laid out with thatch and other waste. Of course, tile is a better choice for some rich people. This arrangement is simple and relatively durable; because of the subtropical monsoon climate zone, the forest in Sichuan Basin is very lush, so Sichuan can build a more stable structure of the housing relative to the thatched *Chuandou* wood structure. The stability and universality of the simple materials ensure that the bucket type structure cannot be shaken in Sichuan.

With a gorgeous voice isolation, low cost and light weight, the wall which is constituted with vacant bricks that are filled with straw, scarp, and mud is widely accepted in the Sichuan area. However, the lack of preservation pushes vacant walls into the edge of extinction.

图 107 传说中的 "神龙见尾不见首"
Fig. 107 The tail of the magic dragon with its hidden head in the legend

图 108 镇江寺和寺前挂满祈愿带的古榕树
Fig. 108 Zhenjiang Temple and the ancient banyan tree with red ribbons over it

图 109 各种传统的耕种农具与灌溉工具
Fig. 109 Many kinds of traditional farming and irrigation tools

歇山顶是在东亚地区广泛使用的一种屋顶形式，在四川地区使用的主要目的是帮助房屋排除积水。黄龙溪的歇山顶有一些装饰，这些装饰与居住者的地位息息相关。

由于成都地区受青城山道教影响较大，所以对于修建的态度更加倾向于返璞归真。与罗泉古镇相似，其颜色大多偏冷色系，没有耀眼的金色或是丹红色，多偏向木头本来的颜色，但是其保护程度远高于罗泉，商业化程度也高于罗泉。

A widely accepted roof form, *Xieshan*, mainly serves as an auxiliary drainage system. There are also some decorations on the roofs; however these embellishments are related to the social status of the dweller.

Similar to Luoquan, there are seldom ornaments due to religious influence brought by Taoism. Most coloration is cold, approaching the original wood color instead of the gold or cinnabar. However, unlike Luoquan, protection of Huanglongxi is much more exquisite, and the commercialization extent is higher.

3. 饮食文化和经济价值

Culinary Culture and Economic Value

图 110 丁丁糖制作现场
Fig. 110 The production scene of Dingding Candy

双流境内的黄龙溪古镇淋漓尽致地展现了四川和当地独有的特色美食。芝麻糕、丁丁糖（图 110）、珍珠豆花、牛皮糖、猫猫鱼、臭豆腐、肥肠粉、黄辣丁、焦皮肘子、土豆豉等满街道都有售卖。其中，芝麻糕是当地最常见且销量较高的特产。当地人不仅将芝麻用于各种美食中，也将它榨碎制成食用油。

当地居民早已形成自己的饮食习惯并保留至今，例如口味偏重，喜爱辣椒和花椒。盐和蒜是每一道菜必不可少的。通过调查，鱿鱼也受到当地人的追捧。多种口味的鱿鱼也得到外来游客的赞扬。所以，当地人民不仅发掘到了用食物体现古镇历史的方法，还发现了利用食物香味来吸引游客的诀窍。这其中的奥秘可能就隐藏在漫长的食物发展史中。

The ancient town located in Shuangliu County has vividly demonstrated the characteristics of unique Sichuan and local culinary culture. Sesame cake, Dingding candy (Fig. 110), pearl tofu, sticky candy, cat fish, stinky tofu, chitterlings rice noodles, Huanglading fish, baked pork hock, local fermented soybeans, etc., are sold on both sides of the street. Among them, sesame cake is the most common and has the highest sales. Local people will not only use sesame in various dishes, but also squeeze the sesame into cooking oil for local people to use.

The local people already have their own eating habits that extend to the present, such as preferring the spicy, salty taste, liking chili and pepper. Salt and garlic are essential in each dish. By observation, local people also enjoy squid, and the variety of flavored squid sold to foreign tourists is welcoming. So, local people not only realized how to use food to show the history of this town but also discovered the secret of attracting tourists through food tastes. The fact that local people are intelligent in business may attribute to the food development of such a long history.

这些年，伴随着社会经济的迅速发展，人们对饮食提出了更高的要求，饮食观念在不断转变，丰富、活跃的饮食文化前所未有。吴克祥曾说过，人们日常生活的基本构成部分包含礼仪、习俗、时尚等文化内容，以及菜品、饮料、服务及饮食文化等构成的综合性商品，而饮食对许多旅游者来说本身就是一种独特的消费商品，具有强大的吸引力，这也使得很多地区的特色饮食成为一种独特的旅游资源，就像黄龙溪一样。

特色小吃并不是黄龙溪的支柱产业，但因其特色多、需求量大，黄龙溪小吃的快速发展无疑也给小镇带来了不少旅游商机，拉动了经济的增长。现在许多旅游胜地都有自己拿得出手的特色小吃，这已经成了一种标杆。为了推动经济发展，小吃的存在必不可少。想想，如果你来到一个地方，吸引你的会是什么？风景名胜，当地文化，历史环境，当然还有不容忽视的特色小吃。

黄龙溪的自然优势，给小镇带来了大量的消费群体。从旅游景点到特色小吃，我们所熟知的黄龙溪在改变，外来的游客不断拉动着黄龙溪的经济发展。无论是餐桌上的小吃还是名胜古迹都是文化的延续。它们在带给小镇居民经济利益的同时，也推动着地域文化的传承。

In recent years, people broached higher standards to their food and drink under the thriving ecological development. People's perspectives towards food culture have experienced great changes in that the food culture appears to be unprecedentedly thriving and lavish. Wu Kexiang once said, "People's daily lives are constructed by cultural elements like rite, convention, fashion, and the general merchandise; the food and drink are also indispensable." For most tourists, food culture is always a great attraction to them, which makes the local diet a considerable tourism resource.

Although the local diet is not the pillar industry of this region, its abundance and large consumption needs bring the region lots of commercial opportunities and thus propel the ecological evolution. The food industry now has striking commercial value to economic development. When visitors arrive at a new place, what they will definitely look at is undoubtedly the scenery, local culture, historic remains, and most importantly—deep food culture.

Natural advantages of Huanglongxi help to bring a lot of consumer groups. From the scenic spots to specific snack food, the well-known Huanglongxi is changing along with the rising economy surged by tourists from all over the world. Both dishes and scenic spots belong to cultural heritages. While they bring economic benefits to the local residents, they also drive the inheritance of local culture.

蜀韵古镇

HISTORIC TOWNS IN SICHUAN:
THE CULTURAL HERITAGE PROTECTION AND UTILIZATION OF
HISTORIC TOWNS WITH DIFFERENT DIMENSIONS AND VISIONS
——多维视野下的古镇文化遗产保护与利用

"一根面"又名"长寿面",是黄龙溪的第一大名小吃(图111)。其特色在于每一碗面都只有一根非常长的面条,寓意人的寿命就像这根面条一样长。以前,人们只在生日或其他节日才会吃"一根面",如今,食客们对"一根面"的喜爱和认可让"一根面"不仅再是逢年过节时才会出现的美味佳肴。俗话说得好,食材是大自然的馈赠,是美食的灵魂所在。正是黄龙溪本地盛产的优质小麦成就了一根面长而不断、韧劲十足、回味甘甜等特点。"一根面"分为干拌面和汤面,两者看起来只是有汤和没汤的区别,但是它们的味型却截然不同。干拌面重鲜美,而汤面则体现了四川美食麻辣的特点。两种调味各有特色,将"一根面"自身的优点烘托得淋漓尽致。

一棵古榕,若是长在黄龙溪,便能见证历史兴衰;一条清流,若是流经黄龙溪,便能见证朝代更迭;一条老街,若是建在黄龙溪,便是鲜活的时间坐标;一座寺庙,若是藏在黄龙溪,便是不倒的信念旗幡。千年水运古码头,桨声灯影夜不收。黄龙溪古镇,前进的步伐永不会停止。

The One Strip Noodle, also called the "Longevity Noodle," means that the bowl of noodle is consisted of only one belt of noodle (Fig. 111). It is the most famous delicacy in Huanglongxi. Previously, such noodle was only served during festival time or at people's birthday celebration. With the rising living standard and the popularity of such food, the One Strip Noodle has become available as everyday food for everyone. As the saying goes, raw material is the soul of the food. It is the locally produced high quality wheat that contributes to the features of length and consistency, tenacity, and sweetness in aftertaste. The one belt noodle has two major flavors: the one with soup is featured in spicy and hot, while the other without soup is featured in freshness with a little sweetness. Despite their differences in flavor, they both turn the one belt noodle into something delicious.

If there is an old tree which grows on Huanglongxi, it can become the testimony of the rise and fall of the history in Huanglongxi. If there is a clear stream which flows past Huanglongxi, it can act as the testimony of the replacement of the dynasties. If there is an old street, it can function as a temporal sign of Huanglongxi. If there is a temple that hides in Huanglongxi, it is the firmly standing flag flying in the sky. Huanglongxi, an ancient wharf which existed over thousands of years, will never stop stepping forward and thriving in the future.

图 111 黄龙溪第一小吃品牌——"一根面"
Fig. 111 The No.1 snack food brand of Huanglongxi: One Strip Noodle

古镇考察报告之二：

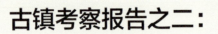

洛带 印象

Historic Town Investigation Report No. 2:
Luodai

1. 背景

Background

洛带古镇（图 115）历史悠久，相传汉代即成街，名"万景街"。全镇 85% 以上的居民都是客家移民的后裔，主要来自广东、江西、湖南等省的客家聚居地。上千年的悠久历史和多种文化相互交融，留下众多民间传说、古老建筑和客家会馆。保存完好的有千年老街、明清民居、客家会馆建筑群和金龙寺等众多历史古迹，一年一度的"水龙节""火龙节"更是几百年来客家人传承下来的特色民俗活动（图 116-118）。洛带镇是全国首批重点小城镇、省级著名历史文化名镇，是中国西部地区最大也是唯一的一个客家古镇，因此又被世人称为"世界的洛带，永远的客家"。2005 年世界客属第二十届恳亲大会在洛带的成功举行，进一步确定了洛带在世界客家文化的中心地位。

The historic town of Luodai (Fig. 115) has a long history. It is believed that the street appeared during the Han Dynasty and was named "Wanjing Street." Over 85% of the people in Luodai are the descendants of Hakka immigrants, most of whom are from Guangdong, Jiangxi, and Hunan provinces. History of thousands of years and the rich culture in Luodai have left lots of folk stories, ancient buildings, Hakka *Huiguan*, and festivals such as the Fire Dragon Festival and Water Dragon Festival (Figs. 116-118). Luodai is one of the first batch of national key towns and provincial key historical and cultural towns. It is the biggest and the only Hakka historic town in West China. Therefore, It is called "Luodai of the world, Hakka forever." In 2005, the 20th World Hakka meeting was held successfully in Luodai, and this international meeting enhances the status of Luodai Hakka culture worldwide.

2. 客家火龙节和水龙节

Hakka Fire Dragon Festival and Water Dragon Festival

图 112 火龙节 *
Fig. 112 Fire Dragon Festival

图 113 水龙节 *
Fig. 113 Water Dragon Festival

早年，客家人因战乱、天灾等原因从中原迁居沿海。沿海雨水充沛，物产富饶，客家人过着丰衣足食的生活。传说客家人与东海龙王交往甚密，为感谢东海龙王适时下雨，客家人每年夏季皆以舞水龙的形式庆祝丰年，而后相沿成习。清朝时期，客家人被迫大批移民四川。刚开始，洛带的客家移民备受干旱煎熬，后得知刘禅"落带"八角井的故事，认为八角井是东海的海眼。受此启发，客家人将老祖宗的舞水龙配合以淘井祈雨，甚是灵验。此后，每年端午节，洛带客家人均以舞水龙的方式来感谢上苍风调雨顺（元宵节则舞彩龙、火龙），庆贺丰年。舞火龙和水龙遂成为洛带客家独特的文化习俗（图 112-113）。

刘氏家族在洛带镇居住了十四代三百余年之久，在吉庆节日由刘家牵头舞龙的习俗，也有三百多年的历史。刘家龙舞直接从中国古代龙舞发展而来，历史悠久，在家族内部传承，一直没有中断。因此，刘家龙舞保存了较多的中国古代舞龙最原始的程序和古朴的仪式。夏日伏旱，水龙大显身手，是为祈雨。舞龙者皆赤裸上身，穿一条短裤，上下腾挪。观赏者用水盆、水枪泼射龙，前后追堵。客家人视水为财，泼得越湿，越旺财，舞者和观者攻防进退，煞是刺激。刘家舞龙也成为客家文化中最具吸引力的一项活动。

In their history, Hakka people moved close to sea because of war and disaster. There are abundant rainfalls near the sea, where the soil is rich and can produce almost everything Hakka people need, and people there live a life with abundant supply. It is said that Hakka residents have a close relationship with the Dragon King of the Eastern Sea. In order to show the appreciation of the Dragon King, who always brings rain at the proper time, water dragon activity is held every summer there, and this tradition is well continued till now. Numbers of people have immigrated to those places near the sea. During the Qing Dynasty, a lot of Hakka people were forced to move into Sichuan. The first immigrants suffered a lot from the drought before they knew about the story of Liu Chan dropping his belt in the Bajiao Well (Luodai). Inspired by it, Hakka people prayed to their ancestors for rain, and it worked out fine. From then on, Hakka people "play dragon" to express the thanks to the god and celebrate for the harvest. Now, water dragon and fire dragon shows have been the unique tradition in Luodai among Hakka people (Figs. 112-113).

While Liu's Family has lived in Luodai for fourteen generations of more than three hundred years, the Liu dragon dance originated from the Chinese ancient dragon dance, also has a long history of more than three hundred years. Because of the great tradition it has, it retains a great many conventional routines and ceremonies. Water dragon mythology would play a great role when praying for rain. Dragon dancers dance without wearing upper garments and jump up and down; the audience would spray water on the dancers with water syringes and basins, and everybody is eager to join and watch. Hakka people believe that water is a representation of wealth and the wetter you get, the more wealth you will get. The dancers and the audiences interact with each other and make this event one of the most attractive activities.

蜀韵古镇

HISTORIC TOWNS IN SICHUAN:
THE CULTURAL HERITAGE PROTECTION AND UTILIZATION OF
HISTORIC TOWNS WITH DIFFERENT DIMENSIONS AND VISIONS
——多维视野下的古镇文化遗产保护与利用

3. 客家美食

Hakka delicacy

图 114 洛带特色美食
Fig. 114 Special food in Luodai

　　客家菜多成系列，最著名的为九斗碗、酿豆腐、盐焗鸡等。现洛带供销社饭店的油烫鹅，新民饭店的野山菌全席和客家酒楼的水酥、面片汤等已成为洛带客家餐饮的特色菜，远近闻名。尤其是夏季，人工无法栽培的野山菌（当地人称"鸡腿菇"）出山之际，慕名前往尝鲜的食客更是络绎不绝。其他客家美食小吃还有伤心凉粉、芜蒿饼、石磨豆花、李天鹅蛋、玫瑰糖、姜糖、张飞牛肉等（图 114）。

　　Dishes in Hakka are ranged in series, in which Nine Dou Bowl, Stuffed Tofu, and Salt-roasted Chicken are the most well-known ones. Special dishes like Fried Goose with Oil from the Gongxiaoshe restaurant, Wild Mushroom from the Xinmin restaurant, and Water Crisp from the Hakka restaurant have been known nationwide. Especially when the wild mushroom, a kind of mushrooms that cannot be cultivated manually, are ripe in summer time, lots of tourists are attracted to enjoy such a wonderful food. Other Hakka snack food include: Sad Bean Jelly, Wuhao Pancake, Stone Milled Tofu Pudding, Li's Swan Egg, Rose Candy, Ginger Candy, and Zhangfei Beef, etc (Fig. 114).

4. 客家山歌

Hakka folk songs

图 115 洛带旧称"甑子场"
Fig. 115 Zengzi Town as the old name of Luodai

客家人喜唱山歌，内容丰富多彩，反映了客家人的生产、生活和情感世界。山歌唱腔婉转优美，唱词生活气息浓郁。每年端午节都有斗山歌的传统，男女对歌尤为吸引人，其中不乏即兴之佳作。《情妹放牛》《情嫂收衣》等，皆为难得之精品。

Hakka people love singing folk songs. The songs include a great many contents, such as their daily life and varieties of emotions. With graceful tunes and lyrics well connected to daily life, singing folk songs has become a tradition in the dragon festivals. The most attractive activity is that boys and girls sing together. Many famous folk songs are created in this way, such as "Sweetheart Grazing Cattle" and "Sweetheart Brings Back the Drying Clothes."

5. 客家街巷

Hakka streets and alleys

图 116 洛带街景
Fig. 116 Street scene in Luodai

洛带古镇由一街七巷组成。一街指的是主街，七巷包括北巷子、凤仪巷、槐树巷、江西会馆巷、柴市巷、马槽堰巷、糠市巷。一街七巷在组成古镇的交通系统的同时，也构成了一个完整的防御体系：上下街口各有一个山门，每条小巷与老街交汇处各有一个栅子门。入夜后大门全部关闭，形成一个完整而封闭的防御体系，以防备土匪、盗贼的袭击。

Luodai is composed of one street and seven alleys. One street refers to the Main Street, and the seven alleys include: the North Alley, the Fengyi Alley, the Huaishu Alley, the Alley of Jiangxi *Huiguan*, the Chaishi Alley, the Macaoyan Alley, and the Kangshi Alley. While composing the town's transportation system, they also form a complete defense system: there is a main gate at each end of the main street, and smaller barrier gates are set up at the joint location when each small alley joins the main street. All these gates will be closed once night falls to protect the town from any brigands and robberies.

图 117 洛带的四大会馆——①广东会馆、②湖广会馆、③江西会馆、④川北会馆
Fig. 117 Four *Huiguan* in Luodai: ① Guangdong *Huiguan*, ② Huguang *Huiguan*, ③ Jiangxi *Huiguan*, ④ Chuanbei *Huiguan*

蜀韵古镇

HISTORIC TOWNS IN SICHUAN:
THE CULTURAL HERITAGE PROTECTION AND UTILIZATION OF
HISTORIC TOWNS WITH DIFFERENT DIMENSIONS AND VISIONS
——多维视野下的古镇文化遗产保护与利用

图 118 五凤楼
Fig. 118 Five Phoenixes Tower

古镇 1000 多米长的老街上有大量客家古民居，基本上保留了清代的建筑风格。屋顶多用小青瓦和茅草覆盖，结构多为单进四合院，正中为堂屋，屋脊上通常有中花和鳌尖等装饰（图 120-123）。

有别于四川其他古镇，洛带古镇虽然沿街店铺繁多，却大多安安静静，无人高声吆喝，游客随意购买，决不拉客扰民，让外来游客感觉说话声稍大些都会不好意思。或许，这就是客家人勤劳内敛的性格特征的外化。

图 119 流水均汇入下场的八角井
Fig. 119 Water all goes into the Bajiao (Octagonal) Well in the lower part of the town

行走在洛带古镇，随处可见沟渠流水、大小水缸。承载都江堰水系文化的清泉从上场龙吻喷发，滋润通街民众，汇聚于下场的八角井（图 119）。

Along the 1000-meter long main street, many traditional courtyard houses are well preserved in their Qing Dynasty architecture style. The roofs are mostly covered with gray tile and thatch, and the structure of them are quadrangle with the main room in the middle, and Zhonghua and Aojian are used as decorations on the ridges (Figs. 120-123).

In Luodai, even though there are a lot of street stores, the streets are rather quiet. Nobody calls loudly to attract attention, nor does anyone speak loudly. Sometimes tourists even feel ashamed and embarrassed when they carelessly speak up in the street. Maybe, this is a reflection of the hard-working and modest characters that Hakka people possess.

Walking around in Luodai, we can see rivers and water vats of all sizes. Pure and clear water comes out from the Longwen in upper town, which flows through all main streets and gathers at the Bajiao Well in the lower town (Fig. 119). This is also a reflection of the water culture of Hakka.

蜀韵古镇

HISTORIC TOWNS IN SICHUAN:
THE CULTURAL HERITAGE PROTECTION AND UTILIZATION OF
HISTORIC TOWNS WITH DIFFERENT DIMENSIONS AND VISIONS
——多维视野下的古镇文化遗产保护与利用

6. 小结

Summary

经过此次实地调查和走访，我们对洛带古镇的发展和人口构成有了初步了解，为下一步研究奠定了基础。总的来说，尽管古镇的开发和旅游业的兴盛促进了当地经济的发展，但是我们在访谈调查中发现了一个不争的事实：尽管洛带以客家小镇著称，但不管是原住民还是外来经营者，他们对客家人历史和文化的了解都十分有限，对古镇未来和个人发展的关系并无太多思考。更让人担心的是，大部分年轻人选择外出求学务工，愿意回来建设家乡的人很少。谁会成为实现洛带古镇可持续发展的主力军呢？我们深知，在经济发展和文化保护之间寻找一个平衡点是不容易的，但却至关重要。

After conducting this survey in Luodai, we have a brief understanding of its development and population structure. All the findings will become the basis for our next step of exploring. Although the booming of real estate development and tourism have brought great benefits to local economy, we also discovered an indisputable fact that neither the local residents nor the business owners know much about the Hakka history and culture, not to mention the relationship of its future development and personal development. What worries us most is that, most young people go out to study and work, with very few who are willing to come back to construct the town. So who could be the main force in Luodai's sustainable development? We know that it is not easy to find a balance point between economic development and cultural protection, but it should be of great concern.

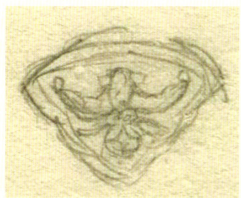

图 120 瓦当速写
Fig. 120 Sketch of an eaves tile

图 121 广东会馆中心建筑屋顶装饰速写
Fig. 121 Sketch of the roof decoration above
the main building of Guangdong *Huiguan*

图 122 洛带常见的歇山
Fig. 122 *Xieshan*-styled roof commonly seen in Luodai

图 123 洛带常见的悬山屋顶
Fig. 123 *Xuanshan*-styled roofs commonly seen in Luodai

古镇考察报告之三：

三道堰印象

Historic Town Investigation Report No. 3:
Sandaoyan

1. 历史

History

　　在望帝和丛帝（图 124）在柏条河治水期间，三道堰，因其用竹篓截水做成三道相距较近的堰头引水灌田而得名。那么在讲述三道堰的历史之前，就不得不讲一下柏条河、望帝和丛帝之间的故事。柏条河为内江水系的干渠之一，起于灌县太平桥，东偏南流经灌县幸福、天马，郫都区唐昌、三道堰等乡（镇），至石堤堰与走马河分支徐堰河汇合，柏条河即止于此，以下称为毗河，为成都供水。在四川历史早期，在三峡一带有淤塞。这时望帝和丛帝出现了，他们为当时的蜀国人民带来了福祉。《蜀王本纪》对两人的记载为：后有一男子，名曰杜宇，从天堕，止朱提。有一女子，名利，从江源井中出，为杜宇妻。乃自立为蜀王，号曰望帝。治汶山下邑，曰郫化，民往往复出。望帝积百余岁，荆有一人，名鳖灵，其尸亡去，荆人求之不得。鳖灵尸随江水上至郫，遂活，与望帝相见。望帝以鳖灵为相。时玉山出水，若尧之洪水。望帝不能治，使鳖灵决玉山，民得安处。鳖灵治水去后，望帝与其妻通。惭愧，自以德薄不如鳖灵，乃委国授之而去，如尧之禅舜。鳖灵即位，号曰开明帝。帝生卢保，亦号开明。望帝去时子规鸣，故蜀人悲子规，鸣而思望帝。望帝，杜宇也，从天堕。古书上虽然只有短短的几行文字，却对这两位先人的生平做了恰当的描述，表达了后人对望帝的悼念之情。其大意为：杜宇从天而降，而他的妻子则是来自井中。杜宇虽尽心力竭地为人们筑堤开堰，还带人们上山避水，但终究"治标不治本"。后来有一个叫作鳖灵的人出现了，带领人们治水。最后杜宇就效仿以前的禅让制让鳖灵当了丛帝，自己就回山中归隐了。人们为了纪念望帝和他的继承人丛帝修建了望丛祠。当然民间关于二帝治水还有各种各样的传言，但毋庸置疑的是，此二人不仅治理了水患，还建造了一座具有千年历史的川西古镇——三道堰（图 125）。

图 124 纪念古蜀国望帝和丛帝的望丛祠
Fig. 124 Memorial Hall for King Wang and King Cong of ancient Shu Kingdom

During the time when King Wang and King Cong (Fig. 124) regulated the Baitiao River, Sandaoyan (the weir with three currents) (Fig. 125) became famous for three irrigation systems consisting of bamboo baskets, as a device for guiding water to fields. Before telling the history of this town, it is necessary to mention the stories of Baitiao River, King Wang and King Cong. The Baitiao River is one of the arteries in Neijiang, originating from the Taiping Bridge in Guan County, flowing through Xingfu, Tianma, Tangchang, and Sandaoyan and meeting with the Xuyan River, which is a branch of Zouma River in Shidiyan. Then the next part of the river is called Pi River as it provides water supply for Chengdu. In the ancient time in Sichuan, there was a siltation in the Three Gorges area. As documented in a world-renowned book *Document of Shu Kings*, Du Yu, named King Wang by his residents, was born from the sky, and his wife, Li, came from a well. Nonetheless, he endeavored himself to construct barriers and guide his men to avoid the danger of the flood; however, the problem of the water was still not solved. Later on, a man named Bie Ling regulated the water so well that King Wang abdicated the throne to Bie Ling, who was named King Cong for his achievement. And King Wang retired into the mountain. In folk cultures, there are so many versions of this legend, but it is undoubted that these two people not only solved the problems caused by such floods but also built such an ancient town in west Sichuan with millennial history.

图 125 复原三道堰
Fig. 125 Replicated three weirs in Sandaoyan Town

2. 水源

Water Sources

在历史上，三道堰不仅仅是著名的水陆码头，还是重要的商贸之地。水对于在这片土地上生活的人来说占据着不可替代的位置。

柏条河 Baitiao River

三道堰镇上最为著名的就是柏条河（图 126）。柏条河作为"穿二江成都之中"的二江之一，属于内江水系，是成都供水的重要通道，全长 44.76 公里，年径流量为 11.76 亿立方米。与三道堰下流的徐堰河相会，柏条河就变成毗河。柏条河上面有两座桥——永定桥和另一座更著名的堰桥。

徐堰河 Xuyan River

徐堰河（图 127），都江堰水系河道之一，为人工开凿的河道，是梁州古江沱的正流。徐堰河流经青城山，沿岸风景优美，是当地村民的"母亲河"。20 世纪工业的迅速发展使得这条河受到了严重的污染，但幸运的是，当地政府及时意识到河流对当地人民的生活是多么重要，并决定加以改善和保护。现在河流整体水质得到极大改善，曾经优美的风景又回到了人们身边。

In history, Sandaoyan is not only a famous wharf and transportation hub in terms of water and land but also an important commerce and trading hub. Water plays an irreplaceable role for people who live here.

One of the most famous rivers in Sandaoyan Town is Baitiao River (Fig. 126). As one of the rivers flowing through Chengdu Basin, Baitiao River belongs to Inner River system and is a water-supplement channel to Chengdu. Its full length is about 44.76 kilometers, and the annual runoff is about 1.176 billion cubic meters. Converging with Xuyan River in the lower reaches, it turns into Pi River. There are two bridges over the river: Yongding Bridge and the more well-known one called Yan Bridge.

图 126 流经三道堰东侧的柏条河
Fig. 126 The Baitiao River running through the east side of Sandaoyan Town

Xuyan River (Fig. 127) is one important channel of the Dujiangyan Weir system. It was artificially dug, forming the main stream of the ancient Tuo River. The river winds through famous tourist sites of Qingcheng Mountain, brings in beautiful scenery, and becomes the mother river that feeds the local residents. This river has been contaminated seriously because of the rapid industrial development during the 20th century, and the picturesque landscape has disappeared. Fortunately, the government soon realized how critical it was and decided to improve and protect it. Currently, the water quality has seen its biggest improvement since the time, and the glittering view of the old scenery has come back.

图 127 流经三道堰西侧的徐堰河
Fig. 127 The Xuyan River running through the west side of Sandaoyan Town

当地人眼中的水利工程 What Local People Think of Hydraulic Works

根据一位在当地生活了 20 年的本地人的叙述我们完成了这部分的报告。他热爱历史，尤其是关于他生活的地方的历史，所以他对三道堰做了大量的调查。因此，我们有理由相信，他的叙述在一定程度上是可信的。

Our report was completed based on a narrative from a local inhabitant who has lived in Sandaoyan for over 20 years. He loves history, especially the history of where he lives, so he has made substantive investigation of Sandaoyan. As a result, his findings should be believable to some extent.

老先生指出，堰的一个功能是弥补两段水的水平面落差，因此水速得以受到控制，与此同时，水流也可以被导向不同的方向。这已经发展为现代水电站的基础结构。通过这样的方法，可以把水流分割开来并最终形成有三道水流的堰口。如何使用堰的另一个有关问题随之而来，假设洪水期到来，由于当时的堰缺少对水流的阻挡功能，用来农耕的田地必定会被摧毁。但是当地居民想到了一个绝妙的办法，他们把一种正六面体木制框架用由黏土填充，堆在水流必经之地来让水流减速。正六面体是自然界最坚固的立体结构，这种有正六面体的堰就是今天大坝的雏形。随着社会的发展，船只也需要通过堰口，但堰在设计之初根本未考虑过船只通过问题。幸运的是，这个问题很快就有了解决办法：人们绕过堰口再挖一条航道，船只便可避开垂直的水平面落差。

综合所有这些提到的因素，老先生说，三道堰最终呈现在了人们眼前。时光飞逝，三道堰越来越多的功能被开发出来。正如我们所见到的，三道堰水流通向一座成都自来水厂，是当今成都最大的饮用水水源。

The gentleman points out that another function of the weir is to compensate the drop of the water level of two different streams so that the speed of the river would be controlled, while at the same time, water can be led to different directions. This experience had been developed to be the basic construction structure of modern hydroelectric power stations, which could disperse the water to different directions to form a weir with three currents in the end. Another problem, however, came out for the usage of weir: during the flooding season, because of the limited function of the weir in restraining the water, agricultural farms would be terribly destroyed. The residents, surprisingly, were so intelligent that they invented a hexahedron cube, which was constructed with ligneous corrugations and filled with clay and put in the middle of water to slow down the speed. Known to be the hardest solid figure in nature, such a weir with regular hexahedrons is the embryonic form of modern dam design. With the development of our society, ships needed to be allowed to go across such dams, but the original weir was certainly not designed to allow the passing of ships. Fortunately, the solution came soon. Another canal was to be dug that bypasses the weir, which allows ships to avoid the vertical difference of the water level.

According to the gentleman's study, Sandaoyan finally appeared in its form by concerning all these elements mentioned above. As time passes, more potential methods of Sandaoyan have been developed. As we see today, there is now a current that goes towards one of Chengdu's waterworks, which is also the biggest resource of household water supplied in Chengdu.

3. 节日和活动

Festivals and Activities

三道堰古镇至今还保留着一个独特的节日——"水节"（图 128）。水节有着悠久的历史，与端午节同时进行。每年农历端午节举办的龙舟会以赛龙舟、抢鸭子、放河灯、歌舞表演、书画展览等活动为主要内容，热闹非凡，人山人海。这是三道堰镇久负盛名的传统文化节日。我们采访了当地一些居民，这些居民告诉我们，他们十分喜欢这个节日，水节让他们相聚在一起，邻里关系也更好了，而且这样的节日也因为游客的积极参与给他们带来了额外的经济收入。

In celebration of its success, there is a very special festival in Sandaoyan named the Water Festival (Fig. 128). Bearing a long history, the festival carries the same date on the lunar calendar as the Dragon Boat Festival. During the ceremony, local people hold the Dragon Boat Festival by competing in various activities such as boating, grabbing ducks, floating river lanterns, dancing, and attending painting and calligraphy exhibitions. The festival is often a riotous affair enlivened by huge crowds of people. We had some interviews with some residents who told us that they really like this festival because nowadays, many people prefer staying at home, maybe they do not see each other for a long time. This festival gives them a chance to better their relationships within their neighborhood. This festival also brings some extra economic profits, for example, the income from tourist expenditures through their festival interaction.

图 128 与端午节同时举行的水节 *
Fig. 128 Water Festival held together with the Dragon Boat Festival

HISTORIC TOWNS IN SICHUAN:
THE CULTURAL HERITAGE PROTECTION AND UTILIZATION OF
HISTORIC TOWNS WITH DIFFERENT DIMENSIONS AND VISIONS
蜀韵古镇 ——多维视野下的古镇文化遗产保护与利用

4. 农业

Agriculture

　　三道堰镇有二十余年的杂交水稻制种历史。勤劳的三道堰人民，依托传统农业，开展水稻制种、川芎和蔬菜种植，把家乡发展成为国家级丰粮工程基地和全县重要的制种基地。与此相结合，农村产权制度改革和新农村建设项目将很快使三道堰成为一个无公害蔬菜基地。总的来说，三道堰的经济作物产量在整个四川省来说都是不可小觑的。

　　The history of hybrid rice has been developing for more than 20 years in Sandaoyan. Depending on the conventional agriculture, the laborious people who live in Sandaoyan carry out a lot of agricultural activities such as producing the seed of rice and cultivating ligusticum chuanxiong hort and vegetables, to build their hometown into a national-level fine rice basement and a seed multiplication basement. Moreover, reforms in property right systems and new countryside construction project will make Sandaoyan a pollution-free vegetables basement soon. All in all, the agricultural economy of this old town cannot be underestimated in its application to modern needs today, as seen in the aforementioned examples.

5. 建筑

Architecture

字库塔 *Ziku* Tower

　　在三道堰的东栅子和西栅子外，分别树立着一座巍峨的塔状建筑——字库，而在东栅子外的二堰沟进水口处河岸边上的那座字库的名声更大。"字库"顾名思义，就是储存文字的一座宝库。从字面上来讲，"库"这个字应该是代表着一个像仓库或厂房一样的建筑。这就是三道堰"字库"的神秘以及迷人之处。其实，这神奇的字库乃是一座中空的高塔，在离地面约一米处有一个透着古老气息的深邃的洞口。三道堰人认为，文字作为中华上下五千年最为博大精深的东西，给予了他们认识这个世界、了解自己和欣赏美好山水的能力。所以他们非常崇敬与仰慕文字。在他们的认知里，文字是神圣的，它代表着上古先贤遗留下来的无上意志，代表着一代又一代精神文化的传承。字库的用处便是焚烧有文字的纸张并收集燃烧之后的灰烬。最后会有专人将灰烬扫出倾倒入柏条河，让它随着漫漫长河长眠于这一方水土。所以这个小小的字库从侧面折射出了三道堰人民对文化的尊崇（图 129）。

图 129 三道堰的字库塔
Fig. 129 The *Ziku* Tower in Sandaoyan Town

There is a lofty towering building standing individually besides Sandaoyan's east barrier and west barrier, which are collectively called *Ziku* Tower. Meanwhile, the most famous one is located at the intake bank of Eryangou Stream. Just as the name indicates, they are warehouses utilized to store documents. Literally, 库 , the character of warehouse in China, refers to a kind of repository or storage. This is exactly the reason why *Ziku* Tower is extraordinarily attractive and mysterious. In fact, this amazing *Ziku* Tower is a towering building which is hollow, and about one meter above the ground. You will find an accessible and ancient hole to put papers with characters into the structure. The people at Sandaoyan regarded "words" as the most essential treasure in their 5,000-year Chinese heritage, which confer them the ability to realize this entire world insightfully, understand themselves, and appreciate the spectacular scenery around the world. Thus, their deference and esteem placed on "words" has reached a height which cannot be overstated. In their cognitive world, words are divine, representing the will left by ancient saints, the psychological and civilization heritage of enormous generations. The usage of *Ziku* Tower is for burning papers and gathering ashes. Finally, there is a person whose job is to sweep the ashes out and pour them in to the Baitiao River, letting them drift with the water and sleep under the continent forever. We can say that the *Ziku* Tower reflects the Sandaoyan people's divine attitude towards civilization with ordinary deference in the above examples (Fig. 129).

牌坊 *Paifang*

从前，孝子牌坊与贞节牌坊竖立在三道堰通往马街的官道上。孝子牌坊俗称为头道牌坊，贞节牌坊又被称为二道牌坊。那什么是孝子牌坊和贞节牌坊？我们就要从头说起了。牌坊作为中国古代的一种特有的标志性门洞式建筑通常用来放在街头路口和园林前代表着"门"。据资料记载，最早的牌坊出现在春秋中叶，叫作"衡门"，它是用两根柱子再搭上一根横梁组成的一种独特的建筑形式。后来这个"衡门"被用在"坊门"上。坊门由衡门改造而来，在侧柱上安装了

图 130 三道堰的牌坊
Fig. 130 *Paifang* structure in Sandaoyan Town

可开合的门扇。古时候的"坊门"与我们现在墙的用途相同，用来分隔两个地方。如今，虽然大名鼎鼎的孝子牌坊与贞节牌坊已经不复存在了，但是还是有几道有名的牌坊在三道堰竖立着，它们是水乡坊牌楼、滨河坊、河坝苑牌坊与永定桥牌坊（图 130）。位于永定桥两个桥头上的牌坊——永定桥牌坊具有一定的特殊性，作为三道堰的入口，它们显得大气磅礴。河坝苑牌坊为两柱一间冲天式牌坊，两个横坊之间悬挂匾额一道，上书"河坝苑"三个大字。滨河坊位于三道堰场镇上，是一个四柱三间不出头式牌坊，同时也是三道堰的路标性建筑物。水乡坊牌楼，这个美轮美奂的牌楼由 8 根柱子组成，并以富有中华色彩的建筑方式建成。水乡牌坊正面立柱上悬挂一联："古蜀情悠绕古堰两岸，水乡春色过廊桥一坊。"背面立柱也悬有一联："三道古堰柳绿花香惹人醉，两河碧波鹭飞鸟鸣待君来。"该对联是三道堰人民智慧的结晶。

In the past, the Xiaozi *Paifang* (Dutiful Son Archway) and Zhenjie *Paifang* (Chastity Archway) were two archways which stood in an avenue leading to the horse street of Sandaoyan. Xiaozi *Paifang* also named Toudao *Paifang* (the 1st archway), while Zhenjie *Paifang* named Erdao *Paifang* (the 2nd archway). But what are Xiaozi *Paifang* and Zhenjie *Paifang*? We have to talk about them from the beginning. *Paifang* is a remarkable landmark and gate-like construction which represented the "door" in ancient China and usually lied on the corner of the street or in front of the park. According to the historic material, the earliest *Paifang*, emerging in the middle of Spring and Autumn Period, is called Hengmen Gate, which was a special structure constituted by two pillars and a beam. Afterwards, Hengmen Gate became to Fangmen Gate. The Fangmen Gate was transformed by Hengmen Gate and added a door which could open and close. Fangmen Gate was regarded as the wall to isolate two places in ancient times. At present, although the famous Xiaozi *Paifang* and Zhenjie *Paifang* have disappeared, there are a few well-known *Paifangs* that stand in Sandaoyan: Shuixiang *Paifang*, Binhe *Paifang*, Hebayuan *Paifang*, and the Yongdingqiao *Paifang* (Fig. 130). Yongdingqiao *Paifang*, the special one, is located at the two bridgehead of Yongding Bridge. As the entrance of Sandaoyan, this *Paifang* conveys a sense of spectacularity. The Hebayuan *Paifang*, an upright archway with two pillars and a room, has a stele hanged between two gates with three words: "He Ba Yuan" (a yard near the river). Binhe *Paifang* is an archway located in the town of Sandaoyan with four pillars and three rooms; meanwhile, it is a landmark of Sandaoyan. Shuixiang *Paifang*, a gorgeous building, was constructed by eight pillars with Chinese characteristics. Moreover, two pairs of couplet attached on two columns of Shuixiang *Paifang*'s both sides reflect Sandaoyan people's wisdom.

6. 研究反思

Reflection of Our Report

随着我们对三道堰文化研究的不断深入，我们发现这样一个千年古镇在视觉上给我们留下的印象是水泥硬道、高齐牌楼、粉饰黛瓦。富有历史古味的古镇如今却充斥着极具现代色彩的事物。和很多"新古镇"一样，那些本属于川西水乡典型古镇的精华在为了拉动经济而整改古镇面貌的动机之下变得面目全非。

图 131 绘制在现代居住建筑山墙面上的线描画
Fig. 131 Linear painting on the gamble wall of modern residential building

经过多番采访，我们想从不同年龄段的人们获得些许有关历史上三道堰的信息，而得到的却极少。看着新建的荡桥，面对普及的美食，我们所想的却是如果政府将古镇的样貌逐一复原，而不是像是在复制粘贴一样用现代的材料做着粗糙的复原工作，那么古镇对于来到这游玩的中外旅客来说，将会更具吸引力。现在大多数古镇都是千篇一律，只有当一个古镇具有它自己的特点，具有因时间的流逝而存在的灵魂，它才会变得独一无二。人们总是钟情于独一无二的事物，前往古镇的人将络绎不绝，同样也能起到更大的促进经济的作用，还能号召更多的对中国历史和文化感兴趣的研究人员参与推进国家历史文化研究工作，促进中国特色文化的发展，一举数得。因此，我们建议，在建设古镇时，应更多地以保护性开发为主，保留当地原有特色，避免千篇一律（图 131）。

Although we did a lot of research on Sandaoyan's culture and dug into it deeply, what this historical town left to us was the concrete footpath and towering buildings, with only some superficial plastering and unscaled roof decoration. This town should have been historical, but it's full of modern things, just like many other "new historical towns." Forms and features of traditional Sichuan historic water towns have been altered and transformed extensively under the motivation to change the scene of the historic town for stronger economy.

We planned in earnest to rebuild the historical image of this town through interviews from people of varying ages. However, the information we obtained was little. Looking at the concrete bridge and eating delicious foods from other places, what we envisioned in our research is still only a dream. If the government in Sandaoyan should restore it into its former condition rather than utilize modern materials to recover it roughly like one copies and pastes images on a computer, we feel that it can be done proper justice in its revamping. Thus, for Chinese or foreigners alike as visitors, it is our hope that they will desire to visit here. Because nowadays, there is a huge sea of duplicated towns. However, while a town possesses its unique history and spirit due to the lapse of time, it will always be a unique one that may leave the greatest cultural imprint. Considering that people's eyes may catch something more unique compared to that of something duplicated for easy visual consumption, it is in this way that if the government tried its best to recover the condition of Sandaoyan, the number of people visiting there will grow by virtue of its standout nature among a sea of soulless duplicated constructions. When business is carried out in such a unique environment where local culture, commerce, history, architecture, and natural beauty are combined, more people are attracted to stay and consume, leading to rapid economic growth. Besides this, it will encourage any researchers who are passionate about Chinese history as well as culture to do more research about it. Hence, we suggest that we should give priority to the protective development of historic towns, such as these mentioned here in the effort to retain local characteristics while avoiding global assimilation and loss of rich thousands of years of valued culture (Fig. 131).

古镇考察报告之四：

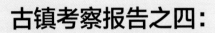

Historic Town Investigation Report No. 4:
Shangli

1. 简介

Introduction

图 132 上里入口的戏台广场
Fig. 132 Opera stage and plaza at the entrance of Shangli

上里古镇（图 132-133），坐落于四川雅安市雨城区北部，位于四县市交界处。古镇形成之初名为"罗绳"，取其昔日古道上的驿站、关隘之意，是南方丝绸之路的临邛古道进入雅安的重要驿站，也是唐蕃古道上的重要边茶关隘和茶马司所在地。历史上的上里古镇依山傍水，东、北、西三面皆为丘陵山地，中南部为山丘围合成的平坝，边缘的东、南、西三面分别有河流小溪围绕。田园小丘，木屋为舍，石板铺街，带有中国古镇特有的宁静与安详。雅安地区夏天通常会下暴雨，城市中有些道路会积水导致堵塞，但上里古镇却不会。它的排水系统充分体现了古人的智慧，利用其上高下低的地理优势，夏天下雨不积水，冬天下雪也不结冰。即使碰上几十年一遇的大雨，积水很快就能排空。

Lying at the intersection of four counties and cities, Shangli (Figs. 132-133) is located in the north of the Yucheng District, Ya'an City, Sichuan Province. This historic town was originally addressed as "Luosheng," which was a vital pass of the South Silk Road and ancient Linqiong Road, leading to Ya'an. It is also as important place where the tea and horse trading took place along the ancient Tangbo Road. Surrounded by small hills in its east, north, and west sides, and rivers and creeks in its east, south, and west sides, Shangli owns a flat field in its central and southern part, which is featured with wood housings, stone streets amidst quiet farming lands and hillocks, full of peace and tranquility. In summer, there are occasional rainstorms in the area of Ya'an. Such rainstorms often lead to drainage problems in the city, but never happen in Shangli. Taking advantage of its natural geographical conditions and the natural slope of the ground levels, the drainage system of Shangli shows the wisdom of our ancestors. As a result, it never accumulates water on the street in summer and never freezes in winter. Even when confronted with huge storms that occur once every dozens of years, the accumulated surface water can be evacuated in a very short amount of time.

2. 历史

History

上里在汉以前为青衣羌人领地，汉至隋归严道县管辖，隋末唐初曾一度隶属临邛郡，而后归雅州府。古时的西蜀称"西南夷"，为开发这片宝地，从先秦到明清间曾有几次大规模的移民活动。他们带来了先进的中原文化和境外文化，同当地文化融合成了统一的汉文化，给后人留下了许多珍贵的文物。上里被民间传为是"财源"汇聚的宝地。

Before the Han Dynasty, the Shangli area was mainly inhabited by the Qing Yi Qiang people. From Han to Sui, it belonged to the administration of Yandao County. From the end of Sui to the beginning of Tang, it was administered by the Linqiong Prefecture. Since then, it belonged to Yazhou Province. In order to develop the vast land of Western Shu (nowadays Sichuan), which was also called the Southwest, several large scale migrations occurred from the Early Qin Period to the Qing Dynasty. Such migrant movements brought the latest cultures of the Central Plains, as well as that of overseas, which were later developed into a single, unified culture after mixing with the indigenous culture. As a result, many precious cultural relics were produced and reserved for descendants, and therefore, Shangli was widely regarded as a precious place and the "source of wealth."

图 133 上里古镇入口的石板桥和河道
Fig. 133 Stone bridge and river at the entrance of Shangli

图 134 刻有抗日宣传标语的石墙
Fig. 134 Stone wall inscribed with anti-Japan slogans

上里古镇还流传着在此聚集的五大家族的趣称：杨家的顶子，韩家的银子，陈家的谷子，许家的女子，张家的锭子。所谓顶子，是说杨家诗书传家，世代官宦；银子，是说韩家世代经商，积聚了大量钱财；谷子，是说陈家田产广阔，粮食丰足；女子，是说许家的女儿品貌双全，勤劳善良，持家有方，各户争相聘娶；锭子，普通话叫拳头，是说张家有习武传统，个个骁勇善斗。如此形象生动的描述，勾勒出了古镇丰富的社会生活。遥想当年，在上里狭窄的石板街上，官场、商场、情场、农场、习武场，也是五大家族的竞技场，有趣的故事一定少不了。

Shangli is also famous for its stories of five great families, each with a respectable humorous nickname: the Yang Family's hat, the Han Family's silver, the Chen Family's grains, the Xu Family's girls, and the Zhang Family's boys. In other words, the Chen Family has been well known for its ascendants' good education, many of whom had become high rank officials. The Han Family was known for its trading and business that had accumulated a large amount of money and wealth. The Chen Family is good at farming and owns a lot of farming lands with high yields. The Xu Family is respected for its education and training over its daughters, who were beautiful with virtue, hardworking and kind, and good at running households, so that they were highly wanted in traditional match-making by other families. The Zhang Family has kept a good tradition of martial art, so that all male members were brave fighters. Such vivid words outlines the rich social life of this historic town. If one recalls the old times, the narrow slab stone streets were also the arena of the five great families, full of interesting stories around politics, business, labor market, love, and martial arts.

蜀韵古镇
HISTORIC TOWNS IN SICHUAN:
THE CULTURAL HERITAGE PROTECTION AND UTILIZATION OF
HISTORIC TOWNS WITH DIFFERENT DIMENSIONS AND VISIONS
——多维视野下的古镇文化遗产保护与利用

1935 年底，红四方面军长征途经上里并驻扎半年之久。驻扎期间，为宣传党的方针、政策，成立了名为"认真""德诚""紫光""崇安"四个代号的政治部，并刻下七十多幅标语，如"中国共产党十大政纲""共产党是穷人的政党""赤化全川""红军是穷人的军队""红军是北上抗日的主力军"等。红军离开后，当地群众用石灰和泥土将石刻标语覆盖保护起来。中华人民共和国成立后再将其覆盖物去掉，这批珍贵的革命文物又重现原貌，也佐证了雅安人民当年对红军事业的贡献。雅安市人民政府于 1985 年 7 月将红军石刻标语审批为雅安市级文物保护单位。当年红军长征时留下的石刻标语现在仍保存完好（图 134）。上里古镇也仍有红军街、红军饭店等，成为当今红色旅游的亮点。

除了红军石刻之外，古镇还有文峰塔、舍利塔、清代石桥、牌坊、民居大院等文物景点，拥有省、市级文物保护单位共八处。上里古镇先后被评为四川省历史文化名镇、革命老区和四川省十大古镇。

Since late 1935, the Fourth Front Red Army occupied Shangli for about half a year. In order to spread the Party's general and specific policies, four political departments were set up, and each with its respected code names, including "Renzhen," "Decheng," "Ziguang," and "Chong'an." Over seventy slogans were carved such as "Ten Great Political Programs of the Chinese Communist Party," "the Communist Party is the poor people's party," "Red the whole Sichuan," "the Red Army is the poor people's army," and "the Red Army is the main force of the anti-Japanese movement up north," and so on. After the Red Army's departure, the locals covered up these engraved slogans with lime and dirt so that they could be well protected until the Liberation War was over. After the founding of PRC, all covers were removed so that such precious revolution relics could be revealed again, providing good evidence for Ya'an people's contribution to the Red Army's great cause. In July 1985, these slogans were authorized by the government of Ya'an to be cultural relics for protection and preservation at the municipal level. Those slogan carvings left by the Red Army during its expedition are well retained even today (Fig. 134), along with the Red Army Street and the Red Army Restaurant, all becoming luminous spots of today's red tourism.

In addition to the Red Army slogan carvings, there are many other site scenes and cultural relics spots, including the Wenfeng Tower and the Sheli Tower, as well as stone bridges, *Paifang*, and courtyard compounds built during the Qing Dynasty. Among them , there are eight cultural relics sites at the provincial and municipal levels. Shangli has therefore been credited as the historical and cultural town, the revolutionary base, and one of the ten great historic towns of Sichuan Province.

3. 活动

Activities

当地的集市大约每周两至三次。人们在集市上挑选自己需要和喜欢的物品、买菜，等等。每年农历二月初二和九月十九这两天当地的人们还会举办庙会、烧香、吃斋饭，用这些方式来表示自己对天神的虔诚。不过，最精彩的活动当属每年农历十一月十二的年猪节。据说这个习俗在当地已有一百多年。在这一天，家家户户都会起个大早，在家中的楼阁上挂上中国结和灯笼，大门外贴上春联。十点半祭天仪式开始，人们用猪做

图 135 一年一度的年猪节游街 *
Fig. 135 Street walking in the annual Pork Festival

祭品在祭祀台上祭供天神。随着祭祀师手中的香火一比画，周遭都安静下来，祭祀师口中唱诵"祈祷明年风调雨顺，祝福上里五谷丰登……"祭天仪式结束后，锣鼓声响起，几个年轻力壮的小伙子抬着一头大肥猪开始游街。之后，四面八方涌来的人们聚集在古戏台前的广场上观看杀年猪。凡是分到年猪的人家都会在中午时分摆好酒席，与慕名前来过节的游客一起共享一年一度丰盛的年猪饭（图 135）。

Locals in the area go to bazaars two or three times a week, choosing what they like, buying food, and so on. In addition, on every February 2nd and September 19th of the Chinese lunar calendar, the locals will hold annual temple fairs for burning incense and eat vegetarian food so that they can express their respects and piousness to gods and goddesses. Nevertheless, the most interesting activity is the annual Pork Festival that takes place on every November 12th of the Chinese lunar calendar. On this day, families wake up early and decorate their houses by hanging lanterns and Chinese knots, as well as posting new year couplets. At 10 o'clock in the morning, the Heaven Worshipping Ceremony, a tradition of more than one hundred years, is to be held. Pigs are placed on the table of sacrifice as sacrificial offerings to deities. As the torch is lit, the surroundings become quiet. The chief priest reads out loud auspicious words such as "pray for favorable climate and weather for the coming year and a good harvest in Shangli..." After the ceremony is over, drums and gongs are played loudly. Several strong men carry a fat pig and parade through Shangli's streets. After that, people gather on the plaza in front of the public opera stage to witness the killing of the sacrificed pig. For those families who are allocated with part of the sacrificed pork, they prepare delicious food and tasty wine to host neighbors and tourists who are here for this festival (Fig. 135).

4. 建筑

Architecture

　　上里古镇的建筑空间以民居大院为特色，建筑风格以明清时期遗存的木结构建筑为主体。古镇内建筑密度较高，古镇整体的建筑肌理与周边的山峦、溪流和田地形成相互依托的关系，和谐自然。古镇的街道呈"井"字状且不宽，主要街道的长度都在 300 米左右。此长度恰好在人体步行适宜范围内，避免了过长的街道给身体和心理带来的疲乏感。街道两旁的建筑排列紧凑，房屋上的花窗、门廊和檐口会随着人的视线发生平缓而微妙的变化，让步行其间的人们感受到古街道和古建筑的视觉美。

The architectural space of this historic town is featured with its residential compounds, which were mostly built in the style of Ming and Qing Dynasties. With buildings densely built along narrow streets, the skyline of the whole town is in quite harmony with the surrounding hills, creeks, and fields, all dependent on each other, well-balanced between the manmade and the nature. Streets are structured in the "井" ("Jing") shape, all not so wide and each no longer than 300 meters, which is just within pleasant walking distance to avoid physical and mental tiredness. Buildings on both sides of the street are compactly and carefully arranged, with gradual and subtle changes among their beautiful windows, porches, and eaves, helping passengers to experience the pleasant visual effects of old streets and buildings.

图 136 韩家大院里的民居建筑与院落
Fig. 136 Vernacular buildings and courtyard in the Han's Family Compound

当地最具独特代表性的民居古建筑群为韩家大院（图 136）。此院始建于清道光年间，历经三代匠人之手建成。不同于一般的川西南建筑自由活泼的布局，韩家大院布局严谨，坐东向西，三进院落，院院相通，最终形成七个四合天井院落，取"七星抱月"之意。从大门进入后，三进院落逐步抬高，每院三级，意为"步步高升"。据说这样的布局主要是因为当时的韩家有钱有权，竭力仿效京城的官宦宅邸格局修建。除此之外，韩家大院的另一大特色就是拥有大量精美的木雕（图 137）。门、窗、枋、檐等皆以浮雕、镂空雕和镶嵌雕刻进行装饰，工艺精湛，具有极高的艺术价值。如今，韩家主人的显赫地位早已不再，但透过大院建筑依然能遥想当年的繁华。镌刻在雕花窗棂上的"淡饭清茶有真味，明窗净几是安居"这副对联，道出的应该是韩氏家族由兴到衰历经 16 代人后悟出来的人生真谛。

Han's Family Compound (Fig. 136) is considered the most unique and representative architecture of local vernacular buildings. Built in the period of Daoguang, it was completed after three generations' successive craftsmanship. Unlike most southwest Sichuan vernacular building styles featured in their free and flexible layout, Han's Family Compound has a rather strict layout, with three-layered courtyards sitting in the east and facing the west. The whole compound is divided into seven courtyards, referring to the auspicious meaning of "seven stars embrace the moon." After entering the main gate, one may find that courtyards on the main axis is built on an elevated ground with a three-step difference, which means "to be promoted step by step." It is said that such a layout and design was deliberately chosen by rich and powerful Han's Family in order to imitate those mansions of high rank officials in the capital of Beijing. Another feature is the wide use of wood carving craftsmanship (Fig. 137), where one may find delicate reliefs, hollow carvings, and inlay carvings on doors, windows, walls, beams, and eaves, all with high level craftsmanship and artistic values. Today, the family's eminent status is no longer present, but one can easily recall its prosperity and glory in the past. The antithetical couplet "true tastes in plain rice and tea, peaceful life in clean windows and tables" carved on the window bars may have well expressed the true meaning of life that Han's Family members have realized from their family of sixteen generations, of family history from rise to decline.

蜀韵古镇

HISTORIC TOWNS IN SICHUAN:
THE CULTURAL HERITAGE PROTECTION AND UTILIZATION OF
HISTORIC TOWNS WITH DIFFERENT DIMENSIONS AND VISIONS
——多维视野下的古镇文化遗产保护与利用

除了韩家大院的精美雕刻之外，在上里古镇大部分建筑上也能找到有精美雕刻的垂花柱。一方面垂花柱是用来支撑南方建筑出挑较深的屋檐。人们在建筑物的檐下寒暄、行礼、殷殷话别都需要一定的空间，如果两根檐柱落地，檐下的活动空间就会受到很大局限。采用不落地的垂花柱，地面空间就宽敞多了。同时，在垂花柱上还可以进行各类题材的雕刻艺术创造，装饰性很强，让这个檐下空间变得更加温馨和美好。

图 137 韩家大院里民居建筑上的精美木雕
Fig. 137 Beautiful wood carving on the architecture of Han's Family Compound

古镇沿河上溯，每隔几十米就会有一座石桥，一共八座，各型各色不会重复。据当地一位老人介绍，历史上一位本地官员就是因为修桥有功而被皇上赏识。最具代表性和识别性的便是二仙桥，属于市级文物保护单位。这是一个有着江南水乡特色的石拱桥，属于高卷拱单孔石桥，形式优美且结构坚固。桥两侧为石栏，正中雕有龙首和龙尾。桥头还有一宝塔，其正面运用了精美的浮雕工艺，刻有"二仙桥"三字，塔壁阴刻文字，记录了此桥在乾隆年间三次重建的历史。桥塔呼应，构图均衡，体现出上里独有的江南水乡韵味（图 138）。

In addition to the elegant carvings well reserved in Han's Family Compound, one may also find beautiful pendant style pillars in most buildings of Shangli. On one side, they help to hold the rather deep eaves commonly seen in southern China. People can chat and say hello and goodbye under such eaves at the entrance of residential buildings. If the pillars were standing on the ground, then there wouldn't be enough space for such activities. By choosing such pendant style pillar, space in front of buildings becomes much wider. At the same time, various artistic carving patterns are very decorative, which help to produce a pleasant and beautiful spatial atmosphere under the eaves.

Sailing from downstream to upstream, there is a bridge every dozens of meters. All together, there are eight bridges, each of which has different styles and colors. According to a local elder, one of the local officials won recognition from the emperor because of his contribution in bridge construction. The most symbolic and identifiable one is the Erxian Bridge, a municipal cultural preservation relic. It is a stone arched bridge built in Jiangnan style with a single high arch, gracefully shaped and solid in structure. There are stone railings on both sides, with the carved patterns of dragon head and tail in the middle. There is also a stone tower at the end of the bridge. Three words, "Er Xian Qiao" (Two Immortals Bridge), are carved on the front side of the tower, while other sides are carved with the history of how this bridge had been rebuilt three times during the Qianlong Period. The tower and the bridge echo each other and compose a beautiful visual balance, bringing Shangli a unique Jiangan water town aroma (Fig. 138).

图 138 上里古镇的二仙桥
Fig. 138 Erxian Bridge in Shangli

图 139 上里双节孝牌坊
Fig. 139 Shuangjiexiao *Paifang* in Shangli

双节孝牌坊和九世同居石牌坊是当地最为著名的牌坊，为朝廷佳赏赐碑而建。双节孝牌坊（图 139）建于清道光十九年（1839年），位于古镇南四家村昔日古道上，是清廷为褒奖韩家姑媳守节敕建的。该坊结构为四柱三间十二翼出檐多脊，镂空石雕彩绘，采用当地优质石英红砂岩石建造。坊前 30 米处还竖立有一对 12 米高六棱四方双斗石桅杆，更显气势雄伟。九世同居石牌坊建于清嘉庆六年（1801 年），该牌坊位于古镇陈家山犀牛望月处，坊前 30 米也矗立了一对八轮双斗雕花石桅杆。牌坊记载了陈氏家族九代同居、人口逾千、共聚一堂的历史，陈氏家族被誉为汉族第一大家庭，因两次受到朝廷嘉奖而立家谱石坊。

居高俯瞰，上里古镇的建筑、石桥和周边的山峦、田野和溪流融合在了一起。宛如一幅悠长而古老的画卷，让人不禁生出一种身在世外、时光倒流、如梦如幻的感觉。

The most famous memorial archways are the Shuangjiexiao *Paifang* and the Jiushitongju *Paifang*, both awarded by the Imperial Court. The Shuangjiexiao *Paifang* (Fig. 139) was built on the old path to the Sijia Village south to the town in 1839, which was to honor the daughter and daughter-in-law of Han's Family for their preserving chastity after the death of their husbands. It is structured in four posts and three archways, with twelve wings reaching out with many ridges. It was built in excellent local red quartzite stones with hollowed-out carvings and exquisite colors. Thirty meters in front of the archway, there is also a pair of 12 meter-high stone spars, making the archway even more prominent. The Jiushitongju *Paifang* was built near the Chenjia Hill in 1801. There is also a pair of stone spars standing in front of the archway. This archway records the history of Chen's Family, who had lived together among nine generations with a total population over a thousand. It was hence regarded as the largest family within the Han Nationality and because it was rewarded twice by the Imperial Court, it was allowed to build such a family genealogy memorial archway.

Watching from above, one may find that buildings, bridges, hills, fields, and creeks all blend into one long and old scroll painting, creating a dreamy feeling of being outside of the world.

参考文献

References

陈益，2001. 周庄：中国第一水乡 [M]. 上海：上海科学技术文献出版社 .

丁浩，叶晓红，2006. 时光影像：36 个四川古镇的瞬间记忆 [M]. 成都：四川科学技术出版社 .

何智亚，2009. 四川古镇 [M]. 重庆：重庆出版社 .

赖武，喻磊，2010. 四川古镇 [M]. 成都：四川人民出版社 .

吕大千，2001. 旅游在中国：周庄，中国江南水乡 [M]. 北京：中国旅游出版社 .

阮仪三，2010. 阮仪三与江南水乡古镇 [M]. 上海：上海人民美术出版社 .

阮仪三，李浈，林林，2010. 江南古镇历史建筑与历史环境的保护 . 上海：上海人民美术出版社 .

ANSFIELD J, 2001. Wake up Wuzhen [J]. City Weekend, May 24-June 6: 8-11.

Department of City Planning and Urban Renewal, 1965. Alexandria Waterfront Study [R]. City of Alexandria, Virginia.

Environmental Law Institute, 1998. Guiding Growth in Virginia: Local Incentives for Revitalization and Preservation [R].

FEI, H-T, 1989. Rural Development in China Prospect and Retrospect [M]. Chicago: University of Chicago Press.

GARREAU J, 1991. Edge City: Life on the Frontier [M]. New York: Anchor Books.

KNAPP RG, LO K-Y, 2005. House, Home, Family: Living and Being Chinese [M]. Honolulu: University of Hawai'i Press.

KOGEL E, MEYER U, and STIFTUNG HB, 2000. The Chinese City—Between Tradition and Modernity [M]. Berlin: Jovis.

MCMAHON E, HOLLBERG S, and MASTRAN S, 2001. Better Models for Development in Virginia [R]. The Conservation Fund.

MORRILL P, 1979. Who Built Alexandria? Architects in Alexandria 1750-1900 [M]. Northern Virginia Regional Park Authority.

PRENTICE, HK, 1998. Suzhou: Shaping an Ancient City for the New China [M]. Spacemaker Press.

School of Architecture and Landscape Architecture, The University of Minnesota Institute of Technology, 1981. Walls— Inside China and Its Architecture [R].

SMITH, WF, 1989. A Seaport Saga: Portrait of Old Town Alexandria, Virginia [M]. Norfolk: The Donning Company Publishers.

Strasbourg Council of Europe Publishing and Documentation Service, 1994. Achieving a Balance Between Historic Preservation and Urban Development [R]. Netherlands.

The ICOMOS International Specialized Committee on Cultural Tourism, 1993. Cultural Tourism—Tourism at World Heritage Cultural Sites: The Site Manager's Hand Book [R]. Sri Lanka Publications Committee.

TREISTER K, 1987. Chinese Architecture. Urban Planning, and Landscape Design [M]. Gainesville, Florida: College of Architecture, University of Florida.

VOGES NA, 1975. Old Alexandria—Where America's Past is Present [M]. EPM Publications.

WALEY-COHEN J, 1999. The Sextants of Beijing [M]. New York: W.W. Norton and Company.

WANG J, 1992. Watertown Zhouzhuang [J]. MIMAR - Architecture in Development: 28-33.

WANG Qijun, 2000. Vernacular Dwellings—Ancient Chinese Architecture [M]. New York: Springer Wien.

XU Yinong, 2000. The Chinese City in Space and Time: The Development of Urban Form Suzhou [M]. Honolulu: University of Hawaii Press.

百度百科 https://baike.baidu.com/.

百度图片 https://image.baidu.com/.

维基百科 https://www.wikipedia.org/.

中国古镇保护网 http://www.zggzbh.com/.

中华人民共和国住房和城乡建设部 http://www.mohurd.gov.cn/.

蜀韵古镇

HISTORIC TOWNS IN SICHUAN:
THE CULTURAL HERITAGE PROTECTION AND UTILIZATION OF
HISTORIC TOWNS WITH DIFFERENT DIMENSIONS AND VISIONS

——多维视野下的古镇文化遗产保护与利用

名词解释
Glossary

穿斗	Chuandou
穿斗是中国南方常见的一种传统民居结构方式。其主要特点是利用穿枋和斗枋把柱子串联起来，形成一榀榀的房架，檩条直接搁置在柱头，由此形成房屋的屋架。	It is a commonly seen vernacular building structure widely used in southern China. Its main feature is that columns are connected by small crossing beams in both directions with purlins rested directly on the columns in forming the entire roof trusses.
风水	Fengshui
风水是中华民族历史悠久的一门玄术，又称堪舆。主要指有关城池、宫殿、村落、住宅、墓地的选址、坐向、建设等方法及原则。	Fengshui is a Chinese geomancy with a long history, with its nick name as Kanyu. It refers to a set of methods and principles in the site selection, orientation and construction of cities, palaces, villages, houses and graveyards.
公馆	Gongguan
公馆特指中国社会权贵家族修建的作为住所的大型离宫别馆。	It refers to different kinds of large-scale residential complexes (mansions) built by influential officials for their families in China.
会馆	Huiguan
会馆是指中国明清时期都市中由同乡或同业组成的团体性组织在各地修建的用于聚会、交流、议事、祭祀等的公共建筑院落。	It refers to building complexes constructed in cities, organized by groups of fellows bound either by same origins or same industries, with many public functions including communications and discussions, meetings and ceremonies, etc.

牌坊	*Paifang*
牌坊是一种特殊的中国传统建筑类型，是由皇家为表彰功勋、科第、德政以及忠孝节义所赐立的建筑物。	*Paifang* is a special kind of Chinese traditional architecture. It was normally granted to be built by the order of the imperial court in honoring virtues such as meritorious service, examination fame, benevolent rule, loyalty and filial piety, integrity and fidelity.
礤墩	*Sangdun*
礤墩是常见于中国南方传统建筑的檐柱与石柱础之间的一种构件，主要用于隔潮，可根据需要进行更换。	It refers to a unique construction component between the wooden peripheral columns and their stone bases that can be replaced when needed. It is used for moist insulation, and is commonly seen in southern Chinese traditional architecture.
歇山	*Xieshan*
歇山为中国传统建筑屋顶样式之一，在规格上仅次于庑殿顶。该种屋顶共有九条屋脊，即一条正脊、四条垂脊和四条戗脊。	*Xieshan* refers to a kind of roof types among traditional Chinese buildings, which is only second to Wudian (hip roof) in terms of building regulations. Such a roof type consists of nine ridges, including one main ridge, four vertical ridges and four hip ridges.
悬山	*Xuanshan*
悬山是中国传统建筑的两坡屋顶形式之一，因其屋面伸出山墙之外而得名。大量用于普通民居，尤其在中国南方，以保护土质山墙免遭风雨侵蚀。	*Xuanshan* refers to a kind of two-slope roof types among traditional Chinese buildings, which is named for its roof hanging over the gamble wall. It is widely used in ordinary houses to protect the earth-rammed gamble wall from erosion caused by wind and rain, especially in southern China.
阴阳	*Yinyang*
阴阳是古代中国先贤创立的一个重要哲学概念，即把宇宙间贯通物质和人事的万事万物概括为阴和阳两个既对立又相互转化的范畴。	An important philosophical concept created by ancient Chinese sages, which summarizes myriads of things in the universe within two opposing categories of *Yin* and *Yang*, who counter pose each other yet can be transformed into each other.

图表说明 *About Illustrations and Tables*

本书绝大部分图片均由编著者拍摄，有明确出处的表格数据和图片均有注明来源，凡标注有＊号的图片均来自互联网非版权图片资源。

*Most illustrations in this book are made or taken by authors, and a few table data and pictures are quoted from clear sources, and only few photos marked with * are from internet with no copyright notices.*